The Fabulists

The Fabulists

The World's New Rulers, Their Myths
and the Struggle Against Them

MICHAEL PEEL

ONEWORLD

A Oneworld Book

First published in Great Britain, the Republic of Ireland and Australia
by Oneworld Publications Ltd, 2019

ISBN 978-1-78607-659-5
eISBN 978-1-78607-660-1

Typeset by Hewer Text UK Ltd, Edinburgh
Printed and bound in Great Britain by Clays Ltd, Elcograf S.p.A.

Oneworld Publications Ltd
10 Bloomsbury Street
London WC1B 3SR
England

MIX
Paper from
responsible sources
FSC® C018072

To Sam, Lorin and Owen

Contents

Introduction: Civilisation Story

Not far outside Brussels, there stands a group of ponds where Belgium's king once kept a human zoo. The well-manicured grounds of the neoclassical Royal Museum for Central Africa in Tervuren are a favourite place for Sunday family outings these days, but the tranquillity hides a dark history. In 1897, seven Congolese people died from exposure suffered while living in makeshift 'villages' set on four sites in the area. Leopold II had created the ersatz settlement as an attraction for the crowds who came to an 'international exhibition' he commissioned to show his wealth and power to the world. Photos of the time show what the 267 Congolese shipped in for the monarch's pleasure were forced to do. Some stand in front of huts, dressed in traditional clothes designed for the tropics. Others ply the lake waters in canoes.

In mid-2018, the site of the villages bore no record of the fatalities, which were mentioned only briefly on the museum's website. They were a tiny fraction of the mass casualties that Leopold's twenty-three-year rule from his little sliver of Europe inflicted on the vast territory of what he named the Congo Free State.[1] As many as ten million people died as the monarch's agents executed a reign of terror and forced labour. The king's rule sucked the wealth from the area's large resources of rubber into the royal coffers in Brussels. Leopold's forces murdered, maimed and drove workers to death by exhaustion, while many other Congolese fled their homes and died from starvation or disease.

Today, despite all that is known about the horrendous abuses that took place under his rule, Leopold still retains his place in the pantheon of Belgium's former rulers. A massive portrait of his thick-bearded figure is hung in a high-ceilinged room in the country's mission to the EU, where the government held briefings for journalists. The room itself was known internally after Patrice Lumumba, the first prime minister of independent Congo until he was murdered in 1961 with Belgian complicity. Which, as statements go, is a bit like honouring Nelson Mandela and then hanging a picture of Cecil Rhodes on the wall.

Nevertheless, changing times have brought some concessions from the Belgian state over Leopold's legacy. The Africa museum shut its doors in 2013 for a long overdue revamp. The renovation was a response to concerns that, as the museum's website understatedly put it, the exhibition was 'outdated' and 'not very critical of the colonial image'. Among the artefacts under debate was a golden statue that stood near the entrance, of an African boy hanging on to the robes of a European missionary.[2] Its inscription read: 'Belgium brings civilization to Congo.'

An old story, for long expedient, had finally become unsustainable. As the museum's online blurb put it, again with some delicacy, a 'new scenography was urgently required'. A fresh version of history – its truth still to be tested – was to be substituted in its place.

After more than two decades as a journalist, in four different global regions, the clash between myth and reality I felt beside the Tervuren museum's ponds seemed all too familiar. Pathologies of denial and delusion appeared the norm. They loomed large, both in the way leaders presented themselves to their peoples and the world, and in a narrative the West told about itself and the rest of humanity. They buttressed autocratic figures in both dictatorships and democracies who were profiting from the growing rip tide of unpredictability, anxiety and anger that coursed through so many societies.

In the previous nine years, I'd witnessed many events that had caused widespread shock. In the Middle East, I travelled from Libya to the Gulf and saw the early hopes of the so-called Arab Spring dissolve into war and repression. In Asia, I charted the end of a royal era in Thailand, the singular durability of another in Brunei, and the role foreigners and international financial institutions played in a vast Malaysian corruption scandal that crossed continents. I returned to a Europe gripped by authoritarian revivalism and ever harsher methods for dealing with migrants whose desperate conditions I had seen at their starting points in southern Turkey and West Africa. For years, I worked to the background drumbeats of Syria's long war, Brexit and President Donald Trump's 'America First' campaign: all events whose significance appears to me still in important respects misrepresented and misunderstood.

This book is the story of one journey to puzzle through the modern age of fabulism, in countries at the centre of world attention and others little thought about by outsiders. The events I witnessed from Bangkok to Bucharest often alarmed me; they didn't surprise me so much. They seemed linked by a style that stretched across cultures, continents and political traditions. All too often, they felt like the predictable, even inevitable, outcomes of the fabrications, wishful thinking and complacency that seem to grip our world ever more tightly.

Some commentators flourish statistics that proclaim humanity is richer and life better than ever before. It often didn't feel that way to me, for all the many moments of grace and inspiration provided by the people I met. I saw precarity wherever I turned, from individuals' struggles to planetary pollution.

Together, the geographically scattered stories in this book highlight crises of legitimacy of one sort or another. They speak of the stuttering credibility of rulers, systems and ideas, many of them born in – or backed by – the West. They expose fundamental fallacies about the spread of liberalism, the potential for benevolence in dictatorship, and the nature of conflict and history itself.

The more I travelled, the more intrigued I was by how national myth-making was both distinctive and in some way archetypal. Every narrative involved winning and consolidating power, either for individuals or – more often – an elite group. Sometimes, outsiders would be told a very different story from that spun to citizens. China's President Xi Jinping, his Russian counterpart, Vladimir Putin, and Narendra Modi, India's premier, all drew heavily on contentious ideas about their countries' backstories and place in the wider world.

The techniques are old but *The Fabulists* argues that the events of the past decade or so have shown that myth-busting has never been more urgent. We are running out of time to deal with existential problems ranging from environmental destruction to sharing the wealth of the world more equitably. What is alarming now is not so much a shortage of truth – sometimes a slippery or shaded ideal – but the abandonment of the quest for it, especially by so many of our leaders. On fundamental points such as making our own societies fairer, ensuring people around the world can live with dignity, or curbing climate change, the strategy is often to avoid the difficulties – or pretend they can be easily solved by crude crackdowns on already victimised groups. At times it seems as if, in some deep sense, we have given up on problems that seem too great to solve, even though the only way to tackle them is to stare them in the face.

The Fabulists in this book are those who push dangerous fantasies about the world around us. Some of these myth-makers are leaders who present themselves as national saviours – or are promoted as such by backers at home and abroad. Those featured here include the hardman Philippine president Rodrigo Duterte, the supposedly reformist Crown Prince Mohammed bin Salman of Saudi Arabia, and the once internationally lauded human rights icon Aung San Suu Kyi in Myanmar. None turned out to be all they seemed.

Autocrats through the ages have spun stories to reinforce their power, but a feature of the modern age of myth is the way this approach has spread to supposed democrats. Elected politicians have become ever more brazen in planting dubious or outright false narratives that have become internalised at home and even convinced observers abroad. If all else fails, these popularly validated leaders simply shrug off legitimate questions and rely on their propaganda to tide them through. Jair Bolsonaro won Brazil's presidency in 2018 on an authoritarian hard right agenda, after making outrageous statements such as suggesting the country's former military dictatorship should have killed more dissidents.

The demagogue's age-old promise to make life easier has also acquired new power in the overworked and atomised societies of the twenty-first century. In this era, characterised by what has been dubbed 'the exhausted majority',[3] worn down by the ever-growing demands of techno-capitalism, the stock of those who offer simple solutions constantly rises. They might be a monarch to worship, a dictator to fix things or an elected politician promising to restore order and security to a chaotic demos.

Unsurprisingly, it is often hard for people to engage deeply with the difficult business of interrogating how they are ruled. For some, it would be dangerous to do so; for many others, opportunities to reflect and dream are crowded out by torrents of data, the pressures of work or the imperative of mere survival. It is a paradox of plenty: while more information is available to us more easily than at any time in human history, never has it been harder to sift and process it all.

What insights I have gleaned over the years are the product of great privilege. Through my work as a *Financial Times* correspondent, and with the great support of that organisation and my colleagues, I have been able both to range widely and to step back and think. I have had the chance to roam and to exchange ideas with people from all over the world. Everywhere I went I was humbled by the accomplishments and durability of people I met, from Syrian writers to Cambodian factory workers. I have tried to pan for golden nuggets of anecdote and experience that reveal something of the way we live now – and throw up parallels and lessons.

The Fabulists is far from a misty-eyed lament for a crumbling Western-led global order. The old system is deeply corrupted and has failed in ways that are becoming ever more apparent. It is something that has long been clear in countries like oil-rich Nigeria, where I once lived, whose troubles were vivid and could be traced in part to the destructive interplay of international power politics and commodity capitalism.

The dishonesty and double standards of democratic countries have powered the rise of autocratic myth-makers elsewhere. On the one hand, wars, financial crises and growing inequality involving the US and European states have discredited their claims that they spread peace, prosperity and fairness. On the other, the Western style of cloaking histories of violence and exploitation in a narrative of benevolence and the greater good finds echoes in the authoritarians who style themselves defenders of their peoples and civilisations.

As the holder of a British passport, I feel the sense of historical reckoning particularly strongly. Most nations have burnished their pasts, but mine has long polished furiously to clean the bloody stains of slavery and empire. The gap between the UK's often indulgent view of itself and how the world sees it is vast – and growing wider still as a result of the way it has dealt with Brexit.

The decade following the 2008 financial crisis has shattered many other illusions in Europe, the US and elsewhere. One accidental effect of President Donald Trump's rise, as this book tries to show, has been to rip the curtain away from many truisms about how Washington has acted in the world during the era of its superpower status. A side effect of Brexit has been to shine greater light on the many flaws of the EU – an institution that, as this book discusses, is wrapped up in its own deceptions about its core values.

Tales of varying degrees of fiction give our lives and communities meaning and purpose. If people stopped loving stories, I for one would be out of a job – and we as a species would have lost one of the defining features of our humanity. As the historian and author Yuval Noah Harari has put it: 'We are the only mammals that can cooperate with numerous strangers because only we can invent fictional stories, spread them around, and convince millions of others to believe in them. As long as everybody believes in the same fictions, we all obey the same laws, and can thereby cooperate effectively.'[4]

But these seductive narratives also need to be seen for what they are – and for the limits of their usefulness. The great danger comes when they shift from being useful social lubricants to means of exploitation. We must all be free to tell our own stories in our own ways for our own comfort, but only to the extent that we are not oppressing others by doing so.

Technology has amplified the present-day turmoil in important ways, but the Internet does not seem to me the root of the problem. As Vaidas Saldžiūnas, defence editor of Delfi, a Baltic media outlet at the forefront of Lithuania's fight against pro-Kremlin disinformation, told me: 'Facebook and other social media are just the vessels. They are not the originators. We look for the primary source. We look for patient zero. Because this is where it starts.'

Stories spread online, in other words, wouldn't capture people unless they were already receptive. Social media companies that have rightly drawn growing criticism for their role in distributing distortions and lies are as much symptoms as causes. Critical audiences should approach all sources with care – and that includes traditional media, as well as Facebook newsfeeds or YouTube recommendations.

We need today to both reaffirm the doctrine of proper scepticism and to reclaim it from conspiracy theorists and self-styled populists. No assertion should be above questioning. It is crucial to be alert to potential biases and conflicts of interest, in areas from media ownership to scientific research funding. But that does not mean every claim is equally plausible. Down this path lies the false idea that empirically supported knowledge is no better than opinion.

The only beneficiaries of the nihilistic view that nothing and nobody can ever be trusted are those who profit from chaos politically, financially or in some other way. It is no coincidence that those who promote this worldview are often to be found on the hard left and right. They have excelled in cultivating a destructive asymmetry of trust. Audiences who rightly approach the arguments of established institutions and individuals with much suspicion sometimes seem to suspend it when confronted with the dodgy claims of demagogues.

From my arrival in Abu Dhabi at the start of the 2010s to my time in Brussels at the end of the decade, I have traced the signature patterns of fabulists and their tales. A common thread between them – whether dictators or democrats – is a lack of accountability for what they do and say. Parsing it all can seem exhausting, but submission carries even greater perils. In this modern age of outlandish stories and snake-oil solutions to real crises, we owe it to ourselves to keep asking the hard questions.

I

THE STRONGMAN BARGAIN

1

All Brave Men – And Women

I met Jamal Khashoggi late in 2011 in Riyadh, as the Saudi Arabian regime grappled with the fallout from the uprisings that had erupted across the Arab world. It was my first trip to the Saudi capital and Khashoggi was a go-to contact for foreign journalists because of his perceptive analysis and high-level contacts. Dressed dapperly in crisp white robes, he received me at his office. He had just been appointed managing director of Al-Arab News, a television channel founded by Prince Alwaleed bin Talal. Prince Alwaleed was one of those impeccable royal connections: he was a grandson of Ibn Saud, the kingdom's founder, and a prominent investor in Western companies including Twitter, News Corp and the Four Seasons hotel chain.

The impact of the regional tumult dominated our conversation. Leaders in Tunisia, Egypt and Libya, who had ruled for almost a century between them, had been toppled during the previous twelve months. Authorities had cracked down on sporadic protests, but there had been no nationwide revolt. Khashoggi, a soft-spoken insider-outsider who was hard to pigeonhole politically, still saw the Arab Spring's fallout as profoundly significant for the Saudi kingdom. He observed strikingly that the Arab world had 'never been as close as it is today'.

'Although Saudis do not themselves see a reason to go on the streets like Libyans and Syrians and Egyptians, I am sure the Arab Spring will have a major effect,' he said carefully.

His modest hints at the need for reform in his homeland proved to be grim foreshadowing. Khashoggi's murder in late 2018 after he had fallen out with the new regime in Riyadh resonated as a signature act of violence in a lawless world. It exposed the fate that autocrats could deal even their highest-profile critics – and it highlighted the limited consequences if the perpetrator led an influential country in the orbit of other powerful states.

Al-Arab news had not lasted long. It was shut down almost as soon as it finally started broadcasting in 2015, the victim of official political hypersensitivity. But Khashoggi's journalism became more and more well known internationally, particularly after the death of King Abdullah in January 2015 triggered a change in the dynastic order in Riyadh. After Mohammed bin Salman was appointed Crown Prince in 2017 at the age of thirty-one, Khashoggi questioned his supposedly progressive credentials with increasing urgency in columns for the *Washington Post* that now serve as a vindication of his views – and his public epitaph.

In May 2018, Khashoggi warned that Saudi Arabia's reformers faced a 'terrible choice' after the arrests of campaigners for greater personal freedoms, such as allowing women to drive. Saudis were expected to 'vigorously applaud social reforms and heap praise on the crown prince' while being asked to 'abandon any hope of political freedom', he charged.

'Is there no other way for us?' asked the columnist, who by now had left the kingdom, saying the government had silenced him. 'Must we choose between movie theatres and our rights as citizens to speak out, whether in support of or critical of our government's actions?'

Less than six months later, Khashoggi was dead. He was murdered in October 2018 during a visit to the Saudi consulate in

Istanbul to obtain papers for his forthcoming marriage. His fiancée Hatice Cengiz waited in vain outside the compound for him to return. When he did not, she raised the alarm.[1]

Turkish authorities immediately said Khashoggi had been killed and later indicated that they had an audio recording of the slaying. Saudi Arabian officials initially said he had left the consulate alive, but kept changing their story. The government then said he had died in a fight, before finally admitting he had been murdered. In November 2018, Saudi prosecutors charged eleven people over what they said was an operation ordered by Ahmed al-Assiri, a former deputy intelligence chief, to force Khashoggi to go back to Saudi Arabia. When the team concluded this would be impossible, they tied Khashoggi up and killed him with a lethal dose of sedative, then dismembered his body and handed the parts on to a local accomplice, the prosecutors alleged.

The case dealt a catastrophic blow to the image of Mohammed bin Salman (often know as MbS). Saudi authorities denied he had approved the hit, but many analysts were sceptical that an assassination of a figure such as Khashoggi did not have approval from the highest levels. On 16 November, the *Washington Post* reported that the CIA had concluded with high confidence that the Crown Prince had ordered the killing.

President Donald Trump denied the CIA conclusion. Instead he issued an extraordinary letter in which he stressed the importance of the US–Saudi relationship and said the full facts of Khashoggi's murder might never be known. 'It could very well be that the Crown Prince had knowledge of this tragic event – maybe he did and maybe he didn't!' Trump wrote.[2]

Trump's crudeness – and the mockery it attracted – hid a deeper truth. His charitable take on MbS was unexceptional in foreign policy circles before Khashoggi's death. As the murder triggered a torrent of criticism branding the Crown Prince reckless and dangerous, it was easy to forget how many Western officials and commentators had previously lauded him. He was feted as the dynamic and liberalising young force the country needed to kick-start changes that had begun modestly under the late King Abdullah but had stalled and sputtered as the Arab Spring raged. In a *New York Times* column in November 2017, Thomas L. Friedman hailed an 'Arab Spring, Saudi style' delivered by a 'young leader who is driving religious and economic reform, who talks the language of high tech, and whose biggest sin may be that he wants to go too fast'.

'Perfect is not on the menu here,' Friedman wrote. 'Someone had to do this job – wrench Saudi Arabia into the 21st century – and MbS stepped up. I, for one, am rooting for him to succeed in his reform efforts.'[3]

Friedman's praise for the young Crown Prince reflected a wider Western weakness for the authoritarian style when used for aims it liked. President Barack Obama showed signs of the same impulse before MbS rose to power, according to an authoritative 2016 piece on his foreign policy doctrine. Weary of various Middle East conflicts, he reportedly joked privately: 'All I need in the Middle East is a few smart autocrats.'[4]

The foreigners who signed up for the MbS fan club after he came to power the following year should have known better. Autocrats oppress: it is in the nature of their power. History is littered with authoritarian 'reformers' who turned to terror rather than tolerate dissent.

There were also plenty of specific warning signs in the Saudi case that made Khashoggi's killing almost a death foretold. The MbS era built on years of repression in the desert kingdom that attracted little criticism from Western allies. Persecution of dissi-dents that rightly would have attracted condemnation in Syria passed by little publicised in its southern neighbour. As I reported from both countries during the Arab Spring, the contrast became increasingly glaring.

Downpours didn't suit Riyadh. The concrete expanses of the Saudi capital flooded quickly because of bad drainage. In the car park of the Granada shopping centre in the north of the city, I leapt puddles and weaved around a group of women in black abayas huddling for shelter at one of the giant complex's entrances. It was 2013 – boom-time in Saudi Arabia – and the mall was rammed. Consumer confidence had been buoyed by high oil prices and the $130 billion of public spending largesse announced by King Abdullah during the early days of the Arab Spring. Out here, though, there was only damp, darkness and the prospect of an unpleasant and perhaps dangerous journey through the city streets. The floodwaters had claimed at least a dozen lives over the previous weeks.

Waiting for me in the car park was Ibrahim, an activist who had become a thorn in the monarchy's side. I have not used his real name or those of his fellow activists I encountered, because I do not want to risk provoking official action against them. Dissent was risky when I met them; as the Khashoggi case shows, it has become potentially deadly since.

As we drove off in Ibrahim's white Toyota, he explained to me the political context of the great rains. Many Saudis saw their country's susceptibility to flooding as linked to the haphazard construction of sprawling cities like Riyadh, where the planning process was undermined by kickbacks. In 2010, King Abdullah himself had called for prosecutions of those responsible for the devastation caused by flash floods that killed more than 120 people and damaged ten thousand homes in Jeddah, even though large sums had been spent on drainage. 'Because of the corruption we have poor infrastructure,' Ibrahim reflected, as spray from the road plumed over a city that is normally one of the world's hottest and driest. 'Everything is full of water.'

Ibrahim had a salt-and-pepper moustache and a way of putting people at ease. He was currently under official investigation, he told me, because of his involvement in a human rights group. The police had informed him of the probe shortly before I'd phoned him the previous day to arrange our meeting. My heart sank at the thought that seeing me would be added by the authorities to his dossier of alleged crimes. As we drove along, I told him that I didn't want to get him into more trouble, but he seemed to relish the confrontation. 'No problem,' he said, with a grin. 'I have nothing to hide.'

Suddenly, the car was illuminated by a series of white flashes as if in a paparazzi ambush. In the scrum of vehicles edging around the paralysed city, we'd managed to jump a red light and trigger a traffic camera. Hundreds of them were now being installed in response to another humanitarian affront. An estimated seven thousand people died on the kingdom's roads each year, a per capita rate about ten times higher than the UK's. I told Ibrahim that I hoped this latest apparent transgression wouldn't be used against him, but once again he shrugged off the concern with dark humour. 'No, I don't think so,' he replied. 'Maybe I will go to jail and so I will not have to pay the ticket.'

I asked him if he was worried about the effect on his family if he went to prison. He had a wife and young children. 'I am sure they will understand,' he said. 'And my big family will take care of my kids and my wife, so I am not worried too much.'

We continued our drive through the Riyadh waterworld, crunching over an unseen manhole cover and then fording a lake in the middle of the carriageway. Moisture hissed from the tyres. We arrived in a suburban district where earth and building rubble lined the streets, turning down an alleyway that petered out amid scattered bottles and other debris. We pulled up next to a patch of wasteland. I realised I had been to this very place eighteen months previously.

The set-up was a far cry from my clandestine meetings with activists in Libya or Syria, who never lingered long in any one place. The Saudi campaigners didn't seem to go for safe houses or concealment. While they might not at that time have faced the same risk of disappearance and death as their counterparts in Tripoli and Damascus, their decision to challenge the government directly still took a lot of courage.

We entered a compound where a floodlight picked out streaking drops of rain. The harsh lighting and sparse surroundings gave the place the feel of a prison exercise area, save for the incongruous presence of a Jacuzzi in one corner. Near to it stood a large tent, and inside the gathering was just as it was when I was last here: about a dozen men in white robes sat on chairs ringed around the walls. Above was a constellation of strip lights fanning from the centre of the tent's roof like a spider's legs. I greeted those present and told them I didn't want to make anyone feel uncomfortable or cause any problems for them. 'It's OK,' Ibrahim reassured me. 'They are all brave men.'

They were fighting for greater rights in a country that by some measures was among the world's most repressive. In 2018, Freedom House, the US think tank, marked Saudi Arabia as one of thirteen countries and territories to receive the worst possible ratings in its annual rankings of political rights and civil liberties.[5] Riyadh's company was dismal indeed, including North Korea, Syria and the West African kleptocracy of Equatorial Guinea.

Persecuted by their own government, often dismissed by diplomats and mostly ignored by the wider populace, Saudi Arabia's rights promoters were playing the loneliest of hands. To be an

activist there was to fight for the right to speak without even feeling the fickle solidarity the West offers campaigners against rival
regimes. Instead, Saudi rights defenders seemed destined to be
picked off quietly one by one. Western powers remained mostly
silent even as they raged against the abuses of the Assad regime in
Damascus.

The Saudi activists' demands fell far short of Libya- or Syria-
style armed insurrection. Many favoured a constitutional monarchy.
Most of their demands could have come off the websites of
multiple Western activist groups campaigning against the policies
of their own governments – these Saudis were for representation
and the right to speak, and against corruption and abuses of power.
They wanted to be listened to, and they wanted to know how the
gargantuan sums flowing each year into the world's largest oil
exporter were being spent.

'These people, they are really intoxicated with power and
wealth and everything else,' one activist had previously told me
about the country's leaders. 'They control everything and look on
the country as private property.'

While repressive Gulf rulers have portrayed the Saudi activists
and others like them as traitors, the rhetoric of these men was of
concern for the country: the patriot as critic. A former Islamist in
the group I met with Ibrahim told me how civil activism had
helped pull him and other fundamentalists back from a dangerous
path that had led certain Saudis towards al-Qaeda.

Another attendee argued Saudi Arabia needed to change to
forestall the violence he feared could follow if building anger was
not allowed a release. He said he did not want to promote a revolution, but to avoid one, hopefully with the help of 'a smart person
in the royal family who could resolve the tension. The idea is to
do what's right, because the street might erupt in chaos against the
regime, like what happened in Egypt and Libya,' he said. 'We
should not take the silence of the people as an absolute situation.

In Libya, people were silent for many, many years, before they erupted in violence.'

There were many points of agreement between these campaigners and US and European liberals. But it would be mistaken and patronising to categorise the Saudi campaigners as 'pro-Western'. In fact, they saw the West as having betrayed them through its mute tolerance of the behaviour of the Saudi regime on which it depends for oil and security support. 'There is no doubt this regime is going to crumble sooner or later – and Western countries are going to lose tremendously,' said one. 'Because the regime that will take over could be an Islamist regime similar to the Iranian regime. It could be a nemesis of the West.'

He urged the West to 'reconsider and recalculate its position' and put pressure on the Saudi monarchy to implement reforms. He pointed out that the West gave strong support – at least rhetorically – to dissidents elsewhere in the Middle East and Asia, making all the greater the moral obligation to do the same in the Gulf. 'Then people could feel that the West is on their side and is not the ally of tyrants,' he said. 'The West could rebuild its relationship with the people, as opposed to the regime.'

As the rain tapped on the tent's roof, the activists drank hot malted drinks and spoke of two prominent detainees. In March 2013, Mohammad al-Qahtani and Abdullah al-Hamid were convicted of spreading false information about Saudi Arabia, setting up an illegal organisation, and rebelling against the authority of the King. Qahtani was jailed for ten years and Hamid for five, plus another six from which he had been pardoned by King Abdullah after a previous conviction. The sentences prompted condemnation from human rights groups – and the usual near-silence from most Western governments. Ibrahim said members of his group had been in touch with the men in Riyadh's al-Hayer prison. They were in high spirits, he said, even though the situation in the jail was 'very difficult'.

A photo of Hamid stood on a small table in the tent with images of other previously jailed campaigners. Another activist described how efforts by Hamid and Qahtani to appeal against their conviction had been hampered by the failure of the authorities to provide them with crucial papers – including the official judgment against them. Hamid had also been sick, suffering from diabetes, high blood pressure and a painful swelling in his back. The two men had appeared for their last hearing with their legs and arms shackled together. 'That was too much,' said the activist. 'It was meant to humiliate them.'

A further four campaigners in the room, including Ibrahim, were now on the 'waiting list' for jail, the activist said. It was part of an attritional official war. Some of the men claimed that this conflict was conducted within certain boundaries; the authorities favoured the mental pressure of opaque and open-ended investigation over arbitrary arrest. But others disagreed, telling stories of people being detained for tweets critical of official policy, distributing leaflets and organising protests. For the government, political activists were 'more dangerous than al-Qaeda', argued another campaigner. 'Al-Qaeda are only a few people and nobody likes them,' he said. 'But the authorities know the population of Saudi Arabia need their freedom.'

A man named Mansour came to sit by me and told me how he'd recently visited Hamid in prison. The jailed activist had complained of a pain in his left shoulder. He'd been trying unsuccessfully for a month to see a doctor. 'He's scared that maybe the pain is becoming more,' Mansour said. 'Maybe a cancer or something. Also, he is losing health generally. When you see his face and skin colour, it's not like before.'

Mansour told me Hamid had eight grown-up children, all except one of whom were in Saudi Arabia. It was a reminder of how one of the most agonising risks for activists in dictatorships is the possibility that their actions will trigger persecution of their families, whether through direct harassment or the blocking of financial benefits and job opportunities. One of Hamid's boys had exams in two weeks, and was worried about his father. Hamid's wife was also anxious about her husband. 'She worries about his health,' Mansour said. 'And now she also worries about his life.'

According to Mansour, Hamid himself was 'happy'. He was used to jail – this was his seventh incarceration. Mansour, a public sector worker, said he had also suffered 'many' problems due to his own activism. He had survived efforts to fire him, been denied promotion, and twice had his salary stopped for more than six months. Recently, he had been moved from a job that involved engaging with the public into an obscure back office role. 'But we will not change,' he said of his activism. 'We will keep going.'

Hamid's family had a long-standing interest in and engagement with political ideas. Like Qahtani, they were from the northern city of Buraydah, which was noted for its independent-minded people – 'some of them with government, some of them against', as one activist put it. Many had farms locally and business interests abroad, giving them both a degree of autonomy and a less parochial perspective than some of their fellow Saudis.

Hamid was an Arabic literature professor and poet. His first big moment of activism – and lesson in its attendant risks – was after the 1991 Gulf War, when he set up a committee on legal rights and wrote to the government asking for political reforms. That had cost him his job at a Saudi Arabian university.

After years of committed – but largely fruitless – activism, Hamid was invigorated by the popular uprisings that began in Tunisia in late 2010, according to Mansour. 'Before the Arab Spring in Tunis, he said: "Maybe our children will see the change,"' Mansour noted. 'But after the Arab Spring, he thought the change would be very soon.'

Only a few people were left in the tent now, gathered around me across from the charred brick fireplace needed to keep the space warm during winter. They laughed at how they were all on an official travel ban – 'because we live in a big jail', Ibrahim said. They were also delighted to have annoyed the authorities by tweeting ten days previously that Hamid was not well. That triggered a barrage of protest calls to the prison, jamming the switchboard.

As I prepared to leave, Ibrahim told me he had a message to the world from Saudi Arabia's pro-democracy campaigners. 'The government will not hear the voices of activists, but they will monitor the international media,' he reasoned. 'The human rights activists are ready to pay the price of freedom. And at the end we will bring all the human rights abuses in our country to justice.

'This is my message,' he concluded, 'before the jail.'

Ibrahim was all too prescient. He would end up being detained as part of a years-long crackdown on dissent in the kingdom that swept up many of its most prominent activists. In 2014, Raif Badawi, a writer and activist, was jailed for ten years – and sentenced to a thousand lashes. Leaked phone footage showed the first fifty strokes being administered in front of a large crowd,[6] in an atmosphere Badawi's wife, Ensaf Haidar, who was living in Canada with their three children, compared to that of a 'beach party'. Later that year, Badawi's lawyer, Waleed Abu al-Khair, who has represented many activists and is married to Badawi's sister Samar, received a fifteen-year sentence, supposedly for terrorism-related offences and disrespecting the court. Al-Khair, a critic of a Saudi antiterrorism law passed in early 2014, was jailed 'primarily for his comments to media outlets and tweets criticizing Saudi Arabia's human rights record',[7] according to Human Rights

Watch. His sister Samar told Reuters that her brother saw the court as 'lacking basic international standards for any tribunal and had objected to trying even terrorists in it, let alone rights activists'.

The regime even jailed female activists who had campaigned for women to have the right to drive – a demand that became government policy under Mohammed bin Salman. Their deten- tion seemed to make no sense even under the brutal logic of autocracy, except as a lesson not to take credit away from the leader who wants to be seen as the author of all things good. One of the campaigners detained was Samar Badawi, Raif's sister, who had sent out regular bulletins on other jailed dissidents.

The sister of Loujain al-Hathloul, one of the detained driving activists, has highlighted the grim situation. Alia al-Hathloul wrote an article describing her alarm and bafflement on hearing the news in May 2018 that Loujain had been arrested at their parents' home in Riyadh. 'I was shocked and confused because the Saudi ban on women driving was about to be removed,' Alia, who lives in Brussels, wrote in the *New York Times* in January 2019.[8]

Alia described how Saudi media branded as traitors Loujain and five other detained female activists. Loujain had already spent more than seventy days in jail after she had tried to drive from Saudi Arabia to the United Arab Emirates in 2014. Then MbS came to power and the government declared in September 2017 that the ban on women driving would be ended in the following year. Alia said that ahead of the announcement her sister received a call from an official in the kingdom's royal court ordering her not to comment publicly on the decision.

Loujain moved to the UAE to study but was stopped by secu- rity officials while driving in March 2018 and put on a plane to Riyadh, according to her sister. She was detained for a few days, released and then rearrested in May, just weeks before the driving ban ceased. Between May and September she was in solitary confinement, before being moved to a prison in Jeddah where her parents were able to visit her.

Alia said Loujain told their parents she had been tortured. She was 'beaten, waterboarded, given electric shocks, sexually harassed and threatened with rape and murder', Alia wrote. 'My parents then saw that her thighs were blackened by bruises.' Her captors, who allegedly included a top royal adviser, made her eat with them during daylight hours of the holy month of Ramadan, during which Muslims are supposed to fast while the sun is up. One of the men told her: 'No one is above us, not even God.'

The alleged abuses appeared to be part of a wider pattern. An Amnesty International report published in November 2018 said several Saudi activists, including a number of women, had reported suffering sexual harassment, torture and other forms of ill treatment while detained arbitrarily at Jeddah's Dhahban prison. The human rights group said it had obtained three separate testimonies detailing how detainees were 'repeatedly tortured by electrocution and flogging, leaving some unable to walk or stand properly'. 'In one reported instance, one of the activists was made to hang from the ceiling, and according to another testimony, one of the detained women was reportedly subjected to sexual harassment, by interrogators wearing face masks,' Amnesty said.[9] The Saudi government has denied the claims.

In March 2019, the Saudi state news agency said authorities were readying themselves for a trial of the women's rights activists. The media report referred to a 2018 official statement that said the detainees were suspected of damaging the country's interests and aiding hostile elements overseas.[10]

Other Gulf countries have also cracked down as the Saudi purge on opposition has played out. In the UAE, the prominent activist Ahmed Mansoor was detained in 2017, sentenced to ten years in jail and fined 1 million dirhams (£215,000). The court found he had insulted the 'status and prestige of the UAE and its symbols', including its leaders, according to the Abu Dhabi government-owned newspaper *The National*. He was also convicted of 'seeking to damage the relationship of the UAE with its neighbours by publishing false reports and information on social media', the newspaper reported.[11] He was one of the 'UAE Five' activists who had been jailed in 2011 – and later pardoned – for insulting the country and its leaders.

It meant many of the prominent activists I'd met or followed during my two and a half years living in the Gulf had ended up in jail. Even more striking was that they'd expected it to happen. In Syria's uprising, you risked imprisonment and even death if you opposed the government – but the combination of opposition-held areas and wider chaos meant you had a chance of survival or evading capture. In a tightly controlled Gulf state, however, there was no escape. If they wanted you, they came for you with a mix of sanctions including asset freezes, travel bans and – ultimately – imprisonment. Instead of the viper's strike on dissent, it was the constrictor's squeeze.

Like their four fellow Gulf Cooperation Council members, Saudi and the UAE were monarchies in which ultimate power lay with hereditary rulers. The Gulf states were forged from the power struggles and alliances between often nomadic clans. The modern countries sprang up over the span of almost half the twentieth century as leaders built authority and British imperialism in the region waned. The new nations ran on old principles attuned to an era of survival in the harsh desert environment and its skirmishes: the power of the leader was absolute and unquestioned, on the understanding that he would rule his people wisely and benevolently.

By 2018, Gulf politics and its international projection were increasingly defined by MbS and Crown Prince Mohammed bin Zayed, his counterpart in Abu Dhabi, the United Arab Emirates

capital. Both men were the driving forces in their countries despite
not being the monarchs. Mohammed bin Zayed – also known in
the west as MbZ – was technically number two to his brother
Khalifa, the country's president. But MbZ had been the de facto
leader for years.

Both Saudi Arabia and the UAE were long-standing allies of the
West. They were the world's two biggest arms importers in 2017
by some measures, with many of the weapons coming from the
US and western European countries – though the totals are much
lower than the economically existential amounts suggested by
President Donald Trump. US general Jim Mattis, who later
became defence secretary under Trump, approvingly dubbed the
UAE 'little Sparta' for its fight against Islamist militants in Libya
and Iraq. Washington, Riyadh and Abu Dhabi grew closer still
after the Trump administration pulled out of the international Iran
nuclear deal in 2018 as part of a much more aggressive approach
to the regime in Tehran.

Since MbS became defence minister on King Abdullah's death
in 2015, he had worked in concert with the UAE on an increasingly hawkish regional foreign policy. The two countries had
blockaded their erstwhile regional partner Qatar, become more
openly confrontational with Iran and prosecuted a bloody war in
Yemen against the Shia Houthi militias there. By late 2018, the
UN estimated fourteen million people – half the country's population – were at risk of famine because they were entirely reliant
on external aid.[12]

Some in the West preferred to focus on MbS's moves to relax
his kingdom's strict social code. He allowed people of different
genders to mix and public performances of dance and cinema to
be held. After years of harsh control, enforced by the country's
feared religious police, these were significant changes, but the
whole approach also had a strong sense of bread and circuses about
it. In a strategy also used by some Western governments,

eye-catching cultural policies left the country's deeper structures of power and wealth intact.

There were early warnings of the harsh authoritarian underlay to the new Saudi veneer of permissiveness. Late in 2017, the regime rounded up more than two hundred royals and prominent business people and imprisoned scores of them in Riyadh's opulent Ritz-Carlton hotel on suspicion of corruption. I had once attended a conference at the hotel, where monstrous chandeliers and soaring bronze stallions loomed over the guests as they networked during the breaks between sessions. A French oilman remarked sniffily that it was 'like Versailles, but in bad taste'.

Those imprisoned there were released only once they had agreed to hand over large sums amounting to more than $100 billion. Authorities presented these as settlements of the allegations. Some of the detainees were members of the late King Abdullah's branch of the Saudi royal family, a rival to MbS's faction. One, a top aide to Prince Turki bin Abdullah, a son of the late king, died apparently after being tortured, the *New York Times* reported.[13] The Saudi government denied ill treatment of any of those held at the Ritz-Carlton. They included Prince Alwaleed bin Talal, the 'Warren Buffett of Arabia', who was Khashoggi's patron. The prince later said his confidential release agreement allowed him to function with 'zero guilt' and 'zero conditions'.[14]

The corruption crackdown won plaudits in Saudi Arabia and abroad but also raised big questions about the lack of due process and the allegations of abuses and killing. The authorities shrugged off the concerns.

In August 2018, further contradictions in MbS's supposed social liberalism emerged. His regime reacted furiously to statements by the Canadian government calling for the release of detained activists. Ottawa broadcast the demand on social media, rather than raise it only privately through diplomatic channels. Riyadh branded it 'a blatant interference in the Kingdom's domestic affairs, against basic international norms and all international protocols'. It expelled the Canadian ambassador, withdrew its envoy from Ottawa and scrapped new bilateral trade.

It showed the dark side of one-man rule, even when put to supposedly progressive ends. It can be capricious – and it is inherently contradictory. While ostensibly modernising in spirit, it requires discussion and disagreement to be stifled.

Most Gulf governments – with the notable exception of Bahrain – hadn't faced any widespread popular uprisings. But the Western silence was disturbing. For all their surface urbanity, the Arabian monarchies oversaw countries where public debate was quelled, activists persecuted and leaders almost never held to account.

These regimes were also not so far from the West in spirit as some might like to think. Transparency in government and access to official information had developed fitfully in Europe, and there were politicians who would like to see those gains reversed. Some Western authorities had infringed increasingly deeply on civil liberties in the name of national security and combating terrorism, through the use of measures such as detention without trial.

The first Western apologia for Gulf repression I heard on arrival in the region came from an unlikely source: a lawyer for a prominent US firm. Based in the heart of Dubai's financial district, this man was a corporate dealmaker rather than a civil liberties specialist, but that didn't stop him offering me some advice on what I should and should not say. He asked me what stories I was planning to do. After I gave a non-committal answer, he suggested that, if I covered conditions in the United Arab Emirates' much-criticised camps for labourers, my newspaper would 'not be very popular' in these parts. As he leaned back in his chair, he warmed to his theme and offered me some advice.

'I know this sounds awful,' he said, 'but I would play it safe.'

Play it safe: three words that seemed to loom large for expatriates who took the Gulf shilling and, as one acquaintance described it, 'put their brains in the freezer'. I lost count of the number of times I'd heard or read remarks from foreign professionals along the lines of: 'Well, if you keep your head down here and don't say anything stupid, then there's nothing to worry about.' The Gulf countries' asphyxiation of debate on any sensitive topic couldn't exist without the support of foreigners, particularly Westerners, who prop up the system either implicitly or explicitly. Some are at least honest about their views: one British public relations adviser to a Gulf monarchy told me breezily over breakfast one day that he didn't really believe in democracy and much preferred the Arabian Peninsula way of governing.

The atmosphere felt all the more disorienting because familiar songs from life in the West had a different tune in the desert. In my first weeks in the UAE, *Time Out* published a guide that stated baldly how the country's laws were 'fair' and 'there to protect you'. The article went on to explain how you could be jailed for bouncing a cheque or having sex with anyone, man or woman, to whom you weren't married.

At a diplomatic level, the same Western powers who had condemned arbitrary political detentions by Libya's Colonel Gaddafi and Syria's Assad seemed much more tolerant of human rights abuses of their Gulf allies. Few were surprised at the lack of concern from Britain, which had been scouring the region for investment to prop up its ailing economy since David Cameron's coalition government came to power in 2010. Cameron swept through the Gulf in late 2012, in an effort to secure multi-billion pound warplane orders from Saudi Arabia and the UAE. He also succeeded in ironing out a diplomatic wrinkle that had seen Britain's BP excluded from the bidding for a huge forthcoming UAE oil concession.

The US, deeply entrenched in the Gulf through oil and military bases, also had soothing words for its Arabian Peninsula hosts after the Arab Spring began. When the USS *Rushmore* docked in 2013 at Abu Dhabi's vast new Khalifa Port, Michael H. Corbin, Washington's ambassador to the UAE, hailed it as a historic moment and 'yet another symbol of the strong bilateral relationship that the United States shares with the United Arab Emirates'.[15] The same week he told a newspaper in an interview that the announcement of the UAE's trial of ninety-four people accused of plotting to topple the government was 'not a human rights issue', as the authorities' evidence would be tested in court. 'When you look at countries that are under the spotlight for human rights,' Corbin said, 'this is not one of them.'[16]

Reading UAE newspapers became a Kremlinological exercise in deciphering the real story between the lines. Articles reported people being sentenced to death, without any details of their names, the evidence against them or details of what they were supposed to have done. Police allegations were routinely reported as fact, with no suggestion they needed to be corroborated or to withstand cross-examination. Foreigners were put on trial for flicking drivers a finger or for kissing in public or having babies while unmarried, while Emiratis who killed people in cars or with guns often received light sentences. Many accounts yelled inconsistencies and suggested potential injustices, yet no journalists ever commented critically on them.

Public life in many Gulf countries embodies the truth that the most effective kind of censorship is the kind that is understood and doesn't need to be enforced. *The National*, the Abu Dhabi government-owned newspaper launched to claims of independence in 2008, was a professionally produced publication with many excellent journalists and plenty of good foreign coverage. But its domestic stories read more like *Pravda*. While some articles did contain mild criticisms of logistical aspects of life in the UAE, such as road safety or urban services, there was naturally a dearth of pieces that criticised the rulers or raised big questions about the direction of the country. 'It's got worse and worse,' a talented *National* reporter lamented to me as long ago as 2013. 'It feels like a vice is tightening ... we were basically ordered to pump out more propaganda and less criticism of Abu Dhabi. Since the [political] crackdown they have been more cagey. They want us to do less of the very little bad news we cover – and more of the press releases.'

The Gulf monarchies' complete social control crystallised during the 2010 trial of Sheikh Issa bin Zayed, a half-brother of the UAE's ruler. He was filmed, in footage later broadcast on US television, as part of a gang that tortured an Afghan trader. The attackers fired bullets within inches of the man's body, beat him with a cattle prod and a plank of wood with a nail embedded, and then drove over him in a 4 x 4. Several men were jailed for their part in the attack, two for sodomising their victim with a stick, yet Sheikh Issa was acquitted on the grounds that he had been drugged by the two men who videoed the assault as part of a blackmail plot. That pair – former business associates of the Sheikh – were each sentenced in absentia to five years in jail. Not only was Sheikh Issa deemed blameless, but he was even held to be the victim and those who had provided evidence against him felons. Sheikh Abdullah, the foreign minister (and half-brother to Sheikh Issa), noted that it was impossible for the government to interfere in the case, as the judiciary acted independently.

The UAE judicial process made international headlines again in November 2018 over the case of Matthew Hedges. The thirty-one-year-old British research student received a life sentence for spying in what his family said was a trumped-up case. The affair triggered a brief diplomatic spat between London and Abu Dhabi. It was fixed after some days when the UAE gave Hedges a pardon – but insisted on his guilt and issued a recording of him confessing to being a captain in MI6, a rank that does not exist in the British foreign intelligence service.

The Hedges case also highlighted the influence of the UAE's growing soft international power. Some fans of Manchester City, which has enjoyed success under the well-financed ownership of Sheikh Mansour bin Zayed al-Nahyan, half-brother of the UAE president, leapt to the country's defence. That sparked a backlash from other City supporters. As a *Guardian* comment piece observed: 'The emirates have spent big to win our affection. Matthew Hedges' case makes us think again.'[17]

Football soon threw up another public relations problem for the UAE authorities' efforts to present a benign face to the world. The Emirates kicked off a 'Year of Tolerance' by hosting the Asian Cup soccer tournament in early 2019. The problem from Abu Dhabi's point of view: the UAE lost heavily to Qatar, its regional neighbour with whom it is in bitter dispute. Qatar then went on to win the tournament. Emirati fans had thrown shoes on to the pitch at the Qatar game; the UAE then unsuccessfully tried to get Qatar booted out of the tournament for allegedly fielding ineligible players. Omani fans gave Qatar vicarious support in the final against Japan, as the regional rift meant there weren't any Qatari fans present.[18] UAE-based newspapers wrote up the match as Japan's defeat, rather than Qatar's victory.

Gulf countries – like every society – are grappling with the anxieties of modernity. They have changed more and faster than most places. The culture of the tough desert Bedouin and their tightly bound kin groups has been overlaid by a kind of hyper-capitalism of industrial modernity and giant mall materialism. Dubai has led the way in selling itself as a place where East meets West, a hub for the world through its Emirates airline. Now main metropolises of the region recall the era of classical city states, importing foreign labour to build their skyscrapers. In the UAE, more than three quarters of the population are estimated to be foreigners, most of them men.

Such seismic social shifts – and the good and bad they bring – naturally spark debate in private. It also surfaces from time to time in public. In an article in February 2013, a respected think tank, the Gulf Research Center, deplored the way the 'tribal concept' of 'Sheikh knows better' had been parlayed by the region's leaders into the running of an industrialised society supposedly governed by institutions. The think tank traced this personalisation of power partly to the way imperial Britain gave leaders special status and interacted with them alone, over the heads of the people.[19]

'The prevailing attitudes, which still apply every day, reflect an enormous disrespect of the people's basic rights and a disregard of their dignity,' the think tank said. 'The concept of "Sheikh knows better" assumes that rational thinking and wisdom is the monopoly of a very few while immaturity and ignorance prevails among the rest of the population.'

The article went on to note how, with the arrival of the Gulf countries' petrobillions, the source of rulers' authority shifted from leadership to ownership. Their near-total control over their countries' resources gives them a crushing political power they never enjoyed in the days when they were trying to eke out an existence in the desert. In some ways, it seemed to me, they operated like the British Victorian pseudo-philanthropists, providing their workers with the basic necessities of life but holding vast wealth back for themselves.

As the Gulf Research Center article put it: 'Satisfying economic needs and demands and maintaining a welfare state cannot, and should not, be a substitute for civil and political rights.'

Those comments highlighted a signal weakness of the supposedly benign strongman rule that Western countries had historically been happy to support. It lacked capacity for self-correction – or self-termination. Five years in power became ten, became twenty, became forty. However young these rulers might be when

they start out, like the millennial MbS, the result tends to be ossi-
fication – with its associated risks of decline and decay.

The fate of another absolute monarchy offered a glimpse of a
possible future awaiting Saudi Arabia. Brunei, an Indian Ocean apart
from the Gulf kingdom, had also once been in the grip of an energetic young ruler. Sultan Hassanal Bolkiah had taken the throne at
the age of twenty-one,[20] a decade more junior even than MbS when
he became Saudi Crown Prince. By March 2019, the Sultan of
Brunei was the world's longest-ruling executive leader and second
only to Britain's Queen Elizabeth II among longest-presiding
monarchs. More than half a century after his coronation, he oversaw
a state that still had oil and peace – but no space for politics or public
debate on how it should adapt to survive in a turbulent world.

I visited Brunei less than three months before the Sultan's Golden
Jubilee. He had ruled since 1967, when his father abdicated and
ceded him the throne of this tiny state, which is almost surrounded
by Malaysian territory on the north side of Borneo. The sultanate
had alliances with the West and particularly deep ties with Britain,
which had played a crucial role in putting down an uprising against
the monarchy in 1962 (a counter-insurgency in which the young
British soldier and future Liberal Democrat leader Paddy Ashdown
had fought). Brunei was one of the last parts of the British Empire
to become independent, staying under London's overall control
until 1984.

The Sultan had become one of the world's richest men, while
his kingdom had remained prosperous and tranquil for decades. So
it should have done. It had oil wealth and a population of fewer
than half a million people to cater for. The question – as for the
Gulf petrostates – was how much more should have been done,
given all that wealth and time. The available evidence suggested
the answer was: quite a bit.

The Brunei monarchy's quiet accumulation of vast wealth blew up into an international scandal in the 1990s. An official report suggested the sultan's brother Prince Jefri had misappropriated billions of dollars for his own personal use – an allegation the prince denied. The affair triggered a bitter fight within the royal family and then urgent action to repair the damage.

The Sultan, who had celebrated his Silver Jubilee in a gilded chariot hauled by dozens of subjects, reinvented his rule along more austere lines. He made it avowedly more Islamic and signalled the possible future introduction of punishments including amputation and stoning to death. He also brooked no questioning. Now, at a moment in history when oil revenues were declining, and the country urgently needed to adapt to social, economic and generational change, the Sultan was tightening his grip.

'That's what it's really all about here – the fact that we can't critique the government and the Sultan,' said one frustrated young Bruneian, whom I'll call Emran. 'Without criticism, how are they going to improve?'

On my first night in Brunei's waterside capital of Bandar Seri Begawan, I had dinner with a group of young local people at an outdoor cafe. They were welcoming and chatty. Some worked, as many Bruneians do, in state institutions, while others were in the private sector. They recommended I sample two culinary mainstays: buttermilk chicken and hot sweet tea. One noted how a typical rich Brunei diet lacks neither sugar nor animal fats. 'That's diabetes in a glass and a heart attack on a plate,' he joked as my food arrived.

The talk turned to the impact of a sugar tax that had been introduced earlier in 2017 and was only now starting to affect prices. It was part of a package of measures launched by the government to mitigate the impact of the sharp fall in the

international oil price. It was a shock in a country where low taxes
meant gasoline was cheaper than bottled water. Pension cuts were
also coming, though slowly. 'Brunei has launched austerity – in as
much as Brunei does austerity,' a young government worker
commented wryly.

The remark hinted at a complacency that some thoughtful
Bruneians wanted the country to shake. While the sultanate is still
among the richest in the world per capita,[21] it has vast disparities
of wealth – and pockets of poverty.It ranked thirty-ninth in the
UN's 2018 world human development index,[22] which uses measures including life expectancy and quality of education. That
placed it equal with Saudi Arabia and just behind Slovakia.

The people with whom I spent my first evening were certainly
privileged. Many of the group had spent some time outside the
country and so had an acute awareness of the wider world and
Brunei's position as a small state within it. The sultanate was one
of several nations in its region that were in dispute with Beijing
over South China Sea territorial rights. It knew it couldn't win in
military terms, so it had tried to turn its silence on the conflict
into leverage for investment. It was part of a delicate effort to keep
the relationship with China close but also at 'arm's length', the first
government worker said. Brunei had tried to push back gently
whenever Beijing came up with more aggressive plans to make
the sultanate more dependent. 'They come and say: "We will build
you a city!" And we say: "But we don't want a city!"' he said.

On the domestic front, there was a sense of scepticism that
things were ever going to change too much. I was told that Prince
Jefri had been partially rehabilitated after his estrangement from
the Sultan over the financial scandal. The once outcast prince was
back in the family fold, though without a formal government
position. The authorities seemed to have accepted the loss of a
good part of the multi-billion-dollar sum at the centre of the
dispute. As one person put it: 'They wrote it off.'

Later, one of the group gave me a lift back to my hotel. As we sped through the capital's near-deserted streets, we talked more about how Brunei was different now from the high-living pre-scandal period. The days of expatriates supping on champagne and strawberries as they watched the Sultan play polo had gone. Brunei had moved into a stricter age, the ruling family's excess now the subject of a kind of organised forgetting. Nor was any foreign country that valued its relationship with this energy-rich and strategically valuable South China Sea foothold likely to make a fuss.

'It's common knowledge what happened in Brunei,' my host reflected of the great royal imbroglio. 'But it's like people pardon it all. It's forgiven.'

The Prince Jefri case had its roots in his fifteen-year stewardship of the Brunei Investment Agency (BIA), a national wealth fund he was appointed to lead on its creation in 1983. The agency was tasked with holding and managing government funds. Between 1983 and 1998, about US$40 billion of so-called special transfers were made from the BIA. The government hired a team of independent investigators to work out what had happened to the money. The probe concluded that $14.8 billion was paid to accounts of Prince Jefri, $8 billion to accounts of the Sultan, while the destination and purpose of a further $13.5 billion could not be established. Just $3.8 billion of the money was used for government purposes.

The government alleged Prince Jefri had misappropriated the funds sent to his account. With the blessing of the Sultan, the authorities demanded Prince Jefri give back assets bought with the money. Prince Jefri resisted and denied any wrongdoing.

The case went global when the Brunei authorities issued a London lawsuit against Prince Jefri in 2000. The subsequent claims and counterclaims alleged both lavish spending and a tawdry lifestyle. It emerged that Jefri owned a yacht called *Tits*, with tenders called *Nipple 1* and *Nipple 2*. Jefri did not deny he had used BIA money to buy 'properties in various parts of the world, as well as valuable works of art, jewellery, motor cars, aircraft and other chattels', as a 2007 judgment by Britain's Privy Council – still the ultimate legal authority over Brunei under its post-independence arrangements – put it. The court ruling also noted that Prince Jefri claimed he only acted on the command of the Sultan and 'at all times had the authority to make the respective transactions'.[23]

Prince Jefri agreed a settlement with the Brunei authorities months after the original court claim. He undertook to hand over assets including seventy properties in the UK, the US, France and the Philippines, according to the Privy Council judgment. Among the properties in the US were the prestigious Palace Hotel in New York and the Hotel Bel-Air in Los Angeles.

Other Jefri assets went for auction in Brunei. The 2001 sale ran to ten thousand lots. It featured gold-plated lavatory paper holders, soap dishes and taps, hundreds of Victorian-style lamp posts and thousands of tons of the finest Italian, Indian and South American marble, according to reports of the time.[24]

The legal slurry and attendant bad publicity from the BIA affair continued for years. There were disputes between the parties over whether the settlement agreement was being honoured. Although Jefri had transferred five boats, nine aircraft, more than a hundred paintings, six hundred properties and two thousand cars to the BIA, he still retained billions of dollars of other assets, a 2008 judgment in the US court of Delaware said. Jefri 'took the position that certain actions by the BIA had violated the Settlement Agreement, thereby discharging him from complying with its terms', the ruling Judge Leo Strine said.[25]

Judge Strine also noted that Jefri had never been prosecuted. Perhaps this was because the Sultan 'still cared for him', the judge mulled drily – or perhaps because he had 'misappropriated funds for the Sultan's use as well'.

'For whatever reason, Jefri escaped a long term in the jailhouse,' Judge Strine wrote.

The dispute spawned further lurid spin-off litigation from former advisers and associates of Prince Jefri. One alleged in a court case in London that the Prince had kept up to forty prostitutes at the Dorchester Hotel – an allegation both the prince and the hotel denied. The case was settled. In an earlier lawsuit, Shannon Marketic, a former Miss USA, claimed she was among seven women held captive and forced to perform sex acts after agreeing to do promotional work in Brunei. The case foundered when the Sultan – who along with Jefri, denied the claims – successfully claimed sovereign immunity.

Bruneians always knew their royals lived well. But the scale and scope of the alleged excesses was shocking – particularly for a Muslim majority country. Most of all, it highlighted how, in normal circumstances and to this day, the people of the country had no idea how money that should have benefited them was being spent.

'Everything is incredibly opaque,' said one long-time Western observer of Brunei. 'The oil revenue is top-sliced for the benefit of the royal family. What you see in the government figures is what's left. So you never really see the full picture.'

I had a little tour one night of the relics of the Brunei royal blow-out. There was a seaside Millionaires' – or Billionaires' – Row of vast royal houses, including former Jefri palaces. An amusement park lay abandoned. 'All the rides, including roller coasters and simulators, used to be free. You just walked in,' one of my hosts for the evening reminisced.

We drove on along the near-deserted beachside roads to the Empire Hotel & Country Club – a signature of the opulence of the late Jefri period. It sat on a tapering peninsula of the country's north-east corner. Sail north from here and you would be in the midst of the reefs, rocks and islands that Beijing is trying to use to cement its claim to more than ninety percent of the South China Sea – even though an international court ruled against it in 2016. These include the Spratly Islands, some of the most disputed territory in the world. No fewer than six territories have claims to some part of the archipelago – China, Brunei, Malaysia, Vietnam, Taiwan and the Philippines.

The Empire Club was opened in 2000, after the royal family legal disputes had already begun. It features a Jack Nicklaus-designed golf course. Nicklaus's corporate website proclaims how 'towering Royal palms, blossoming bougainvilleas and other exotic shrubs provide a stately arrival at a property which is regarded as one of the finest in the world.'[26] The club's own publicity declares: 'The Empire has become synonymous with Brunei: reflecting the country's majestic and cultural heritage.'[27]

The Emperor suite offered guests 'access to privacy and security unrivalled anywhere else', according to the club website. It had its own elevator, swimming pool, steam room and sauna. 'The private movie theatre and grand piano round up a beautiful private night in,' the blurb added.

A vast conical chandelier in the main lobby set the tone for visitors. I gazed round the cavernous atrium and thought of the air conditioning bill. A glass cabinet offered 'Unexpected Treasures', including a B$570 (about £325) perfume, to the few locals and tourists drawn by curiosity. We saw only a handful of people, as we toured the pools, dunes and restaurants on this Friday night. 'Crazy place', my host said. 'Even crazier that you can just drive round it.'

I asked why Prince Jefri was remembered, indulgently it seemed to me, for these colossally wasteful projects. 'People are quite shallow and superficial. They come here and think it's really grand,' came the answer. 'It would be a lot more effort to start an uprising than to sit back and enjoy the free theme parks and nice bonus and good pension.'

But there was certainly anger as well as apathy in Brunei. How much existed of each was hard to gauge, as strict sedition laws stifled dissent and deterred people from putting their names to criticism. Anonymous social media users posted pointed material such as a graph showing how Brunei's gross domestic product had fallen behind that of its regional neighbour Singapore. 'Without welfare many might have difficulties standing on their own,' commented one poster on Reddit. Another condemned the country's 'idiotic government system'.[28]

After the Jefri debacle, the Sultan had radically revamped his rule. In 2014, Brunei put in place a tough Islamic criminal penal code. This threatened fines or prison sentences for failing to perform Friday prayers and becoming pregnant while unmarried. Authorities planned a year later to introduce whipping and amputations for stealing or for Muslims who drank alcohol, followed after another year by the death penalty for acts including adultery and sodomy. The Sultan said: 'We are not doing this just for the sake of it, we are doing this by order of Allah and what is in the Koran.'[29]

The surprise change drew immediate condemnation from international rights groups. It quickly spawned a campaign to boycott Brunei state-owned properties, among them the Dorchester Collection hotel group that includes the Beverly Hills Hotel. Foreign government officials said privately it risked driving investment away, since multinational companies would be under both legal and ethical pressure not to expose LGBT employees to such risks.

The Brunei government in turn appeared taken aback by the strength of the criticism. It delayed implementation of the second and third phases of the law changes, though it did not cancel them. In early 2018, local media reported that the religious affairs minister had promised the next phase of the code would be carried out at 'the right administrative time'.

Some were sceptical about the reasons for the Sultan's religious zeal. Emran observed a trend – which I'd also noticed in the Middle East – of people who partied hard and slept around in their youth growing pious as they aged, in what almost seemed to be a kind of penance. 'When they are young they have a lot of entertainment,' he said. 'When they get older they need to make up for it.'

The Sultan now had to distance himself from his past extravagances. It was also a useful stance to appeal to the country's strong strand of social conservatism. 'He's done a complete 180,' Emran said. 'It's not enough for him to make up for his sins. The rest of his country has to do it alongside him.'

What goes on underneath the surface of a superficially strict society is of course another matter. One night in Brunei, Emran took me to a speakeasy in the capital. I waited self-consciously at the entrance to the building until he arrived with a friend. Inside, we walked down a corridor to a door that looked like any other. We knocked and after a short delay heard the sound of a lock being turned.

Inside was a large low-lit room that reminded me of a cheap and cheerful student bar of my youth. The air was thick with smoke that recalled club nights in the UK before the smoking ban in 2007. The main feature of the room apart from the bar was a wall of four electronic dartboards. A group of ethnically Chinese people drank cheerily nearby, while an older white guy sat at the counter on his own. As dens of illicit debauchery went, it was, in truth, a little underwhelming.

The three of us settled down at a small round table and took the cans of beer offered by the barman. I asked Emran if the authorities knew about this place. He looked at me with amusement. 'Are you kidding?' he said. 'Government officials and executives come here – it's a great place to network!'

His friend was a Chinese-Bruneian who worked in finance. People of Chinese descent were treated as 'second-class citizens' in the country, he said, articulating a common complaint both here and in Malaysia. Chinese investors and Bruneians of Chinese descent were popularly seen as dominating economic life. The friend noted how 'we' – a revealing choice of words to describe Chinese companies – were building two of three big bridges then under construction.

In Brunei, authorities had made it hard for Chinese-Bruneians to own land and shareholdings in companies, he said. The post-Jefri Islamicisation of Brunei life had also had an impact: the government had cracked down hard on daytime eating during Ramadan the previous year. It had also banned the celebration of Chinese New Year in public and restricted the famous Lion dances.

'The royal family is using religion as a way of controlling people,' he said. 'The pattern is that they make a law change that gets us worried.'

We left multiple cans later, after the barman called last orders in the early hours. I realised then that Emran intended to drive us home – and I didn't really have any other option. Taxi drivers in Brunei were few, generally worked by appointment – and the two I knew were unlikely to appreciate being woken in the early hours by a half-cut customer. Emran had drunk too much and drove too fast: for the middle-aged me, it was the wrong kind of wild. It also seemed a manufactured thrill in a country of few natural ones. As Emran's financier friend had observed wistfully earlier: 'The thing is, in Brunei, we are too comfortable.'

★   ★   ★

Brunei's rigid status quo would never have existed had it not been for British support. UK troops including the famed Nepalese Gurkhas had foiled the putsch launched in 1962 by Indonesian-backed rebels against Sultan Omar Ali Saifuddien III, the present ruler's father. A state of emergency enacted in Brunei at the time remained in place when I visited more than half a century later.

The bond between Britain and the ruling Bolkiahs forged by those events was evident in Brunei's modern security arrangements. The present Sultan maintained a military unit that included Gurkhas who had retired from the British army. Dozens of UK officers and other troops were also seconded to the Brunei military.

Even more striking was that the Sultan funded a battalion of active British Army Gurkhas. The soldiers were based near some of the country's main oil industry operations, in which Royal Dutch Shell dominated. They rotated in and out from active duty in Afghanistan and other conflict zones. The British military also used the forest that still covered the majority of the country for jungle warfare training.

The relationship suited the UK well. It got a paid-for strategic base in Asia during an era of British military cuts. It was also London's strongest diplomatic relationship among the ten countries of the Association of Southeast Asian Nations. Those links seemed likely to become still more important once Brexit left London searching for friends in the world.

But the financing of an active British military unit by the head of a foreign state raised obvious questions. It was unclear what would happen were the Sultan to request it to deploy in an external security crisis, such as a South China Sea territorial confrontation – or if he were to call for it to fight another domestic uprising. The terms of the UK–Brunei deal were confidential and it seemed likely that London's response to any threat would be ad hoc.

One British former government official conceded that it was possible to argue that the relationship was 'very unwise'. Any uprising might have foreign support – or the Brunei government might claim so – leaving London in a difficult political position. 'You could see some sort of external influence leading to internal unrest. How could you separate these out?' the former official asked rhetorically.

The uneasy Western foothold in Brunei has become still more important because of the rise of China and its assertion of its power in the region. Beijing-backed investment in the sultanate has grown sharply, including bridges, a spice export factory and a $3.5 billion petrochemical plant. Guangxi Beibu Gulf Port arrived in 2017 as a partner in operating Brunei's largest container terminal, as part of China's 'Belt and Road' project to build infrastructure across Asia.

All this has left Western governments in no mood to rock the boat. One Western official insisted Brunei was not a kleptocracy – though the sums in the Prince Jefri case were almost inconceivably large. 'The corruption you see in Angola or Venezuela or Russia doesn't exist here,' the official said. 'That said, there is an absolute monarchy, it's a large family – and they don't live in poverty.'

It was a similar story to the Gulf petrostates. There was no clear accounting, so it was never evident how much the family was taking for itself – and what percentage of the total this was. 'You have to look at the way a royal family, particularly when it's spoiled by oil wealth, has a completely different set of standards to everyone else,' said the British former government official. 'And if there's profligate spending, it's just something the royals do.'

The Sultan did enjoy a level of trust and esteem. But for all the devotion, I also noticed a certain chafing – especially among younger people – against an old order that was becoming still more conservative. Some sensed a country retreating from modernity rather than grappling with it.

I chatted over coffee one night with a group of young LGBT Bruneians. They were a mixture of men, women and one transgender person. None, of course, could be publicly open about their sexuality, so I have not used their real names.

Abdul, who sported a pile of slick black hair and had a background in public relations, surprised me when he opened up by saying that Brunei had been 'misrepresented' in the media over its application of Islamic criminal law. His point was that, as long as you didn't reveal your sexuality in public, it was 'not really' a problem. 'Not really' didn't seem to me very comforting – and of course it meant that LGBT people were forever forced into secrecy. 'You just keep it to yourself,' he said. 'You don't hold hands in public.'

Hussein, a slim young man in ripped jeans, agreed the practical point that it was possible to have relationships discreetly. He'd been able to hook up with men on the Grindr app. He saw the authorities' application of the tougher laws as political. 'Maybe it's one of the ways the regime wants to keep a grip on this country – by telling its people to be religious,' he said.

Nour was transgender and lived a double life. At work and in the family home, Nour wore big sweaters and hair tied up to present as the man she was born as. Outside of those circles, she presented as a woman. She explained the divide as a necessary artifice in a conservative society. 'You have this understanding in this culture that if you don't see and you don't say, then it's not real,' she said.

The conversation segued into broader worries that the country was not changing fast enough from its strict paternalistic model. Sharper business people from countries such as China and South Korea were reaping the economic benefits, members of the group said. Bruneians were too dependent on government, several agreed. The group, none of whom was older than thirty, also worried that the leaders were all 'veterans', as one put it diplomatically. Efforts to diversify the economy beyond oil and gas seemed to lack urgency.

'It's too late. This should have been done many years ago,' Hussein said of the reforms. 'Now the oil price has gone down and everyone is scrambling. It's unfortunate it happened this way.'

As the evening wore on, the conversation became darker. Abdul said the Islamic legal clampdown 'kind of made me feel I don't want to work for the government' – even though the state had paid for his educational scholarship.

Hussein, who had experience in the media, pointed to the harshness of censorship. Journalists were advised to consult before publishing on subjects that would 'stir things up', such as South China Sea territorial rights – or Islamic law. 'The government is tightening its grip on us,' he said. 'You will get a call the next day if it's something negative. You will be invited in for a meeting.'

The *Brunei Times*, one of two main English language newspapers, had to shut down abruptly in mysterious circumstances in 2016. Shortly before, it had published – and later apologised for – an article that suggested economic problems lay behind the Saudi Arabian government's decision to raise visa fees for foreign pilgrims travelling to Mecca. Hussein picked up an edition of the *Borneo Bulletin*, the surviving paper, which is largely a mouthpiece for officialdom. 'Let's just face reality. The mainstream media in Brunei is boring,' Hussein said, brandishing his copy to knowing laughter from the others.

Zainab, a private sector worker dressed in a flowery top with flowing sleeves, said, 'We are under a microscope. It feels like there is CCTV everywhere here.' Her neighbour, a student in white T-shirt and jeans who was the youngest of the group, nodded: 'Constantly monitored'.

Zainab pointed also to a friction in government policy of a kind that often troubles authoritarian regimes, including in the Gulf. Brunei wanted people to be better educated to help diversify the economy, but it did not want to encourage questioning of the political order. 'They want you to be a thinking person. At the same time, they want to limit that as well. It's a contradiction,' Zainab said. 'It's very dangerous for them to have a thinking generation in Brunei.'

Younger Bruneians' best hope – and one far from certain to be realised – was that exposure to the wider world would make a difference. The Internet had allowed for more public discussion of LGBT people's situation in Brunei – although caution was still needed and a government crackdown could come at any moment. 'The younger generation are comfortable on social media telling their stories. That makes people understand more,' Zainab said. 'There's a greater visibility. When people see more of you, you are the next norm. We are the next norm – the new norm.'

Some of the six acknowledged they were insulated to a degree from possible official sanctions because they were from relatively privileged backgrounds. Nour, whose mother and father both had high-status private sector jobs, said she was 'not scared'. Hussein pointed out how hard traditional Islamic law made it to secure a conviction. 'What you need is four witnesses who saw the actual penetration thing,' he said.

But Brunei's version of a sexual 'don't ask, don't tell' is very dangerous. It makes it impossible to report a sex crime against you, for example, if it would involve divulging to the police you are LGBT. There is also no way to set up organisations to advise LGBT people on sexual health and other matters, as all non-governmental groups have to be registered with the authorities. It is a precarious existence – socially restrictive, psychologically claustrophobic, and with the lurking threat of draconian punishment.

'I feel like we are in this safety bubble,' Zainab concluded. 'But we are walking on eggshells.'

In April 2019, Brunei's government enacted the law that made anal sex and adultery punishable by stoning to death. It reminded me of a similar power play during my time living in Nigeria in the years after 2000, when some states in the mainly Muslim north had introduced the same penalties. I'd covered the case of Amina Lawal, a young woman condemned to be stoned for adultery – but who was reprieved on appeal, as have been others who have received the same sentence.

People whose judgement I trusted thought the new punishments – which also included amputation for stealing – were unlikely to be carried out in Brunei. The country's mission to the EU sent the same message in a memo to the European parliament, saying that it was 'extremely difficult ... in this day and age' to find witnesses of the piety needed to testify against the accused.[30] But the menace of the new law was there, whatever the official policy on enforcement.

The introduction of the punishments triggered an outcry in the West. Celebrities including the actor George Clooney and the pop star Elton John called for a boycott of Brunei-owned hotels. In May 2019, the Sultan said an existing Brunei moratorium on the death penalty would extend to the new law.

I had left Brunei wondering if it would still be governed by the Sultan's successor in another fifty years' time, when the young people I'd met would all be pensioners. No one foresaw imminent revolution, or anything like it – but it is equally a mistake to assume that longevity equals eternality. As one of the group had put it to me: 'Give us, the new generation, a chance to try. Don't stop us.'

My final act in Brunei was a bit of tourism: a weekend in the rainforests of Temburong. The place was stunning – and still relatively untouched. There was a helicopter pad for royals and others who couldn't be bothered with the speedboat, road and pirogue. I watched as a Draco lizard glided from tree to tree, camouflaged entirely against the trunks between puffs of its orange throat fan. A gibbon whooped in the distance.

Yet even here, in this remote idyll of a tightly controlled micro-state, it was possible to hear rumblings of frustration. I chatted to a Bruneian student and noted how we'd had to arrive that morning via a detour because both connecting bridges were out of action. Her riposte served as an indictment of the decay that even self-proclaimed benign absolute monarchies seem invariably to over-see. 'They don't repair,' she shot back without missing a beat. 'They just let things rot.'

2

Don't Insult the Dog

The shouts began as soon as the prisoners started their slow shuffle from prison bus to the Bangkok court complex where they were to be tried. Relatives and friends behind the mesh fence cried out at loved ones among the brown-uniformed cohort. The detainees jerked their way awkwardly past, dragging the shackles on their arms and legs. To my left, a stylish woman in a short black dress balanced her handbag and iced coffee on the handrail as she strained forward against it, the backs of her feet rising up from silver high-heeled shoes. Looking around me at the wave of humanity that had just risen from the wooden visitors' benches, I reflected that there were probably enough stories in this one sultry waiting room to keep a half-decent author busy for a lifetime.

The prisoners' loose-fitting garb and close-cropped hair brought to mind the lines of Buddhist monks that snaked elsewhere through the Thai capital. Among the last of the accused to arrive was Prawet Prapanukul. Slender and sharp-chinned, he was a lawyer who had defended people accused of insulting the country's monarchy. Now he was himself facing a possible record 150-year jail sentence for the same offence. Prawet's brother Pravit and sister Janjira pressed towards the gate for a glimpse of their sibling. His sister broke into tears and fell into the comforting arms of a friend.

Prawet himself seemed composed and defiant. He started to yell out messages for his visitors to pass on to friends and families of other inmates. I thought it might be my only chance to talk to him, so I started to call questions via an interpreter through the two wire fences and ten-foot corridor that separated us. It was one of the more bizarre interviews I have conducted. Prawet said he was fine and in good mental shape, neither sad nor depressed. He spoke of the strength of his spirit to continue. 'I am going to fight the case,' he called out. 'No matter how long it takes, I am going to fight.'

His rhetoric was bracing. Few people fought *lèse-majesté* cases in Thailand – for the good reason that they were almost impossible to win. Those who did resist all too often found themselves in a Salem witch trial bind. Whatever the facts, authorities would not dare drop the matter in case they triggered accusations that they themselves had disrespected the monarch.

This is a side of Thailand largely invisible to the millions of tourists who visit the kingdom each year. Most are charmed by all that there is to be charmed by: the markets and food, the temples, the easy if practised warmth of the welcome. The many public portraits of the monarchy are a small part of the tapestry of pictures on holidaymakers' smartphones by the end of their trips.

Thailand's monarchy had also seemed to exert a spell on politicians of the democratic world. For decades, Western governments had lauded the supposedly stabilising influence of King Bhumibol Adulyadej, who became the world's longest-ruling living monarch. Yet Bhumibol's death in 2016 exposed illusions behind his supposedly benevolent stewardship and triggered fears about the country's future under his son and successor.

Prawet's case offers a view into this darker parallel world. It is a realm in which repression underpins the monarchy and the wider system of elite political control. The lawyer was accused of defaming, insulting or expressing malicious intentions towards the king, queen or wider royal family in thirteen separate Facebook statements in early 2017, according to his indictment. He called for the replacement of the monarchy with a republic, said the *lèse-majesté* law was stupid and also insulted the king personally, the charge sheet said.

These were dangerous allegations, given that the new king Maha Vajiralongkorn had a reputation for capriciousness. His wife Srirasmi once told the US ambassador how Vajiralongkorn had made his pet poodle an air chief marshal, according to a US diplomatic cable published by WikiLeaks. When Srirasmi later fell out of favour, her family was purged. Vajiralongkorn divorced her, she was stripped of her royal name, and her parents and three brothers were jailed for *lèse-majesté*.

It was part of a stifling political atmosphere that had intensified around the monarchy during the epic reign of Vajiralongkorn's father. King Bhumibol (pronounced roughly Poom-ee-pon) had died in October 2016 after seven decades on the throne. Scores of people had been investigated and many jailed for *lèse-majesté* during his last years. A taxi driver was imprisoned for two and a half years after being reported by a passenger over remarks he made about social inequality.[1] Another person was arrested over graffiti scrawled on a toilet wall in a shopping mall. In one notorious case, a man was even probed over a Facebook post that allegedly mocked Tongdaeng, Bhumibol's favourite dog and the subject of a bestselling book by the king widely seen as a manual for how he expected the Thai people to behave. As an appreciation of the text in the *Bangkok Post* newspaper put it: 'Tongdaeng is a smart dog that has a deep gratitude towards His Majesty as its owner. The book teaches people to express loyalty and gratitude for the ones who feed and support them.'[2]

Some of the sentences handed down to those found to have insulted the monarch were typical of those given to political prisoners in tyrannies. Each instance of *lèse-majesté* carried a potential jail term of up to fifteen years. Combined with other draconian laws, such as those on sedition and computer crime, dissenters could be put away for decades. In June 2017, a thirty-four-year-old ex-insurance salesman received a thirty-five-year sentence.

The clampdown passed with little criticism from outside. Thailand was one of a group of countries around the world designated major non-NATO military allies by the US. The country of 65 million people was a big destination for Western tourists and an important market for its companies. Western diplomats always paid careful homage to the royals, as they must.

In 2018, the US embassy in Thailand marked two hundred years of relations with the country with an exhibition entitled 'Great and Good Friends', a reference to a 'salutation used by US presidents in addressing the kings of Siam'. The commemoration featured gifts from four former Thai kings and Queen Sirikit, Bhumibol's wife. These included a golden turtle for President Lyndon Johnson's grandson and diamond-embellished purses given to then first ladies Hillary Clinton and Laura Bush. A website devoted to the exhibition described the 1931 visit to the US by King Prajadhipok, when he 'stood atop the newly completed Empire State Building'.[3] He also met the baseball player Babe Ruth and the pilot Amelia Earhart during a trip that 'endeared him to the American public', the account noted. Decades later, his successor-but-one, King Bhumibol, addressed the US Congress.

The longer I spent in Thailand, the harder I found it to reconcile this respect and Thais' supposed universal affection for the monarchy with the cruelty of the *lèse-majesté* laws. Many Thais would say – and many expatriates would parrot – that the whole country loved Bhumibol. They meant it – and it had a degree of truth to it. But it also failed to capture the complexity of the feeling towards a man – and more precisely an institution – that had the power to punish severely those deemed to be showing it insufficient regard.

Democracy in Thailand had been in retreat since the military seized power – again – in May 2014. The arrival of King Vajiralongkorn underscored a pertinent question that applies to all supposedly benevolent dictatorships, particularly monarchies: where did love end and dread begin? And that raised another even more vital point: how long could a modern monarchy remain stable if its authority stemmed in part from intimidation?

Prawet disappeared for so long from the prisoner group that I began to wonder what had happened to him. A friend of his surmised that he was being pressed into a bargain to accept a guilty plea in exchange for a halving of his sentence. This is how most *lèse-majesté* cases ended, mainly because defendants thought no court was likely to acquit them. So ran the circle of fear around Thailand's most venerated institution and proclaimed bedrock of national stability.

I settled back to wait underneath ceiling fans wholly inadequate to the task of keeping this sweaty July day at bay. A smell of fresh pineapple wafted temptingly past my nostrils, suggesting someone was breaching rules against visitors bringing food for prisoners (the last regulation on the list of ten regulations for inmates was: 'Always keep clean'). As the hours ticked on, staff arrived carrying plates of lunchtime rice and soup.

Finally, Prawet reappeared and waited his turn at the well-worn speaking booths. Visitors and inmates separated by the corridor had to talk into microphones and strain to hear the replies broadcast through small speakers. I stood next to a woman whose toddler, dressed in a Mickey Mouse T-shirt, squirmed under the counter. At one point the little boy escaped and had to be recaptured.

Prawet crossed his shackled legs and cupped his left ear to hear. I asked him how his case was going. He said he had turned down the offer of a nineteen-year sentence in exchange for a guilty plea.

He said he had no regrets. For him, his stance was all about an idea, not personal animus. 'I posted to disagree with the system, not a person,' he said. 'What I posted wasn't meant to harm anyone personally. I just expressed my opinion and disagreement.'

'This is what I am,' he continued. 'This is what I thought it was right to do.'

He said he hadn't applied for bail because he knew it wouldn't be given. It generally never was in *lèse-majesté* cases. He said he was putting together a statement to the UN to complain about the *lèse-majesté* law. He echoed the argument made by other campaigners that the harshness of the punishment risked damaging the very institution it was supposed to protect. 'The only way to solve this problem is to do away with this law,' he said. 'It has more downsides than upsides to the institution and the people.'

He noted how the rules had proved a useful way for politicians to silence opponents. This was particularly so under the generals who had taken power in a coup more than three years previously – although he pointed out how it had the downside of making them look repressive, particularly internationally. 'This is used as a political tool to hurt opponents – especially under the military,' he said. 'But it's a *daab song khom*' – a double-edged sword.

He said he had no complaints about the authorities' behaviour towards him in jail. He seemed prepared for a long stay. 'Life in prison is not good but I still get treated a bit better than the other inmates,' he said. 'Because I am a lawyer so I know how to conduct myself.'

Soon visiting time was up. It was somebody else's turn at the booth. With a wave, Prawet was gone.

I went back upstairs from the detention facility to the main exit. In the central lobby there was a large display in honour of the late Bhumibol. Passers-by deferred to the montage with the traditional palms-together honorific known as the *wai*. One panel was devoted to Bhumibol's favourite flowers.

I had visited Prawet's family home just a week or two before, on another dank rainy season day when the threat of a downpour loomed constantly. His sister Janjira and brother Pravit lived in one of a row of tall pastel-painted houses off King Rama IX Road – Bhumibol's honorific, as the ninth king of the Chakri dynasty that began in the late eighteenth century. Behind the dwellings lay a waterway and marshy ground covered in thick grass, a reminder of the swamp into which the sinking metropolis of Bangkok may one day revert. A tortoiseshell cat stalked outside and a dog barked in the distance.

The siblings were welcoming hosts. They had pictures in the downstairs sitting room of Bhumibol, Queen Sirikit and King Chulalongkorn, the most honoured of the country's previous monarchs. We moved to an upstairs area where the blinds were drawn, giving the feel of a house in mourning. A brown divider curtain at the top of the stairs rippled in the current from the air conditioner. I sat on a sofa next to a desk on which a Bhumibol calendar was perched. A table lamp stood beside it, augmenting only feebly the dim light from the single bare bulb on the ceiling.

Janjira, the older of the two by several years, was a handsome woman in her late fifties. She wore purple-rimmed glasses and a tie-dyed top of white hearts on a blue background. She had once run a street stand selling noodles, but found the work too exhausting and so now did odd jobs instead. She spoke of the trauma of

Prawet's arrest almost three months previously. 'I was shocked,' she said. 'I love the monarchy. I warned him. But he didn't listen. He had studied the law, so he gave his opinions.'

At first, Prawet's family had no idea what had happened to him. He lived on his own in another part of town. Suddenly, he just disappeared and couldn't be contacted by phone. Pravit, a slender software designer, described the stress as they spent days searching for his brother. There was no system of habeas corpus in *lèse-majesté* cases: authorities did as they pleased. Eventually, they revealed Pravet's predicament.

Prawet, Janjira and Prawit were part of a family of seven brothers and two sisters. Their parents came to Thailand as part of the generational wave of immigration from China during the first half of the twentieth century. Their father left his home city of Shantou in Guangdong province so he wouldn't be drafted into the army during the Second World War. His mother fled the same region during the conflict.

Prawet's father died young in the late 1960s, leaving the full burden of raising the family on their mother. She sold sweets and groceries on a *soi* – side street – high up the long Sukhumvit Road, now dominated by offices and shopping malls. Janjira started crying as she recalled how she had once had a younger sister, whom she raised because her mother was busy working and looking after her ill father. Her mother gave the girl away to another family after her husband died, because she felt she couldn't afford to provide for her. Prawet played a crucial role in supporting the rest of the family, through a variety of jobs including as a bus conductor, bag packer and bookseller. 'He was a really smart kid and he lived to help our mother,' Janjira said, drying her tears on a paisley patterned handkerchief. 'During the school holidays he would always earn money to give to her.'

Prawet studied law in the late 1970s at Thammasat University in Bangkok. A massacre had taken place at the institution in 1976.

It was a time of official paranoia about communism in the region: the previous year, the Laos monarchy had been toppled and the US chased out of Saigon by North Vietnamese forces. Thammasat students mounted a protest for greater political freedoms, during which they staged a play involving the mock hanging of two actors. Far right royalist counter-demonstrators claimed that one of the pair was supposed to be Crown Prince Vajiralongkorn. The students denied this but the media spread the story, helping provoke an orgy of retaliatory violence.

Security forces and royalist mobs killed dozens of protestors in a slaughter broadcast around the world. Some were lynched from trees on Sanam Luang – or 'royal turf' – a great grassed expanse next to the Grand Palace. A photo that later won a Pulitzer Prize shows a man using a folded chair to beat a student strung up from a branch, as a mob of mainly young men and boys look on and, in some cases, grin with delight. I stood on the same lawn in the pouring rain almost exactly forty years later, talking to people as they queued to pay tribute to the recently deceased Bhumibol. The king never condemned those killings perpetrated in sight of his home – and supposedly to protect his family's honour.

The young Prawet emerged from Thammasat with a strong streak of social concern. He had almost got into serious trouble as a student by demanding identification from a plain-clothes police officer he saw making an arrest, Janjira recalled. Now, as a graduate, he took on cases pro bono, including one against a loan shark. He used to work intensely and come from time to time to stay with his brother and sister to 'sleep and be fed', Janjira recalled. People whom he had helped way back had sent him money since he was detained, Pravit said. 'He always helped poor people who didn't have money to fight,' he said. 'When he finished school he barely had enough money for himself – but he always helped people without taking money from them.'

Prawet's legal career soon began to take off. He got married, travelled around the country – and for the first time started to represent people accused of *lèse-majesté*. Some of his relatives immediately saw the danger.

'One of our brothers said:"If you keep helping people with this, you are going to get into trouble."' Pravit said, as he played nervously with a fingernail. 'Some of these people didn't say anything about the king. They just didn't know the law.'

Prawet also defended people who were pushing the boundaries of *lèse-majesté*. One was Daranee Charnchoengsilpakul, better known as 'Da Torpedo'. She was jailed for fifteen years over a speech she gave at a 2008 political rally about the 2006 military coup that had deposed Thaksin Shinawatra, the prime minister who later briefly owned Manchester City Football Club. Da Torpedo served eight years before she was freed in August 2016 under a general prisoner amnesty. Before her conviction, she said she was not a republican but favoured 'a sustainable monarchy like in the United Kingdom and Japan'.[4]

Now Prawet was no longer a defender of the accused but a target himself. Janjira lamented that he wouldn't have taken such risks if their mother were still alive, as he wouldn't have wanted to worry her. But Janjira was still perplexed as to what, exactly, her brother was supposed to have done wrong. 'He didn't kill anybody, he just helped people,' she said, tapping her now folded handkerchief with her free hand for emphasis. 'He's not a bad person. He just had an opinion.'

Pravit said his positive feelings about Prayuth Chan-ocha, the general who had taken power in the 2014 coup and arranged for himself to be installed as prime minister, had evaporated since his brother's arrest. Janjira fretted that there was nothing they could do for Prawet except 'go to the temple and keep praying'. 'I keep getting headaches,' she said. 'I just try to think: he chose his own path.'

The two siblings produced some family photos for me to look at. Janjira began to cry again as she leafed through the pictures of Prawet as a boy. 'He did his work without corruption,' she said. 'He helped society. He's a good person.'

One picture showed all of the siblings together. Janjira was holding the little girl their mother later gave away on account of poverty. 'I have already lost a sister,' she said tearfully. 'Now I feel I have lost a brother too.'

Janjira's pain was part of a landscape of repression that had been decades in the making in Thailand – and had been amply supported by foreigners. The present-day power of *lèse-majesté* was the result of a masterclass in parlaying survival into supreme authority. During Bhumibol's epic reign, Thailand's military, administrative and business elite had quietly entrenched their control into a position of near-impregnability.

It is a striking version of a familiar story. Many royal houses, not least Britain's, give a sense of permanence that belies the power struggles they had to win to assert control. Laws and ideas of *lèse-majesté* also linger long, even in constitutional monarchies that are supposedly only ceremonial. In the Netherlands, which prides itself on its social freedoms, insulting the king is still punishable by a jail term.[5]

Bhumibol's Chakri dynasty had wrested power from a previous ruler of Siam and in 1782 they founded Bangkok as their capital. They instituted a feudal system of absolute monarchy that ruled without challenge until a 1932 uprising by military officers and bureaucrats influenced by democratic ideas. The coup's authors cornered King Prajadhipok and had the chance to dethrone him. Instead, they let him stay in exchange for the introduction of a parliament and other constitutional changes.

After the war, another hammer blow fell on the monarchy. In June 1946, King Ananda Mahidol, Bhumibol's brother, was found shot dead at the Grand Palace in circumstances that were never explained. He was killed by a shot from a Colt 45 revolver that he kept by his bedside. The circumstances left open the possibilities of murder, suicide and accident. Few believed in the guilt of the three men, including two palace pages, who were later executed for plotting to kill the king. Even the palace later distanced itself from a verdict most outsiders saw as a travesty aimed at saving the royal family embarrassment. Bhumibol had been with Ananda that day and may have been the last person to see him alive; the two brothers were both fascinated by guns. When Bhumibol died, so did the final witness with direct knowledge of those events.

The eighteen-year-old Bhumibol inherited the throne and with it a massive job to rebuild the monarchy's damaged prestige. He was a slight presence in the early years of his rule, not least because he returned to Switzerland to finish his education. But Thailand's powerful military, who dominated the country's post-war politics, realised that a venerated monarchy could be a strong ally and source of credibility. Both shared an interest in entrenching the established hierarchical social order, an aim reinforced by the rise of communism elsewhere in South-East Asia.

This plan meshed with US ambitions in the region. Thailand had cemented its alliance with Washington in 1954 through the creation of the Southeast Asia Treaty Organization. As conflict grew in Vietnam and Laos in the 1960s, the US dispatched troops to Thailand. It used the country as a base for its B-52 bomber missions and 'R & R' time off for its forces – a driver in the development of Bangkok's sex industry.

Washington also sought to bolster the US-born Bhumibol's image as an enlightened monarch offering an attractive alternative to communist rule. The US hosted the Massachusetts-born king and his charismatic wife, Sirikit, on a month-long 1960 tour to eight states and Washington, D.C., including a ticker-tape parade in New York and an appearance on a chat show. They met Elvis

Presley in Hollywood and Bhumibol jammed on his saxophone with Benny Goodman. President Dwight Eisenhower hosted the royal couple at the White House, where he and Bhumibol swapped recipes for Thai noodles and ice cream. In 1966, *Time* magazine purred that '[the] men who run Thailand are well aware that their youthful King is their – and the nation's – greatest living asset.'[6]

Domestic and international efforts to buttress the king intensified as war, revolution and genocide engulfed Thailand's Mekong region neighbours. At home, he was portrayed as the 'developer king' who brought progress to impoverished rural areas. He epitomised noblesse oblige as he travelled the country with his camera slung round his neck, directing irrigation projects and other efforts to help the country's farmers. He even became known as the 'rainmaker', because of technology he allegedly invented to improve cloud seeding in areas short of precipitation. An officially approved documentary explicitly invoked the idea of godlike powers, noting that the late king was seen as a 'semi-divine monarch who could harness the weather for the benefit of the people'. The Thai government even has a Department of Royal Rainmaking and Agricultural Aviation.[7]

Thongchai Winichakul, a US-based Thai academic, has described the Cold War-era promotion of Bhumibol as the birth of the modern style of 'hyper-royalism'. Once the perceived threat from communism had eased, this remained vital to the Thai establishment as a means of social control.

'Hyper-royalism generates the concept of the ideology of modern monarchy – a charismatic king who is sacred, righteous and cares for his people, and who is indispensable to Thailand – and the belief that royalist democracy is best for Thailand,' Thongchai said in a 2016 paper. 'Hyper-royalism also generates the illusion that the monarchy is divine, thanks to visual performances and objects, especially through television and majestic pageantry.'[8]

Bhumibol's international connections helped him ride out the bad publicity after the 1976 Thammasat University massacre shocked the world. The king and his family gave unprecedented access for a 1980 BBC documentary about them, an investment that paid back handsomely when they were depicted in glowing terms. Entitled *Soul of a Nation* and narrated stirringly by Sir John Gielgud, the two-part film broadly endorsed the Thai monarchy as a beacon of civilisation and moderation in a dangerous neighbourhood. The director, Bridget Winter, has written of how she was enchanted by Queen Sirikit when they met in 1978, discovering that the two women shared an interest in the paranormal. Winter described her first dinner with Sirikit and Bhumibol as an epiphany.

'What I shall never forget from the conversation that flowed on that remarkable evening was the Queen saying, "You know, Bridget, we love you. We feel we know you,"' she wrote. 'I heard myself replying "I feel the same way" – and meaning it with all my heart ... It was a dazzling demonstration that miracles can happen, even between kings and commoners who live on opposite ends of the earth.'[9]

Despite its hagiographic overall tone, the documentary does contain revealing moments, some unintentional and some thanks to the questioning of the reporter, David Lomax. The king is clearly not comfortable discussing the mysterious death of his brother. He refers darkly to how evidence has been 'shifted' and crucial facts 'suppressed by influential people in this country or in the international politics'.

Another dissonant note is the brief appearance of Crown Prince Vajiralongkorn. He is introduced as a brave army officer who has put behind him 'a not very happy time' at school in England. Vajiralongkorn is seen dressed in military uniform. His unsettling manner is already apparent. Asked about what the personal pressures are on him as Crown Prince, he fiddles with an object on his desk as he replies cryptically.

'The first second of my life, I'm a prince,' he says. 'It's difficult to say what is it like to be a fish, when you are a fish. Or what is it like to be a bird, when you are a bird . . . They don't know what it's like not to be a fish, or a bird.'

Concerns about Vajiralongkorn mounted during the decades that followed. The prince qualified as a pilot and joined the Thai military, but established a reputation as a playboy. His own mother, Sirikit, famously once described him as 'a bit of a Don Juan' and suggested her 'good boy' might have to change his ways or quit the royal family, if the public disapproved of him. Top members of Thailand's Privy Council, a powerful royal advisory body, made 'quite negative comments' about the Crown Prince during a meeting with the US ambassador in Bangkok, according to a 2010 US diplomatic cable published by WikiLeaks.[10]

Vajiralongkorn's white poodle Foo Foo – the one allegedly made an air marshal – played a central role in another source of the prince's notoriety. A video leaked in 2009 opens with a fully clothed Vajiralongkorn seated at the table with his third wife, Princess Srirasmi, who is wearing only a thong. A staff member produces a cake and the couple sing 'Happy Birthday' as the prince clutches the dog. The trio pose for pictures before the topless Srirasmi crouches on the floor in front of the prince and offers him a piece of cake from a silver salver.

Vajiralongkorn attracted further comment in 2017 after photos surfaced of him wearing a crop top at an airport and shopping mall in Germany, where he had spent much of his time in previous years. Thailand's generals clashed with Facebook in May of that year as they attempted to scrub the Net of the images. The dispute ensured the story went viral internationally, generating ridicule of the king outside Thailand – but no coverage, still less criticism, in mainstream Thai media.

After Vajiralongkorn became king, long-standing palace staff members were dismissed via scathing announcements in the *Royal Gazette*. Some officials with decades of service were branded 'lazy' or 'arrogant'. Such humiliation broke what foreigners are often told is a central taboo in Thai culture: never make people publicly lose face.

Other episodes were even more disturbing. In 2015, two people had died in murky circumstances after working on 'Bike for Dad' and 'Bike for Mum', cycling events headed by the Crown Prince in honour of his parents. The pair – a senior police officer and a famous fortune teller known as Mor Yong – were part of a group of event organisers accused of using the monarchy's name for personal gain. No credible explanation was ever given for how the men died.

A few days before his formal coronation in May 2019, Vajiralongkorn married Suthida Tidjai, an ex-Thai Airways cabin crew member whom he had in 2014 appointed deputy commander of his personal bodyguard. It was the first official acknowledgement of the long-rumoured relationship between the two. Thai media published pictures of Suthida, whom Vajiralongkorn gave the title Queen, prostrating herself on the floor in front of him as other officials present did the same.

In private, the new monarch provoked a mixture of anxiety and disdain among many of his subjects. One office worker told me he 'doesn't have the potential to be king'. Asked what she would do under the new reign, she laughed and replied: 'Live somewhere else.' She added, after a pause, 'We will have to be more careful.'

None of these fears could ever be expressed publicly. As another person put it to me: 'We cannot speak the truth from our heart.'

Vajiralongkorn has previously argued he is unjustifiably maligned. In a rare interview in the 1980s, he said he was sometimes the subject of false rumours and unfair criticism. He has shown interest in conflict resolution in restive south Thailand, urging efforts to end a long and bloody conflict there that has pitted security forces against ethnic Malay Muslim separatists.

Vajiralongkorn took significant fresh powers after becoming king. He intervened to change a constitution that the military junta had ordered to be drafted. The amendments meant he could now travel overseas, notably to Germany, without appointing a regent to act on his behalf. He also acquired greater authority to intervene in the country's political crises.

Another big change concerned Thailand's tentacular Crown Property Bureau. This fund was a national treasure chest whose huge landholdings and stakes in industries ranging from banking to cement were estimated to be worth tens of billions of dollars. It was a vehicle for enormous patronage, offering prized property in central Bangkok to those in favour. It demanded only peppercorn rent for a sprawling plot it leased to the US government for the ambassador's residence.

Thai authorities had long rejected suggestions the bureau was the monarch's piggy bank. In a September 2011 letter to the *New York Times*, a Thai diplomat in Washington insisted the assets of the Crown Property Bureau were 'held in trust for the nation and not at the king's personal disposal'. But a person familiar with the bureau's operations told me in June 2017, six months after Vajiralongkorn came to power, that the institution was in flux and it wasn't clear who was running it. He declined to discuss either the bureau's history or basic workings. He referred to the perceived danger of speaking out of turn about any royally linked institution.

'Even talking about the past and mechanics is potentially problematic at this point,' he said.

Within weeks of that conversation, a new law gave Vajiralongkorn direct control of the bureau. It allowed him apparently unlimited authority to manage the fund, just as he has acquired control of other institutions previously considered to be under the aegis of the government, police or military. Again, no explanation was offered for these profound changes to a source of wealth that could have had a transformative effect on many Thais' lives, in a country still marked by significant urban and rural poverty.

Vajiralongkorn also benefited from a lore of obedience to their royal betters drummed into Thais from their earliest years. The national anthem has long been played twice daily in some public places, including on Bangkok's BTS Skytrain urban railway, at 8:00 a.m. and 6:00 p.m. People are expected to stop what they are doing in the middle of morning and evening rush hours and stand still and straight.

The greatness of the monarchy and its central role in protecting the country are staples of the Thai school curriculum. At a 2017 visit to a rice farm outside Bangkok, I watched as the owner offered children prizes of swords carved from bamboo if they could answer questions about the monarchy. These included reciting the full honorifics and names of the late Bhumibol. Those ran to thirteen words and 140 characters in the Roman script, according to the web page of the Thai embassy in Washington.[11] Another rice farm task was to describe the main features of Bhumibol's 'sufficiency economy' theory of development.

I found the iconography around Bhumibol revealing of the monarchy's relationship with its subjects. It seemed to me more authoritarian than paternalistic. One popular image after Bhumibol's death was of him dressed in military uniform, looking down at a child crouched, head bowed, at his feet. In another context, it could have depicted the citizenry's abasement before the head of a junta in a totalitarian state.

A second favoured picture of the king after he died was a close-up of him – again, in a military cap – bending down towards a wizened old woman. She did not (dared not?) look straight at him. He was not lifting his deprived fellow citizen up: he was, for a brief moment, condescending to her. It recalled the days when Thais were not even permitted to gaze at their monarchs.

The portrayals of the king also made clear that the days of him appearing accessible were gone. After he and Sirikit made thirty-one trips to twenty-nine countries between 1959 and 1967, the overseas travel – and informal mingling with foreigners – stopped abruptly. During the remaining near half-century of his reign, Bhumibol officially never left Thailand, save for one overnight stay in Laos.

All this was consistent with the monarchy's steady move in a more conservative direction under Bhumibol. His palace signed off on coups, some against elected governments. Under his rule, old rites like ploughing ceremonies were enhanced, while prostration – abolished by his nineteenth-century predecessor Chulalongkorn as undignified – was restored. Perhaps most significantly, he also bequeathed the country to his son, despite the many concerns about his suitability for the throne. Bhumibol appointed Vajiralongkorn as his heir in 1972 and declined ever to reverse his decision.

Any system based on extreme conformity to an idea like the godlike status of Thailand's monarchs cannot only work top-down. It has to be reinforced by the wider populace. I could understand why generals and politicians pushed *lèse-majesté* cases for nakedly political reasons. I could see why the police pursued complaints that they felt were too hot to drop. What intrigued me the most were the people who enthusiastically supported the system for no obvious advantage of patronage to themselves. Some were so zealous they had become royal vigilantes, actively helping to bring to justice those they felt had insulted their king. These were the people who perpetuated the system – and made it self-perpetuating.

I met one of these royal enforcers during the first year of Vajiralongkorn's reign. Our encounter took place in far from regal surroundings: a roadside cafe at a terminus of Bangkok's elevated Skytrain rail line. The coffee shop where we talked was sandwiched between a petrol station and a green and white liveried branch of Tesco Lotus, the British supermarket's brand in Asia. Pork skewers sizzled on the griddle cart of a street vendor just outside the window where my contact awaited.

Songwut Romyapan was dressed simply in a lumberjack shirt in red, white and blue, the colours of the Thai flag. His only adornment was a golden necklace with a Buddhist amulet. His weathered face spoke of a tough early life, but he was still handsome and fit at forty-eight. He was friendly and approachable – though his words were stern.

'People of my age are different from young people nowadays,' he said, explaining his devotion to Thailand's royals. 'We have been seeing the late king and the monarchy working for the people. As Thais, we have to love three things: nation, religion and monarchy. You have to be grateful for whatever people have been doing for you. And the monarchy has been working a lot for the people.'

Songwut was an engineering equipment dealer by trade but I was more interested in his hobby: upholding the honour of Thailand's royals. For him, as for many of his compatriots, Bhumibol was an awe-inspiring figure. During his seven-decade reign, Bhumibol had – according to the official narrative – been a uniquely reassuring force in a country buffeted by political conflict and military coups. He was the spiritual guide who was not afraid to get his hands dirty, helping improve agricultural output in the country's vast rice-growing heartlands. In short, he was both above politics and better than politicians.

'With governments you always hear about corruption and doing things for their [favoured] people,' Songwut said. 'But the

Thai king did things for all the people. That's why Thais love him as a father.'

Songwut recounted his troubled early life. He said he was raised from the age of three by an adoptive mother and father after his blood parents gave him away because they couldn't afford to look after him. It didn't seem a great psychological leap to speculate that the king became some kind of paternal surrogate to him. Indeed, the birthdays of Bhumibol and Queen Sirikit had been designated Father's Day and Mother's Day in Thailand.

'I had all the basic needs,' Songwut recalled of his childhood. 'But I didn't have the love and care I wanted. Father's Day and Mother's Day were two days I didn't want. They made me feel hurt. In those days, fathers and mothers came to school. But I didn't have them.'

As if reading my thoughts, he added: 'The king didn't replace my real parents. I just respected him.'

Songwut's earliest royal memory was from when he was eight or nine years old. He recalls waving a Thai flag when the king and queen passed by on a visit to his home area. That was a different age: those visits became rarer over the years, as the royals' health failed and the monarchy became more elevated and remote.

Songwut's difficulties continued. He said that he shot someone when he was seventeen years old and went to jail for four years for the crime. He was vague on the details – although he said his victim survived. The one constant in his otherwise turbulent life was the monarch.

'When you are born in Thailand, there is always the king,' Songwut said. 'It's something you hold on to and find heartwarming.'

Songwut's mood darkened when he came to consider Thailand's modern politics and in particular the great rupture brought by the rise of Thaksin Shinawatra. Thaksin had won two landslide

election victories in 2001 and 2005 on the back of heavily subsi-
dised healthcare, rice subsidies and microcredit schemes for the
country's rural heartlands. He also had many and severe failings:
corruption and rights abuses flourished under his rule, including a
war on drugs that killed thousands of people. He has stayed out of
Thailand since he was convicted in 2008[12] of a land deal corruption case he says was politically motivated.

Thaksin posed a very particular threat to the status quo and the
role of the monarchy in it. By lavishing state funds on neglected
areas and – perhaps even more significantly – ostensibly dealing
with people there as equals rather than serfs, he showed that the
old royalist neo-feudal model was not the only way. This was why
his critics began to accuse him of *lèse-majesté*, which he denied.

Songwut said Thaksin's so-called 'red-shirt' supporters had got
away with all sorts of coded insults against the monarchy. He said
they made pointed references to the so-called Blue Diamond
scandal, when jewels allegedly stolen by a Thai gardener working
at a royal palace in Saudi Arabia apparently ended up in Bangkok
around the necks and wrists of high society figures. Thaksin
sympathisers would refer to the king and queen in code as 'Uncle
Somchai' or 'Auntie Somchit' – much as some expatriates wishing
to maintain at least a fiction of discretion used to refer to Crown
Prince Vajiralongkorn as 'Charlie Parker'.

Songwut said the *lèse-majesté* problem had worsened during the
digital age. He thought the government had been lax in forcing
websites to take down anti-monarchy postings. 'Even primary
school students can access all those clips,' he complained. 'As a
citizen of Thailand I couldn't take it any more – that people could
insult the heart of the nation. So I felt I needed to use my own
voice to make the Thai people wake up.'

In fact, social media companies have often proved helpful to
Thai authorities' efforts to censor discussion of the monarchy, for
all their proclaimed commitment to free speech. Companies such

as Facebook and Google routinely block material in countries if governments make what they deem valid complaints that the posts break local laws. Facebook acknowledged in 2017 that it had geoblocked fifty items of content the previous year because they were alleged to have breached Thai *lèse-majesté* rules. The company reported that in the first half of 2018 it blocked 285 items due to local laws – although it did not say how many of these were linked to the monarchy.[13]

Songwut still wanted the censors to do more. About four or five years previously, he had met a group of people who shared his anger at what they perceived was a lack of official protection for the monarchy. This cadre was known as the Rubbish Collection Organisation. Led by an army officer who was also the director of a general hospital, they launched online campaigns against people they alleged were insulting the throne.

Songwut said he worked with the organisation but pulled back when he started being cited in public as a witness in *lèse-majesté* criminal cases. People he knew started asking him awkward questions about whether he was working for the police. So he shifted focus to the less public task of searching for potentially illegal posts online. As he spoke, I found myself wondering where offence ended and desire began in this search for transgressive material.

Songwut seemed an interesting sort of zealot. He lacked the pious self-assurance that often characterises those who take it on themselves to preach to others. He admitted he was no saint in life. He also acknowledged the personal anguish his freelancing in defence of the royals had caused his targets. 'I made a lot of people miserable,' he said, of the people he had helped jail for *lèse-majesté*. 'There's one who is serving thirty years in prison.'

He said he didn't like to talk about the cases he worked on directly. But he acknowledged one of them was the well-known affair of a play called *The Wolf Bride*. Two students were jailed over the satirical production, which featured a fictional kingdom, monarch and aide-de-camp. It was put on for the anniversary of a deadly 1973 crackdown on student protests.[14]

Songwut saw a video of the production on YouTube and reported it. His description of why he thought it merited punishment seemed almost the definition of thoughtcrime.

'In the play, they didn't directly mention the monarchy,' he said. 'But the *lèse-majesté* case happened because of how people perceive and interpret the play.' He continued, 'It's the same thing as your family. If somebody insults your parents in front of you, what would be your reaction?'

I said that surely a person should not be jailed just for criticising someone. Songwut became agitated, his hand gestures more expansive. 'What they say is not true,' he said of the students and their supporters. 'Some of them falsely made a story. That's why we need to use the law.'

He insisted he was reasonable in his approach. He said he sometimes even warned people whom he believed were breaking the rules, to give them a last chance to stop. 'They do not stop. I tell them to stop. How do you solve this problem?' he asked. 'Every day people come to shout at your family. You send them messages but they ignore it.'

For him, it was axiomatic that people should not be able to attack the monarchy. His tone towards offenders often tended to the kind of exasperation you might feel with a misbehaving child.

'They do it every day until it becomes normal,' he said of the *lèse-majesté* suspects. 'When you want them to stop, they never stop. How do you take any measure against that? It's about the same person doing the wrong thing – repeatedly.'

He said he accepted diversity of opinion on the monarchy. He just drew the line at insults and false information. 'Opinion we accept,' he said. 'Making stories we do not accept.'

I asked him why he didn't then see *The Wolf Bride* as an example of a legitimate difference of view on the monarchy. He closed his eyes in thought for a moment.

'You have to be Thai to understand it,' he replied eventually. 'When you watch it, you will understand what it means. Often, they don't say things directly. They do it indirectly. But you add one or two things together and you understand what they mean.'

He seemed to view debate on the monarchy as an objective rather than a subjective activity. In other words, since the royals were *a priori* good, it followed that it had to be false to say they were bad. 'Thailand is open for opinion,' he added. 'But it has to be the truth. And you have to have evidential backup on that. People have to say things that are based on the truth.'

I asked him if he felt sympathy for people who had ended up in jail for *lèse-majesté*. He said he did, noting that the punishment was 'very severe'. But the same law applied to everyone, he added. His empathy for the relatives of *lèse-majesté* convicts was also qualified. 'The families should have told them not to do it,' he said.

I was asking these questions in part because I knew that in one respect his work had taken on a very personal dimension. He had fallen out with his son over his alleged disrespect for the monarchy. I asked gently about this. He replied elliptically.

'In my family there is a family member who does not accept the monarchy,' he said. 'I told my son: "You should love the king as your father." He said: "I only have one father."'

I asked if he would report his own son for *lèse-majesté*. He thought for a moment and seemed perturbed. 'It's a tough question,' he said. 'Definitely I would do it. But if it happens in the family, I would give a warning.'

He went on: 'But my son did it. So that's why I cut him off. It's really difficult, but that's why I did it. I taught him. I said: "You are no longer my son in this life."'

He was now warming to his theme, his certainty returning. 'My son stopped. Because if he didn't, the first person who would file a report against him would be me,' he said. 'I didn't raise my son to be someone who attacked the monarchy.'

Songwut and I talked about the qualities of Bhumibol that had inspired him. He cited attributes ranging from making rain to conflict mediation, as in a famous 1992 intervention after dozens of people died in a crackdown on pro-democracy demonstrations against the military government. The king summoned both the prime minister General Suchinda Kraprayoon and the protest leader to the palace, where they sat on the floor as the monarch gently but firmly chastised them from his higher position on a sofa. The premier resigned a few days later and Bhumibol was widely acclaimed in the country for restoring peace. Some more sceptical observers pointed out that his action had the additional effect of draining momentum from the political reform movement.

I asked Songwut whether he felt the new king would assume his predecessor's mantle. He closed his eyes again and thought a while. 'He's following in his father's steps,' he said carefully. 'From what we have seen of the current king, he is following in his father's steps.'

Like many Thais, Songwut's discussion of the new reign was founded on nostalgia for the old one. Vajiralongkorn had little positive presence in the public consciousness. During his early days on the throne, there were strikingly few photos or videos to show in public places, such as cinemas when the pre-film national anthem was being played. Pictures of poolside frolics and crop-topped visits to German shopping malls would not fit the bill.

I appreciated Songwut's candour. He recognised the dangers in it. He ended with a warning that showed how stifling the atmosphere around Thailand's royalty had become. In these uncertain times, even the *lèse-majesté* hunter could become the hunted. As Songwut put it: 'Be careful about repeating stuff that could get us both into trouble.'

Here was the sinister absurdity of *lèse-majesté* laid bare. Even the act of talking about the monarchy loyally carried risks. Nobody was above suspicion because – for the system to be effective – nobody *could* be above suspicion.

Lèse-majesté was like a genetically engineered creature that was breaking even the bonds its creators had imposed. It had acquired its own impulses and the ability to grow and multiply. There was nothing to hold it in check because nothing *could* hold it in check, save the monarch himself. It would continue to mutate and grow stronger, rendering ever wider landscapes of politics off limits – and even requiring history to be rewritten.

Sulak Sivaraksa had been in trouble for *lèse-majesté* before, but his latest skirmish had reached a new level of the bizarre. This time the public intellectual and self-styled critical friend of the monarchy was under investigation over a piece of sixteenth-century royal folklore.[15]

His difficulties had begun two and a half years previously. Sulak had suggested in a university seminar late in 2014 that a famed elephant battle between Thailand's ancient King Naresuan and his Burmese counterpart might never have happened. His timing was certainly mischievous: Thais had been enraptured that year by the latest in an epic series of films about Naresuan, rather as Brits gorge on movies harking back to the Second World War. What's more, the Naresuan series had enthusiastic backing from the military authorities in Bangkok, who gave out 35,000 free tickets. Colonel Winthai Suvaree, who played the king's brother in the latest film, had even become a spokesperson for the junta that had seized power earlier in the year.

If Sulak knew he was treading on sensitive ground, even he might have been shocked by the fallout. After all, it was hardly controversial that the Naresuan films were an artistic interpretation of a period for which written records were scant. The saga's director, Chatrichalerm Yukol, had admitted the movies were a 'blend of history, plausibility and imagination'.

The octogenarian Sulak had also long enjoyed a certain leeway to play the provocateur. He had written a memoir whose title in English was *Loyalty Demands Dissent*. But in the febrile atmosphere of Bhumibol's last years, even this semi-licensed gadfly found he could not avoid the official swat. A military officer filed a *lèse-majesté* complaint against him and police called him in on suspicion of questioning the Naresuan elephant battle 'in a way that insults, defames, or threatens' the current king.

The cloud was still hovering over Sulak when I met him almost three years after the initial complaint against him. It was in the pitiless nature of *lèse-majesté* cases for them to grind on. Sulak had been at the police station only the week before. They were 'very nice' to him after he'd paid his 300,000 baht (about £7,500) bail, he said with the ghost of a smile. 'And, the police said, "Well, since you're a good boy, we will return you the bail money,"' he said. 'But they don't know what to do, you see, because we have no rule of law in this country.'

We were talking in Sulak's traditional wooden house in the dense mercantile area between the Silom and Surawong roads in Bangkok. It was one of the last old-style residences standing amid the shops, street vendors and entertainment establishments of varying degrees of respectability that now dominated the surrounding area. Sulak shook his head in regret as he told me the news that a condo was due to be built next door. It was another small wash in the tide of construction that had turned Bangkok from sleepy backwater to overbuilt megacity in barely half a century.

Sulak cut an instantly recognisable figure with his signature wooden cane and red-and-white chequered sarong. A beautiful cat from the next-door shop-house dropped by to join us, hunkering down on the kitchen counter to enjoy the cool offered by the dwelling's dark wood design. The old ways clearly still had their advantages.

Sulak was born into a life of privilege in Thonburi, the former Thai capital across the Chao Phraya River from Bangkok. His father worked for British American Tobacco. The young Sulak studied at what is now the University of Wales and then returned to Thailand to become an academic there. He founded a publication called the *Social Science Review* and became a prominent speaker and author on human rights and the accountability of government. He also carved out an international profile: his best-known book, *Seeds of Peace*, had a foreword by the Dalai Lama.

Sulak was no revolutionary. Indeed, he was pro-monarchy and conservative in his wider social vision. His emphasis on the importance of material restraint and Buddhist-inspired spiritualism closely echoed the rhetoric of King Bhumibol himself. He had said that the king's death left him with a hole in his heart.[16]

But Sulak's questions about the role of royalty, including whether it should be more like constitutional monarchy and more open about its finances, had brought him problems. He went into self-imposed exile for a time in the late 1970s after his bookshop in Bangkok was burned down amid the bloody political crackdown and military coup of 1976. He had been accused of *lèse-majesté* several times over the decades, including a case in the mid-1980s that was stopped after heavy international pressure. Other complaints against him had been discreetly withdrawn, after what Thai media sometimes diplomatically described as the 'intervention of somebody' – code for the palace and its agents.

Sulak relished his role as a debunker of received wisdom. We talked about the shaky claim that Thailand, unlike all its Mekong region neighbours, was never colonised. This is an article of faith in Thai official history (and an irritating boast to some other countries in the region). But it ignores the way Europeans – particularly the British – pressured the monarchy into offering preferential trade terms and power over key institutions. Many in the Thai monarchy had also spent formative years in Europe, absorbing practices from there. As one Thai author put it to me, Thailand was 'internally colonised', even if not formally occupied.

'We were told to imitate the West blindly,' Sulak said. 'We were forced to wear neckties. And we were not allowed to chew betel nuts. We were not allowed to eat with our fingers. And we used to have floating houses along Bangkok. That was abolished in the name of progress.'

My host went further in his critique. I'd noticed that he habitually referred to Siam, the old name of the country before the military junta rebranded it Thailand in 1939. Sulak thought Thailand a 'dreadful name', because it did not take into account the Malay Muslim population of the south, where a bloody battle had raged for decades between a secessionist movement and the Thai military. Sulak further deplored what he called the 'Nazism' of the Thai national anthem, with its 'ethnocentric' focus on how the country belongs to those of Thai 'blood and flesh'.[17]

He saw the current case against him as another example of official propaganda. It was an attempt to 'brainwash' the people by not only exaggerating King Naresuan's achievements, but covering up allegations of his despotism (itself from partial sources, such as a Flemish gem merchant[18]). It was all part of the military's bigger argument that it was indispensable to the survival of the nation. 'Naresuan became a great king because the army needs him,' Sulak said. 'The army say: "Without us you cannot survive." So, they can't accept that he's a sadist. And, in fact, you look at history, it's quite plain.'

Sulak consequently styled his Naresuan *lèse-majesté* case not as a question of loyalty, but a question of truth. He agreed that historical enquiry was generally not encouraged in Thailand. He said liberal arts universities taught with a similar philosophy to military academies. 'You have to all agree; no questioning,' he said.

Sulak said he often received visits from politically aware young Thais. One was Netiwit Chotiphatphaisal, a skinny student in natty red specs who made national headlines with a protest at Chulalongkorn University in 2016. At an induction ceremony, Netiwit refused to follow what had become the modern practice for students to drop to the ground before a statue of Chulalongkorn. He was criticised by conservatives when he pointed out – accurately – that the former monarch himself had abolished prostration almost a century and a half previously.

It was revealing that even such established matters of historical record should be considered contentious. Still more sensitive was the more recent and relevant matter of Bhumibol's legacy. A critic of his rule could make some serious charges: he had pushed the monarchy in an ultraconservative direction; he had chosen his unpopular son to succeed him; and he had allowed *lèse-majesté* to become the monster it is today.

I asked Sulak if Bhumibol should have said more clearly that he thought *lèse-majesté* prosecutions were wrong and should stop. 'He did mention it, you know,' said Sulak, a little more defensively than I'd expected.

He was talking about an oblique remark by Bhumibol in a 2005 speech, when he said he was ready to be criticised, but did not explicitly suggest changing the *lèse-majesté* law.

It was a rather subtle reference, I said. 'Well, that's the way he speaks,' Sulak replied.

I noted how the way the monarchy related to the people had changed during Bhumibol's reign. The institution had taken on ever-growing overtones of the 'sacred', as Sulak put it. I asked him if he thought that was right. 'I don't think the late king believed in that but he did not destroy the myth. He kept the myth going,' Sulak said.

But why did Bhumibol do that? I asked.

'Well, it suited him,' came Sulak's straightforward reply.

I put it to Sulak that he seemed to be fighting against a trend in politics worldwide towards comforting historical fictions. I asked him whether he accepted that at some level the urge for people to believe in a great authority as an escape from daily struggles was just too powerful. In the end, people would always prefer a simple morality tale to the complex truth.

Sulak said it didn't need to be so. Myths could be tamed, made useful and their potential to damage limited. He told the story of receiving the Right Livelihood Award – sometimes called the 'Alternative Nobel prize' – at the Swedish parliament in 1995. In his acceptance speech, he doggedly referred as usual to Thailand as 'Siam'. He recalled talking to Swedish MPs who said that, while they themselves didn't believe in the monarchy, King Carl XVI Gustaf was a unifying symbol and was 'cheaper to keep' than a president – as long as he had no formal authority. It is perhaps no coincidence that the emasculated Swedish king liked visiting Thailand and enjoyed vicariously the aura of Bhumibol, who gifted him two elephants. 'He loved to be pampered in this country. In Sweden they ignore him,' Sulak observed mischievously.

I asked Sulak what made him think that, while a dash of royalist mystique worked in Stockholm, it was damaging in Bangkok. He framed the answer as the difference between the Nordic model of monarchy as a public distraction and the Thai version of public dependence on the throne.

'There was one verse from the Buddha. It's very important,' he began. 'He said when people are afraid, people will stick to separate house, big trees, whatever is sacred. That helps you temporarily. Like a person who cannot swim, you will cling on to the coconut or banana stem. It will help you temporarily. But ultimately you have to learn to swim to get across the river.'

Sulak credited his father with encouraging him to ask questions from an early age. He even told the young Sulak not to make the traditional Thai palms-together *wai* gesture of respect to people if he didn't want to – a bold break with custom. 'So, in a way, he helped me to be a rebel,' Sulak said. 'I think that's my starting point, although he died when I was very young. I'm very grateful that he was my first friend and I have been lucky like that all the time. The Buddha said the best thing in life is not power, not money, not fame but good friends. And good friends are those who tell you what you don't want to hear.'

Sulak said he had little time for personal hagiography. He told a story of a funeral he had attended the previous day. The son of the deceased man had distributed a book he had written, in which he discussed how his father was an enthusiastic financial gambler. Sulak was delighted. 'I told him, "Well, you are excellent, you speak the truth,"' Sulak said. 'He said: "I was proud my father was a gambler. Marvellous." And he said: "The best gamble my father made was marrying my mother."'

One of the central official tenets of the Bhumibol era was his universal brilliance. The late king was exalted as an expert practitioner in every field in which he dabbled, from the saxophone to painting to yachting. The embellishment extended to his development projects, which were never independently assessed for their success or usefulness.

'None of them accountable,' Sulak said, before mimicking the official narrative: '"Everything is wonderful. Everything is good." For me, that's lies, not truth.'

In private, many Thais were more knowing than the public eulogies to the royals would suggest. There was genuine respect and even reverence for Bhumibol, but also an awareness of the monarchy's chequered history and an increasing consciousness that the throne was far from apolitical. Some people spoke of the significance of the palace's endorsement of the 2006 putsch against Thaksin Shinawatra in provoking a realisation that the king was not afraid to act against the elected choice of the people. As the country's growth slowed and its population aged, others asked whether the kingdom should have done more with the long postwar peace it had enjoyed while its neighbours lurched into war and genocide.

The rise of Vajiralongkorn had sharpened the questioning. One indicator was the subtle differentiation between people's heartfelt tributes to Bhumibol and the often more reserved praise for Vajiralongkorn. The seeds of discontent were there, although so was a deep fear of the consequences of speaking out. The more Vajiralongkorn flexed his authority, the greater the tension became. 'He's taken what was barely a constitutional monarchy and turned it into almost a Saudi Arabian-type situation,' a contact of mine lamented of the tilt towards monarchical absolutism. 'And the royalists don't see it . They don't see what the system has become.'

Sulak suggested that the public worship of the royals concealed a deeper, more pragmatic attitude. He compared the situation to the furore the honesty of his own autobiographical writings had caused within his own family. His relatives had been 'very, very angry' with him, not because they disputed the facts, but because it was embarrassing to have them publicised. 'I said: "This uncle was put in jail, the other uncle was corrupt." They said: "Why did you write that?" I said: "Is it true?" They said: "Yes, it's true but it should be in the family. It shouldn't be in the open."'

In his outspokenness on the monarchy, Sulak seemed an island, an outpost, almost one of a kind. He lived in a house that was out of time and gradually being suffocated by the modern city. It was also literally sinking. It suffered from a phenomenon that afflicted other old buildings in Bangkok: as the roads and sidewalks were built up around them, their lower-lying foundations became basins into which the rains would settle.

Sulak was also unusual – and not just in a Thai context – in his proclaimed preference for cold fact over romantic story. As his own writings about his family showed, the results of that approach could be brutal. He rejected the idea that, sometimes, it could be kinder – or at least more bearable – not to tell the truth. His animating fear was that myths infantilised and stifled progress.

'The point, you see, is we are now in the twenty-first century,' he said. 'Do we go by fact or by fiction? Are we still clinging to superstitions? If you regard it as myth – accept it as myth – it's okay but you make myth become history. It's very dangerous. Your people never grow up.'

In January 2018, the Naresuan charge against Sulak was dropped. It was another reminder of how, for all his intellectual courage, he still benefited from a measure of protection from a system he sought to amend rather than destroy. Authorities made no comment about their reasons for abandoning the case. Sulak told reporters tactfully that it was because of the 'grace' of King Vajiralongkorn, whom he had petitioned about the affair. The news came on the eve of the alleged elephant battle's anniversary, which is marked each January as the Royal Thai Armed Forces Day.

Prawet Prapanukul, with his edgier history, was not so lucky. In June 2018, he received a sixteen-month prison sentence for sedition. The sentence was much lighter than expected because the *lèse-majesté* charges were dropped. It meant he was released within a couple of months, because of the time he had spent on remand. No public explanation was given for why his case took the course it did.

The outcome was barely a footnote in the media. It made a four-paragraph report on the Associated Press. It was another sign of the international normalisation of Thailand's draconian approach. When people were receiving sentences of thirty years and more, sixteen months looked lenient.

Prawet's conviction came less than two weeks after Vajiralongkorn had made his most significant move yet as king. An announcement appeared on the Crown Property Bureau's website saying that all its assets would from now on be held 'in the name of His Majesty'.[19] The change – a further contradiction of years of official insistence that the bureau's assets were held in trust for the Thai people – was presented as a progressive move. Tax would now be payable on the previously exempt holdings, 'in line with His Majesty's wishes', the statement said. The argument found its way into a *New York Times* headline. Its report was headed: 'Thai King Now Owns Monarchy Assets. He'll Have to Pay Taxes on Them.'[20]

It didn't seem to me that taxes were the real story here. It is worth reflecting on the magnitude of the shift in the control over the bureau. Thailand had reversed years of custom and practice to sign over wealth possibly amounting to tens of billions of dollars to the king. Once again, as in the Gulf and Brunei, it seemed a monarch had near-limitless leeway on money, more even than that enjoyed by non-regal dictators. As throughout history, royals played by their own rules.

Thailand's governing generals seemed to have tentatively found a modus vivendi with the new ruler. They were helped because the international pressure on them over their coup had eased. In December 2017, as the junta approached its fifth year in power in Bangkok, the EU announced it would resume contact 'at all levels' with the Thai government.[21] Soon after, the generals announced that their timetable for holding elections – originally promised in 2015 – had slipped yet again. The military stifled opposition and finally held tightly controlled polls in March 2019 that maintained ex-general Prayuth's grip on the premiership.

The new king also continued to assert himself, although that required reading between the lines of both local and international media coverage. Bangkok's Dusit Zoo was shut down as part of a move to take a large area of prime capital real estate under the monarch's control. One academic who visited the zoo reported how he had 'spotted through the fence newly erected signs proclaiming the adjacent area around the Dusit Palace a "royal zone"'.[22]

Even as Thailand had thrown itself into technological modernity, it had a king who could flex the same kind of untrammelled power as his nineteenth-century predecessors. It had been almost a century since Siam came within a whisker of overthrowing its monarchy. Now many outsiders appeared to have more or less accepted that Thais wanted nothing more than subjection to their king.

The spectre of *lèse-majesté* receded a little in 2018 as authorities brought fewer cases, perhaps in a tacit recognition of the bad international publicity they brought. Then, right at the end of the year, came a ghastly discovery on Thailand's Mekong River frontier with Laos. Authorities retrieved the bodies of two Thai anti-monarchy campaigners whom police later said had been disembowelled and stuffed with concrete.[23] The pair had fled Thailand after the 2014 coup, along with a third activist, who had disappeared. The Thai military denied any responsibility for the deaths. As of February 2019, no suspects had been identified.

In the same month, Vajiralongkorn made a very public intervention in Thailand's long-delayed elections. The polls scheduled for March appeared to have been transformed when his sister Ubolratana Rajakanya announced she would be a candidate for a party affiliated with self-exiled former premier Thaksin. The declaration triggered a wave of excitement and appeared to create a big problem for Prime Minister Prayuth as he attempted to use the polls to reinforce the military's sway in politics. Could he be seen to stand against a royal – even one like Ubolratana, who had been stripped of her status when she married an American commoner in 1972?

Vajiralongkorn weighed in less than twenty-four hours after Ubolratana had put her name forward.[24] In a statement read out on national television, he denounced his sister's act as 'highly inappropriate', condemning her to one of the shorter candidacies in electoral history. The declaration added, without apparent irony, that the monarchy shouldn't be involved in politics.

A fascinating archive photo that I occasionally saw in official contexts in Thailand was of the event to mark Bhumibol's sixtieth anniversary on the throne in 2006. It was an auspicious anniversary, because multiples of twelve are significant in the Buddhist life cycle. Dozens of royals from Europe, the Middle East, Africa and Asia are gathered in it, dressed in clothes ranging from military garb to the white dishdashas of the Gulf. They include absolute monarchs and nominally powerless figureheads. But the picture is a recognition of their shared common interest in maintaining the mythos of monarchy. If that sours – as the Thai establishment has understood very well – a crucial lever of authority will have been lost.

Bhumibol and his allies had managed a rare trick in the second half of the twentieth century. As more liberal political ideas spread bumpily but gradually in many parts of the world, the Thai establishment took the monarchy in a more traditional direction. By the end of Bhumibol's reign, the king was not only formally inviolable but impossible to discuss. It was a model for how to apply centuries-old instruments of social control to the modern age. It was also a template for the rise of illiberalism elsewhere.

The adoration of the Thai throne had proved an effective tool for the country's military, administrative and business elite. But the death of Bhumibol had revealed a fundamental problem. Monarchy's great organising strength – the concentration of authority in a person who has a veneer of legitimacy that coup-mongers lack – was also its weakness. When it fell into the hands of someone who ignored the old conventions, the creation suddenly looked much more precarious. The climate became stifling and paranoid for everyone, the stuff of medieval witch-hunts.

Now Thailand was caught in a trap barely apparent to the ever-growing numbers of visitors that had elevated it among the world's most popular holiday destinations. One well-connected acquaintance said the monarchy under Bhumibol and Vajiralongkorn was 'like religion'. Unquestioning loyalty was the only way to survive, however unworthy the object of that commitment. As my contact put it: 'If you are pinpointed as the person who does not believe, you are the heretic.'

3

Enter the Punisher

Ellen hadn't expected to be caught up in Philippine president Rodrigo Duterte's war on drugs. But now, fearful and angry, she wanted the world to know how her husband had ended up dead. The need to talk had brought her to this joyless room with peeling walls in an office building in Manila. She was worried about reprisals and didn't want her real name used, nor to appear full face on camera. Instead, I focused on her hands, her blue-painted fingernails clasped together on her lap and moving fretfully from time to time as she told her story.

Ellen lived with her husband and children in one of the deprived areas of the capital that were central to Duterte's bloody campaign. She didn't present her spouse as a paragon. She said he had in the past made money as a courier of small quantities of '*shabu*', or crystal meth, the stimulant whose use had exploded across Asia during the previous decade. But she insisted he had stopped once Duterte took office in June 2016. He was afraid because the new president had pledged to slay drug dealers and feed their corpses to fatten the fish of Manila Bay.

Whether or not Ellen was right about her husband being a changed man, the events she recounted some months after Duterte took office were horrific. She said she and the children were asleep when police raided the house and opened fire. 'The police went to our house and shot my husband repeatedly,' she said. 'They dragged me and the children out, and we heard more gunshots.'

The police, as usual, insisted the slaying was in self-defence. It has been their explanation for thousands of deaths in drug operations since Duterte came to power.

Ellen had no faith in achieving any accountability for her husband's death. But she wanted to nail what she saw as a lie at the heart of Duterte's claim to be dismantling the narcotics industry. As she saw it, influential drug kingpins were being spared, while innocents or anonymous small-time players such as her husband were being slaughtered.

'I know that we will not get justice during the tenure of Duterte, because his war on drugs is really a war on the poor,' she said. 'They intentionally kill the poor, rather than jail and punish powerful people.'

Claims like Ellen's had become a common refrain from victims' relatives, rights groups and cops turned whistle-blowers in Duterte's Philippines. Yet none of this appeared to have gained much public traction. The president enjoyed sky-high approval ratings for his 'clean-up'. He also traded heavily on a tendentious creation myth: that his hard-line approach had transformed his home city of Davao during more than twenty years as mayor there.

Duterte's first years in office bore hallmarks of totalitarianism, as his administration launched its scorched-earth drugs policy, repressed dissent and built a cult of personality around its chief. The leader, who traded in offence and threats of violence, was a repudiation of a discredited old order and harbinger of a dangerous new one. He was also a prototype for political earthquakes that would follow over the succeeding years, in countries from the US to Brazil.

The rise of Duterte is a case study in the growing autocratic style among elected leaders worldwide. He sold himself to voters by

offering a superficially plausible backstory and then promising easy
solutions to a real problem that he hyped until it seemed an existential threat. It worked as long as few people had the time or inclina-
tion to analyse either the evidence or the morality too deeply. Those
who did found the image of Duterte the redeemer grotesque.

Many journalists, Filipino and foreign, have gone deep into the
drug war gore. Some have taken great personal risks. They had
described a campaign in which the ideology was almost as disturbing as the violence. In particular, the president's supporters appeared
to discount or dismiss the testimony of Ellen and many others
who had suffered from or documented the drugs crackdown.

It seemed the more alarming because this was no hidden
campaign of terror in a secretive dictatorship. The Philippines can
make a good case to be the most democratic country in South-
East Asia. Institutions, some of them government-funded, did raise
concerns about the death toll. Duterte himself made no secret of
the slaughter during his frequent tirades, even if he claimed the
deaths were justified. He once likened himself to Adolf Hitler and
vowed to kill millions of people if needed to stamp out narcotics
in the Philippines.[1]

Critics of his blood-soaked presidency noted how the pursuit of
drug suspects had the hallmarks of a tyranny's pogroms. The lists of
targets were drawn up by local officials in districts known as
Barangays, leaving all sorts of scope for grudges to be indulged and
scores settled. 'Due process' was supposedly a warning by authorities
to leave the area or face the consequences. It was known in the
Philippines as *tokhang*, meaning 'knock and plead'. If a suspect didn't
respond to the calls to surrender, the gunmen could come for him
or her at any time. Activists said some people were killed without
even receiving the *tokhang* deterrent. You might die, in Kafkaesque
fashion, without even knowing you were on the hit list – or why.

★   ★   ★

Duterte's notoriety in the West extended beyond his drugs war. His speech was sprinkled with violence and misogyny. His rhetoric had led some to brand him the 'Trump of Asia', although that had things the wrong way round. It would have been more accurate to call Trump the 'Duterte of the Americas', since the Philippine leader took office six months earlier.

More grievously, the comparison was misleading because Duterte had gone far further than Trump – and he operated under fewer constraints. Duterte's story was more of a cautionary tale for the US in how far erratic and instinctively autocratic elected leaders can go if they manage to shrug off the checks on their behaviour. Trump used his inauguration speech to summon a dark vision of rampant drug crime and 'American carnage'; Duterte portrayed the Philippines even more apocalyptically as a virtual narco-state. While Trump boasted he could shoot someone on Fifth Avenue in New York and still not lose voters, Duterte had bragged about actually killing people. Trump called for political opponents to be jailed; in Duterte's Philippines it actually happened.

Duterte soon became a liberal bogeyman and one of the names regularly cited in think pieces about the rise of autocracy. He not only sloughed off criticism, but appeared to thrive on it. Because he appeared instinctive and uncensored, he gave his supporters permission to be so, too. He often seemed not merely willing but delighted to say things that offended people.

Duterte embodied other themes of the new age of authoritarianism. He swept away an old dynastic technocratic elite. His predecessor was Benigno Aquino III, son of both a former president and an assassinated political hero. Like Trump, Duterte sold himself as someone who could be trusted because he said what he thought and worked in plain sight. It was a winning strategy because it created the impression of openness: 'you might not like him, but at least he's honest.' But of course important parts of his

story were always concealed – most crucially, the details of the
drug killings.

It is perhaps no surprise that Duterte serenaded Trump with a
Filipino love ballad at a South-East Asia regional summit dinner in
November 2017. When I saw the picture, I wondered who was
the master and whom the pupil. 'You are the light in my world, a
half of this heart of mine,' the Philippine leader sang, in what he
said was a performance requested by the US president.

It marked a new phase in a notable – if sometimes volatile –
bonding between the leaders of the two Pacific allies. Trump had
quickly highlighted a change in approach from the Obama
administration, whose criticisms of Duterte over the drugs war
had triggered the Philippine leader to brand his US counterpart a
'son of a whore'. Trump instead praised Duterte for 'fighting very
hard' against the 'scourge' of narcotics.

Perhaps Trump envied Duterte's mandate. Unlike the US
president, Duterte actually received more votes than any of his
opponents (though still not a majority). His 39% tally in a five-
way race easily beat the 23.5% of the runner-up – Mar Roxas,
grandson of another former president. Duterte also proved much
better than Trump at expanding his popularity. His approval ratings
stood at more than 71% after eighteen months in office.

The Philippine leader rode out failures and difficult questions. His
financial affairs came under scrutiny, but he simply denied wrongdoing and moved on. His promise of peace to his restive home
province survived the debacle of a city there being occupied by ISIS-
inspired militants, triggering a months-long siege to recapture it.

Duterte's mastery of public opinion reflected a personal history
that – unlike Trump's – was steeped in politics. Davao is the
Delphic centre of Duterte's legend. It was as mayor of the city, the
most populous in the country's south, that he honed his tough-
guy modus operandi. His nicknames included The Punisher and
Duterte Harry.

Davao is also where the story of Duterte the anti-establishment
maverick fighting on behalf of the common person starts to fray.
In Manila, he's the outsider bothering the elites. But in Davao, he
was the ultimate insider.

Duterte's home town is a world away from sprawling and traffic-
choked Manila, whose crowding sometimes felt like Bangkok on
steroids. Davao is the capital of the vast southern island of
Mindanao, a land of succulent fresh tuna, giant grapefruit-like
pomelos and mixed Christian and Islamic heritage. The variety is
typical of a country of more than seven thousand islands whose
cultural influences are a melange of Asia, Europe and the Americas.
Outside the cities lie lush forests and banana plantations, with
glimpses of flattened buildings that speak of the region's vulnerability to typhoons and other extreme weather.

The greater Davao region is home to the Philippine Eagle sanctuary. The great bird's preservation was a cause championed by the
American aviator Charles Lindbergh, a notable supporter of the
original America First movement. That historical connection is a
reminder of the Philippines' history as a US colony. The occupation – which lasted for most of the first half of the twentieth
century – was one root of Duterte's frequent criticisms of the US
when he clashed with Obama.

My flight to Davao in late 2016 yielded another brief Philippine–
US intertwinement. A pair of evangelist pastors from the American
South and their wives sat in the seats next to me. I chatted to one
of the churchmen about the US election, which had taken place
just a few weeks earlier. I asked him why so many evangelicals had
ended up supporting Trump, given that so much of his behaviour
seemed to conflict with their stated core moral beliefs.

The pastor answered carefully that many evangelicals weren't
strongly drawn to either Trump or Clinton. He said he hadn't

voted for either of them. But, he went on, a good number of religious believers had decided to overlook Trump's personal flaws in favour of his wider agenda. Clinton, on the other hand, was seen by a good number of the faithful as beyond the pale. 'Many of them', he concluded, in words that might have come from Duterte's own mouth, 'just saw her as a *Jezebel*.'

From the moment I arrived in Davao, it was clear I had entered Duterte's domain. A sticker on a passenger's bag on the carousel showed the president's trademark symbol of a clenched fist punching towards the viewer. It felt like I couldn't escape him in a city where he was idolised in posters, stickers, cups and T-shirts. Life-size cut-outs of him were scattered around business premises. The only other person who loomed larger was the late Pope John Paul II, who was immortalised in a huge sign down the road from Duterte's favourite piano bar. The president still liked to go there and sing.

Duterte's father moved to Davao when Rodrigo was a boy. He soon made it big in politics. He became a provincial governor and ended up serving as a minister in the cabinet of Ferdinand Marcos, before Marcos turned himself from elected president to dictator for the rest of his more than two-decade rule. Duterte studied law at the prestigious San Beda College in Manila, whose alumni – in another neat bit of triangulation – include Jose Antonio, Trump's business partner in the project to build the fifty-seven-storey Trump Tower Manila. (Antonio's representatives said he didn't know Duterte at the time.) Duterte became a state prosecutor and then went into politics himself in the 1980s.

Some say Duterte junior ran for mayor in 1988 partly because his mother, a teacher and civic leader to whom he was devoted, deflected pressure to take the job herself. Duterte ran the city as mayor or vice-mayor for the following twenty-seven years, barring a three-year spell when he was constitutionally forced by term limits to stand down. He became a member of the House of Representatives instead. When I visited, his children were perpetuating the family political dynasty: his daughter Sara was mayor and his son Paolo her deputy.

One of Duterte's oldest Davao associates was Sonny Dizon, a maverick local business person. He invited me to meet him at the crocodile park he owned outside the city, where Duterte had held a post-election celebration party. I found the inevitable lifesize cut-out of the president, grinning from among crowds enraptured by the animal shows. A young staff member caressed and kissed a python, while another made a cockatoo ride a miniature bicycle. Billboards advertised crocodile steaks and nourishing skin creams made with reptile extracts.

Dizon was friendly and informal. He sported a ponytail and was dressed in jeans, boots and a designer crocodile-skin belt. He was a fidgety sort of tycoon, all the more flighty that day as he fielded calls to wish him a happy birthday. He was also indiscreet, to a point, bragging about the well-connected people he knew – and flashing me text messages to prove it.

His personal history also gave him an interesting insight into the world of drugs. He told me that he used to take *shabu*, which he described with feeling as 'so addictive, so overwhelmingly powerful over people'. He told me he had kicked that habit and now campaigned for the legalisation of marijuana as a pain reliever.

We moved outside in front of a pen where two saltwater crocodiles were having a midday snooze. Dizon's own experience with drugs did not seem to have given him any great empathy for other users. He turned out to be a staunch supporter of the drugs war and a forthright defender of its deadly prosecution.

'Well, of course when you clean up dirt, the dirt has to be thrown away,' he said of the high casualty rate. 'I don't know who is killing who.'

He continued: 'Like the president says: order the policeman, "Whenever you feel that your life's threatened, fight it out and kill your enemy."'

When I asked who was dying, Dizon replied that it was a 'big puzzle'.

What if even more people were killed? 'So be it,' he said, seeming a little irritated by such an obvious question. 'Because they are destroying the next generation.'

Then the hyperactive Dizon left for his next appointment. His giant crocodiles slept on, dormant with menace.

Duterte's Davao was not a place to question authority or step out of line. Outside the imposing City Hall, where young boys were doing backflips under the narrow-eyed gaze of decorative stone eagles, a faded sign reminded visitors of a ban on public smoking. The board – which carried the Coca-Cola logo – threatened a 5,000 peso (about £75) fine. People who wanted to carry on puffing were corralled in little pens away from buildings, like criminals ritually shamed before their fellow townsfolk.

Two soldiers milled about on a busy shopping street across the road. They were from the Davao Task Force, which patrols the city and runs checkpoints coming in and out of it. It's a legacy of a bloody decades-long history of bomb campaigns and other clashes between authorities and Muslim and communist insurgents. When I visited, a peace agreement was more or less holding, but the conflict continued and had left people with a higher tolerance of a security state than might otherwise have been the case.

Across from City Hall, I bumped into Duterte's sister in a furniture showroom (it was one of three occasions during my Davao stay when I met a relative of the president by chance). Jocellyn Duterte was clearly enjoying the celebrity that her brother's rise had brought. She readily agreed to an interview and reeled off other media organisations to which she had talked lately. A nephew scurried around after her, acting as her personal assistant.

We chatted sitting somewhat incongruously on one of the shop's display suites. Jocellyn was poised even as customers browsed around us. Her floral dress, yellow shawl and multicoloured beaded bangle combined with the garish purple sofa to deliver a vivid retinal burst. She watched me attentively from beneath sharply etched eyebrows.

Jocellyn admitted to a 'love and hate' relationship with her older brother. She said she found him autocratic and used to number herself among his critics. She noted how, at seventy-one, he was the oldest person to be elected president in the modern era – an existential factor that might be driving his search for quick fixes. 'The mayor has a very authoritarian manner,' she said. 'I think the opposition right now thinks he is going to be a dictator, you know.'

She said she became more sympathetic to her brother the leader when she returned to Davao after fifteen years away. She was impressed with how it had changed from the 'killing fields' she had left behind. I was not surprised to hear this: in my experience, expatriates of many countries are often among the first to sign up to hard-line rule. They're not around to see the suffering of those crushed – and then they can come back home once it's done.

Perhaps, Jocellyn went on, Filipinos were due a dose of authoritarianism. It was the age-old autocrat's bargain: tough love to save us from ourselves. 'We can talk about democracy, but before we can go to democracy I think we should have discipline,' she reflected. 'And I think that's what the Filipinos needed. And that worked in Davao.'

A pattern was emerging from my encounters in Davao. Members of Duterte's circles would offer praise, but at the same time – wittingly or unwittingly – raise doubts about him. Whether it was Dizon's offhand ruthlessness or Jocellyn Duterte's now suppressed concerns about authoritarianism, what was emerging was hardly a bland puff for the city mayor turned national leader.

Jocellyn Duterte's host at the furniture store was Samuel Uy, the owner and another long-time compadre of Rodrigo. Uy's grungy white T-shirt and well-worn face gave little sense of his status as a leading Davao magnate. Uy said he used to rent the future president videos from a store he ran in the 1980s. Duterte liked action flicks such as the *Indiana Jones* series. He also loved movies about justice. *Walking Tall*, a minor cult hit from 1973 starring Joe Don Baker, was a particular favourite. It's based on the true story of a Tennessee man named Buford Pusser who is beaten up by gangland thugs and exacts his own revenge on them. He is put on trial, stirringly acquitted and then elected as town sheriff. He goes on, as the IMDb movie database puts it, to almost single-handedly clean up his small town of crime and corruption – but at a great personal cost.

Uy, who had been a classmate of Duterte's brother at school, said he didn't charge the president-to-be for the film rentals. He saw something he admired in the man. 'I noticed he is a very sincere person,' recalled Uy, in an interview in his messy office at the back of the store. 'So I tell him, you don't have to pay me, because of our friendship. That's where our friendship started.'

Uy – whose business interests ranged from office equipment to cockfighting – said he had helped the president financially for decades. He did it because he noticed Duterte sometimes seemed 'short of money' because of his generosity to others. Uy fished out a pocket book showing a ledger of what he said were acknowledgements of money he gave to Duterte ahead of his first successful mayoral campaign. Headed 'Victory 88', one page showed twelve entries dated between 25 November 1987 and 8 January 1988 totalling about 150,000 pesos (£2,250). A handwritten note on a separate page relating to another payment was initialled 'RD'.

At the end of *Walking Tall*, Sheriff Pusser's wife is killed and he is seriously injured in an ambush. After his wife's funeral, he rams his car into a gambling parlour and kills two of his antagonists. People of the town arrive and ransack the establishment, in a kind of cleansing of the temple. The camera pans to the badly injured Sheriff Pusser, who weeps tears of gratitude amid the violence.

I asked Uy why he though Duterte enjoyed films like *Walking Tall* so much. He answered without hesitation. 'Because he always said to me that evil will prosper if good men do nothing,' the businessman said. 'That's what he is doing now. He is doing things just to lessen the evil.'

In the real world, Buford Pusser died in a car accident in 1974, aged just thirty-six.

There was little doubting Duterte's heroic status in Davao. But there were also few illusions about his methods. They might be violent, the logic seemed to go, but they worked. Or, at least, they seemed to work for the city's elite.

Elsewhere, there were hints of more ambivalence – and more compassion. They just needed to be teased out.

Albert Hernandez, the taxi driver who took me to Davao airport for my return flight to Manila, told me at the start of the journey that he was a big Duterte fan. Hernandez, a wiry twenty-seven-year-old, deflected a question about whether he thought innocent people were being killed: 'It's not like I investigate,' he said. But he did acknowledge the point that 'people can change if you give them a chance.' Then he went much further: he volunteered that five years previously he had been addicted to *shabu*. 'I am selling coffee and I use the money to buy drugs. Every day drugs, every day drugs,' he recalled of those times. 'One day I saw my mum and she was crying and said: "What are you doing, my son?" I was crying also and I decided to leave that place.'

He moved out of his home town of Cotabato to be free of the social circle that was into drugs. He got a job as a security guard, started a relationship and stayed clear of *shabu*. Other addicts were not so lucky and needed help. 'When I see people on the street, I am crying because they don't know what they are doing,' Hernandez said.

Now he talked of his devotion to his adopted daughter of eighteen months, who was suffering from a heart defect.

'I give life to that child,' he said. 'Before I was not proud of myself. But now I look at the changes and I am so happy for what I am.'

The ride had turned into an uplifting coda to a dispiriting trip. The chat was an example of what I took to calling the 'Duterte dialectic'. A person I spoke to would express strong support for the war on drugs. After a bit of talk, a more nuanced view would emerge. In a quarter of an hour, Hernandez had turned from condemnation to sympathy informed by personal experience. As so often, a person's views turned out to be much more nuanced than the crude currency of soundbites, opinion polls or referendums suggested.

Hernandez had also hinted at something deeper. In some fundamental sense, I didn't think many Duterte supporters I spoke to really believed the police protestations that they only killed in self-defence. They knew the force's huge corruption problem. Instead, they simply avoided looking too deeply into the matter. What they weren't forced to confront they could ignore.

Back in Manila, I went to look for a man who had little faith in the story of the Duterte Davao miracle from the start. He worked in Intramuros, the walled Manila city built by the Spanish imperialists in the sixteenth century. It is a place of atmospheric stone buildings and epigrammatic signboards. 'Remember that the squires of today will be the knights of tomorrow,' read one.

After lunch at the Mitre restaurant, where each dish was named after a churchman, I walked round the corner to the headquarters of the Catholic Bishops' Conference. The offices of the individual priests gave on to a well-shaded courtyard where an icon of the Virgin Mary stood next to the main building's door.

Father Amado Picardal had a certain world-weariness about him that could have come from a Graham Greene novel. He had seen the Duterte drugs war up close in Davao, where he was a priest for fifteen years. He said he twice had direct experience of the Davao killings, including one person who was shot in a car park outside a church where he was conducting a service. He and fellow activists had examined the activities of death squads that operated in the city for many years.

'For a period from 1998 to 2015, we monitored 1,424 killings perpetrated by what we believe were the members of the Davao death squads,' Picardal said, with unnerving precision. 'Many would believe this has been inspired, supported and even organised by Mayor Rodrigo Duterte.'

Duterte had never given a clear account of how his crackdown on crime in Davao worked. At times he denied the existence of any Davao Death Squad (DDS), the collective name often used for the armed groups that enforced the clampdown. At other times, he apparently revelled in his involvement in killings. He denied allegations aired at a 2016 Senate hearing, where a self-confessed hitman claimed he was part of a DDS unit that killed about fifty people on Duterte's orders. But, when mayor of Davao, Duterte had told reporters in 2015 that an Amnesty International report claiming he was responsible for seven hundred deaths during the anti-drugs campaign had actually underestimated the true number by a thousand. He went on to inform an audience of business people at a function at the presidential palace in December 2016 that he used to personally hunt down drugs suspects to kill when he was in charge of Davao.[2]

Father Picardal's critique went still further than accusing Duterte of complicity in mass killings. He said the depiction of

Duterte's stewardship of Davao as having turned the city from bedlam to paradise was misleading. A presentation by the Davao police force in 2015, Duterte's last full year as mayor, said there were 363 murders (plus 252 other unlawful killings) in the first half of the year. That was a slight rise on the same period in 2014 and more than in the much larger New York City during the whole of 2016. It also wasn't clear whether the Davao statistics account for the 'liquidations' by police that were often reported on the force's Facebook feed, complete with pictures of the dead in pools of blood. The city also had high numbers of rapes, which Duterte once said reflected the presence of 'many beautiful women' there.[3]

Nor was the vision of Davao as an emblem of good administrative governance under Duterte borne out by evidence. Questions loomed over whether the city had ranks of 'ghost workers', who received salaries for doing nothing. A 2015 report by the Philippines' Commission on Audit said fewer than a quarter of the 14,499 people on the city's payroll held regular, verifiable positions. The commission raised concerns about the lack of documentation, including daily time records and attendance logs, to prove people were doing what they were being paid for.

Picardal was also worried that the Philippines' drugs problem, while serious, had been 'highly exaggerated' by Duterte and his supporters. While Duterte had claimed there were more than 3.5 million users in a country of about 105 million, the Office of the President's Dangerous Drugs Board in 2015 estimated the number at barely half that. It also said that significant numbers of those were either very occasional users or used only marijuana.

Picardal said Duterte and his backers had successfully changed the narrative so that people now parroted that drugs were the worst threat facing the Philippines. It followed that, if it was so bad, a war was needed to stop it. In a war, just about any action by government could be justified – and not only in the fight against drugs.

'It seems to me that all of these things are a myth, the myth of Duterte,' said Picardal of the various claims made on the president's behalf. There was an even bigger myth, he added: 'That what he did for Davao he will do for our entire country. There is a belief among so many people that President Duterte is a saviour of our country.'

As Picardal left the office on his bike at dusk, I thought about the reversal of fortunes exemplified by Duterte's rise. A man like Picardal who sat at the heart of the Catholic establishment in a highly religious country was now in a lonely fight against public opinion (Duterte's popularity on the campaign trail had even survived calling Pope Francis a 'son of a whore'). Picardal looked small as he waited in the fading light for a break in the early Friday evening traffic: a man on a pushbike off to take on a juggernaut.

Others were to make even more direct allegations about murders in Davao under Duterte's mayoralty. A chief accuser was Arturo Lascañas, a self-confessed hitman who claimed to be a member of the Davao Death Squad. Lascañas had gone into hiding after his revelations, fearing that his life was in danger.

A *Financial Times* colleague was able to arrange for us to interview Lascañas at a safe house in Manila. We waited in a cafe for a contact who took us a short drive away to a nondescript block of flats where the man himself waited. The interview took place in a room with the curtains permanently drawn for privacy.

The ex-cop looked a lot more tired and stressed than when he had testified before a Senate inquiry months earlier. Then, he had appeared in a crisp white shirt and black jacket, looking well groomed and younger than his fifty-six years. Now he gave a good impression of a man dishevelled by guilt. He said a tipping point was remorse at his involvement in the killing of his own brothers. Dogged by that and other crimes, he said he had vowed to make a full public confession. 'If I violate this promise, I will die carrying all these secrets to my death,' he said. 'Until the end I will be condemned by God. I can't keep this secret any more. Whether people believe me or not, I will tell my story.'

It was a terrible tale. Lascañas claimed he had been involved in more than two hundred murders during a thirty-four-year police career that ended in 2016 when Duterte left the Davao mayoralty to become president.

Lascañas said he was part of an anti-crime task force that was initially set up by Duterte to take on drug suspects, kidnap-for-ransom groups and other criminals, but later targeted personal and political rivals. Lascañas said his team was paid between twenty thousand and three million pesos (£300–£45,000) per killing. One job was to murder an entire family, including a five-year-old boy and a pregnant woman. The biggest fee was for the notorious murder in 2003 of Jun Pala, a well-known journalist and Duterte critic.

Lascañas said his loyalty to Duterte was so great that he did not stop an operation targeting his own brothers, Cecilio and Fernando, who were both *shabu* users. 'I allowed my fellow police officers to arrest my brother, kill him if he resisted,' he recalled of Cecilio's death. 'He died. Of course, the records say he fought back.'

He continued: 'I was indirectly involved in their deaths because of my blind obedience, my blind loyalty to [Duterte's] campaign against illegal drugs – only to know later that it doesn't apply to everyone.'

Lascañas acknowledged that there was an intense campaign to discredit him. He had broken into tears at a press conference a couple of months previously when he said he lied previously to the Senate investigators by denying his death squad involvement. He insisted he had not been paid to change his story, pointing out that his claims were self-incriminating. He said he had come to realise he had been 'blind' in his previous belief that he could justify the killings because it made the public safer. 'I thought it was serving the greater majority, for the best interest of more people, and there's nothing wrong with that,' he said.

Now he hoped to stop the bloodshed under the Duterte presidency, 'even if I am imprisoned or killed'. He wanted to expose the truth: 'What's happening in Metro Manila and the entire Philippines, everything is patterned from what we did in Davao.' Of Duterte, he said: 'He will be accountable for everything, not just I. Both of us will be accountable.'

A Senate committee took fresh testimony from Lascañas after he recanted his previous statements. It then promptly shut down the probe after a single hearing. Asked what had happened to the claims, Panfilo Lacson, committee chair, who is a former police chief and Duterte ally, replied simply: 'Filed and noted.'

Days after I met him, Lascañas fled the Philippines for Singapore. Another source of domestic criticism of Duterte had been abruptly silenced. In June 2017, Philippine authorities announced they were seeking the help of Interpol to catch the remorseful hitman.

Duterte's Davao years – and the political messaging around them – have served as a blueprint for his presidency. He sold the public a Manichean view of a country split between decent people and a criminal class that threatened to overwhelm them. He used the rhetoric of extreme violence, often personalised. On the eve of the November 2017 summit where he had his choral tryst with Trump, he claimed he had stabbed a person to death as a teenager because the guy had been giving him a strange look.[4] He had previously claimed that he once threw a Chinese man suspected of rape and murder out of a helicopter mid-air.[5] As so often with the frequently self-contradictory Duterte, it was hard to tell where macho fantasy ended and horrific fact began.

Duterte was also a skilled politician, capable of turning apparently negative events to his advantage. When a shocking case emerged of the murder of a South Korean businessman by a gang that included police officers, he theatrically denounced the force as 'corrupt to the core'. The killers allegedly arrested the man on trumped-up drugs charges, murdered him at police headquarters and then extorted money from his widow by pretending he was still alive. The police said they would suspend anti-narcotics operations to clear out 'scallywags' from their ranks. Yet the cops were soon back on drugs duty – until they killed a high-school student and were once again relieved of their command.

The drug war death toll became ever murkier as authorities gradually restricted the flow of information. Official documents I saw that had been prepared in early 2017 said more than 2,500 people had been killed at the hands of the police in narcotics operations, with more than 3,500 further killings unexplained. By early 2019, authorities said more than five thousand people had died during the drugs war, while some activists believed the true number was several times that.[6]

The crackdown was truly a nationwide affair, as outlined in a scathing report by Amnesty International in January 2017.[7] The research was based on scores of interviews and covered twenty cities across the country. It said police officers were paid a bonus for every kill and also enriched themselves by stealing from victims' homes. They even earned commissions from funeral parlours where the corpses were sent, according to witnesses. Two contract killers said a police officer gave them five thousand pesos (£75) for each drug user slain and ten thousand to fifteen thousand pesos (£150–£225) for each 'drug pusher', Amnesty alleged. The rights group claimed the scale and scope of the wrongdoing could constitute crimes against humanity before the International

Criminal Court, whose prosecutor had already registered concern about the drugs war.

As I moved around Manila, the drugs war seemed like a zombie movie in which the terrors came out at night. During daylight hours, you would see the signs in the news of a killing, a relative's testimony, or the fear of those who flocked for rehabilitation to escape death. Then fresh ghastly events would arrive after sunset.

A private addiction rehab centre in the capital provided a particularly unnerving sideways glimpse of the carnage. The facility – called Roads and Bridges to Recovery – was full of motivational signs that exhorted patients to stay drug-free. The strict regime included disciplines such as silently facing a wall in contemplation for twelve hours or more.

From the office where I chatted with my hosts, we could hear the shouts and howls of residents from elsewhere in the facility. Staff explained that patients were encouraged to release their frustration. The atmosphere was primal and the tension evident.

Even quitting drugs gave no guarantee of safety to these people once they were out on the streets again. Chester Ligtinen, the centre's programme director, explained that he was even worried his own history could come back to haunt him. He had previously been a drug addict, although he had been clean for six years.

'For now I am not really sure of my own safety,' he said. 'There is something in my mind, saying, "You should be cautious of the things you are doing, of the places you go."'

His words highlighted an apparent paradox at the heart of the drugs war – and indeed Duterte's popularity. People claimed to be hugely supportive of his clampdown, yet they also feared being caught up in it. A December 2016 poll by the respected Social Weather Stations non-profit research institution found a net sixty-three percent public approval rating for the president. But it also found that almost four fifths of respondents were worried they or someone they knew would become a victim of the anti-narcotics crackdown. It seemed to distil again how people's feelings about the drugs war were mixed and more nuanced than superficial opinion poll numbers or vox pops suggested. It appeared to me that one of the reason pro-Duterte trolls were so vehement online was precisely because they knew public support was conditional and precarious: hence the need to give the impression that no one had any doubts.

The vicious pro-Duterte social media campaign was one reason so few people had been prepared to stand up publicly to the president. The online network was known as DDS, which stood for Duterte Diehard Supporters. These were also, perhaps not coincidentally, the initials of the Davao Death Squad. One prominent troll target was Maria Ressa, the co-founder of Rappler, a popular news website. She had been targeted with death and rape threats after her site ran stories that questioned the government spin on events. Ressa and Rappler were indicted in October 2017 on tax evasion charges they said were politically motivated.

Duterte and his supporters also had their sights on other high-profile public critics. These included Senator Antonio Trillanes IV, a charismatic former naval officer. Trillanes claimed Duterte, relatives and friends had amassed tens of millions of pounds in unexplained wealth while he was Davao mayor. Trillanes said he had transaction records to show that funds totalling 2.4 billion pesos (£36 million) were transferred into accounts in the name of Duterte, family members or close associates between 2006 and 2015 – a year when Duterte's official salary and benefits as Davao mayor came to less than £25,000. Duterte denied any wrongdoing and dared Trillanes to launch a court action against him.

Trillanes acknowledged he had something of a chequered past on the rule of law. He was once detained for more than seven years after leading an uprising of fellow military officers against alleged corruption under a previous president. But he pledged to resign as a senator if his allegations about Duterte were proved wrong. In

September 2017, the Philippine Office of the Ombudsman launched an inquiry into Trillanes' claims, but this was terminated in less than three months.[8] Duterte's spokesman said the president welcomed the investigation and had nothing to hide. In September 2018, Trillanes was arrested and bailed after Duterte scrapped an amnesty under which he had been released from detention in 2011.

Duterte's biggest opponent – and the closest he had to a nemesis – was one of Trillanes' fellow senators. Leila de Lima was an ex-human rights lawyer and activist who was among the first to raise fears about the official violence promoted by the man who would become president. I first met her in February 2017 in her parliamentary office (Manny Pacquiao, the boxing champion turned senator and Duterte cheerleader, had his headquarters just down the corridor). De Lima had denounced what she said was a politically motivated campaign against her. Television crews were stationed outside her door, ready for the predicted police raid to seize her – a swoop which happened just a couple of days later.

Some months later I went to see de Lima in prison at the sprawling Camp Crame police headquarters in Manila's northern reaches. I was a little nervous of discovery at the detention centre, because I hadn't revealed to the authorities that I was a journalist. The officers didn't show much interest beyond a cursory bag search. A list of about twenty inmates, including de Lima, was posted at a second reception area inside the complex.

The visiting room was decorated sparely, a fan whirring at full power in a vain attempt to lessen the stifling late-afternoon heat. I took a friend's advice and set up the room's fold-up chairs so that they minimised the viewing scope of the CCTV camera mounted on the ceiling. I made sure also that I sat with my back to the device, to conceal my note-taking as much as possible.

De Lima appeared, looking a little slimmer than before but still healthy. She was colourfully dressed in red trousers and a patterned red, white and blue shirt. She wore black-rimmed glasses and a brace-let she had been told was blessed by Pope Francis. She tried to appear cheerful and stoic. 'I just have to weather the storm,' she said. 'I know it will pass. But I don't know how long I will be detained here.'

The senator was accused of accepting money from jailed drug dealers – claims she described as 'simply surreal'. She was scornful of what she said was the government's reliance on the evidence of 'drug convicts' who were, in some cases, part of a gang she targeted during a previous stint as justice minister. She rejected as betrayal the testimony against her from past associates, including a senior National Bureau of Investigation executive and Ronnie Dayan, a man who had been her driver, bodyguard and lover. Duterte supporters had used her relationship with Dayan in a smear campaign based on sexual innuendo.

De Lima had already been in jail for almost five months with-out any sign of her case being moved for consideration by a court. Amnesty International had declared her a prisoner of conscience, while the European Parliament had passed a motion denouncing her detention. 'As long as the attention of the world is on my situation, I will be okay,' she said, with an optimism I hoped would not prove misplaced. 'It's that international attention and that international interest that – more or less – prevents them [the authorities] from doing something else.'

The senator didn't have any complaints of ill treatment by prison authorities. She wasn't allowed access to electronic devices, but could still get physical newspapers. She even found reason to be glad of being cut off from the Internet. 'It's actually a blessing also to some extent,' she said, 'because I am now able to concen-trate on reading, meditations and reflections.'

She had become 'more prayerful' but was also deep in John Grisham's *The Confession*, which is about a man wrongly sentenced to death for the murder of a cheerleader. Miscarriage of justice seemed to be a theme: a visitor had brought her a copy of *The Count of Monte Cristo*, Alexandre Dumas' adventure about a man who hunts down the people who conspired to have him wrongfully jailed. Dumas' mid-nineteenth-century hero stops just short of self-destruction, although he feels troubled by the impact of his campaign of ruination on innocents linked to his targets. 'He exacted revenge on everyone who betrayed him, but it seems there was collateral damage,' said de Lima. 'So he felt rather empty in the end.'

Duterte's enmity towards de Lima seemed worthy of literary epic treatment. She believed he had never forgiven her for her actions when she was the chair of the Commission on Human Rights, a government-funded body.[9] In 2009, she opened a probe in Davao into the drug war killings during Duterte's mayoralty. 'He's rather obsessed with me,' she said of the president. 'It's a personal vendetta. This is very personal to him because I dared call him out and I dared investigate him in 2009. And I did that to him in his own territory – his own kingdom of Davao city.'

She added: 'No one, let alone a woman, can do that to him. He's a misogynistic character.'

Critics of Duterte have long condemned his attitude to women. He notoriously joked about not getting the chance to rape an Australian missionary who was gang-raped and murdered in Davao in 1989. He has claimed he has a video of de Lima having sex with her driver and has said he might show it to Pope Francis.[10] The senator has denied such a video exists and has noted with distaste Duterte's apparent sexual preoccupation with her. 'I cannot resist asking the president, what do you see in me that you find so sexual?' she once said. 'Why is your mind so fixated on my sexual aspect?'[11]

Duterte had also attacked de Lima with his own version of the cry of 'lock her up' Trump and his supporters used against Hillary Clinton. In September 2016, a few months after taking office, the president said evidence existed to charge de Lima and that she would end up going to jail. Weeks after she was arrested, he gave a joint press conference with the House of Representatives speaker, who declared de Lima the 'number one drug lord' in the country: or, as Trump might have put it, 'crooked Leila'.

De Lima argued her case was a 'microcosm, really, of how Duterte has managed to coerce key institutions' in the Philippines. She noted the slowness of the Supreme Court to consider a challenge she had made to the charges against her (it would eventually throw out her case in October 2017, by a 9–6 majority).

'He threatened me and he made good on his promise – one of the very few promises he was able to make good in his first year in office,' she said. 'The killings – and putting Senator de Lima behind bars. Those were the only two promises he was able to fulfil so far.'

De Lima said she and her Liberal Party hadn't seen The Punisher coming. They 'never really thought anyone like Duterte would be president', she said, in an assessment that will be familiar to many US Democrats. The Philippine Liberals were also wrong-footed by the intensity of the social media campaign for Duterte, much of it 'garbage', she added. 'With all his braggadocio, he was only good for local governance, not national scale. We never thought a majority of the Filipino people would go for someone like him.'

Her honesty continued with an assessment that – intentionally or not – risked sounding condescending in the way some anti-Brexit and anti-Trump campaigners do. It also seemed politically exactly the wrong way to persuade the electorate that it should vote for someone other than Duterte next time. Many people had been 'duped', she said. 'I don't know if it's naivety on my part, the idealist in me. I would like to think Filipino voters can still be trusted to make the right choice.'

Her predictions for the future also seemed to be from the anti-Trump and anti-Brexit playbook. She ticked off the talking points: his popularity wouldn't last; the economy would suffer; there would be buyers' remorse. 'It will hit the masses sooner or later,' she said. 'And once that happens there is a time they will start realising they made a mistake. They will. It's just a matter of time.'

If that analysis seemed to take too little account of what people's preoccupations and prejudices were when they voted for someone like Duterte, then de Lima was more convincing when she turned to the impact of the killing spree. The many thousands of deaths would have a wider knock-on effect, she predicted, as people saw it happening to those they knew – and then started to ask why.

'More and more people are being killed, even if they stopped reporting the official figures,' she said. Families so far untouched would inevitably see relatives killed. 'They haven't experienced yet being victims. But if they do become victims, I'm sure they would have a change of heart.'

Like other Duterte critics, de Lima seemed to be trying to convince herself that the nightmare would soon end. She listed the mounting problems during his tenure: corruption, unfit people in government, martial law imposed on the whole province of Mindanao after a militant group aligned with ISIS took over the city of Marawi. 'There ought to be disillusionment,' de Lima said. 'There ought to be general frustration. There isn't. Not yet. But there will be.'

Visiting time was starting to run out. De Lima said she didn't think she would get out as long as Duterte was president. If he served his full term, that would be almost another five years. She was getting people she knew to bring food, for fear she might be poisoned via prison rations. She added that she would feel vulnerable even if she were freed. 'I still feel I am not safe here, inside or outside, as long as he's the president,' she said.

Propaganda on de Lima's fate was flying about the Internet. 'There is even fake news about me,' she noted, showing how the phrase has permeated global English. One story said she had committed suicide, another that she had been released and was now under house arrest. There were different falsehoods for different readerships, the vengeful Duterte supporter and the worried liberal. Each would be happy to read their own bespoke version of events.

De Lima's arrest attracted only muted public protest from high-profile Philippine politicians and the wider public. She called the response 'lacklustre'. It is not as if the Philippines is politically inert. The 'people power' movement that in 1986 ousted Ferdinand Marcos, the dictator of two decades, is the stuff of folklore. But every uprising has a tipping point, especially if there is the possibility of change at the ballot box. Paradoxically, it can be easier to mobilise people against the hard wall of full-blown dictatorship than against the spongier autocracy of an elected leader.

De Lima described how her world as a successful lawyer and lawmaker had now shrunk to an overheated cell and a small exercise yard. She walked it every day exercising with a weight – which, if nothing else, had been good for her abs. For now, she was physically well enough, if lonely. 'I feel like I am healthy,' she said. 'I hardly get colds and coughs because of less pollution. And . . . I am fully rested because I have enough sleeping hours. I sleep soundly. But I am all alone from five o'clock in the afternoon to eight o'clock in the morning. My only companions are the stray cats.'

Her aide appeared to tell us time was up. 'I just have to survive this,' the detained senator concluded. 'But I think I am getting stronger.'

As I came out, the combination of repression and openness seemed bizarre – and the more unnerving for it. I'd been able to visit de Lima without difficulty and had encountered no official suspicion. Yet there was a good argument for saying the senator was a political prisoner. At the very least, due process seemed to have broken down in her case. If the jail-visit policy seemed typical of a democracy, the prosecution of the case against her was more reminiscent of a dictatorship.

Duterte had found a way to establish an authoritarian style in a state supposedly governed by institutions and the rule of law. As Trump has also discovered, if you are shameless – or at least give the impression of being so – your critics' excoriation has little effect. The drug killings went on, and Duterte enjoyed the prestige of hosting world leaders. Duterte's soaring approval ratings faltered a little as inflation climbed, but by the end of March 2019 Social Weather Stations put public net satisfaction with him at sixty-six percent – the highest since he became president.[12]

There was a potentially important nuance. People defined as 'extremely poor' – typically those at the sharp end of the killings in slum areas – marked the president lower at fifty-eight percent. It was still a comfortable majority, but it also showed how Duterte's support was strongest among the middle classes and wealthy people who were mostly insulated from the drug war's immediate impact.

By January 2018, de Lima was approaching the first anniversary of her arrest. She was unable to attend an event organised by the US magazine *Foreign Policy* to honour her as one of its Global Thinkers. Her aides issued a bleak but defiant statement on her behalf:

President Duterte and his minions have not stopped demonizing, slut-shaming, and persecuting me.

State-sponsored extrajudicial killings, fake news, and lies continue unabated.

As no succor from pliant courts is forthcoming, with our democratic institutions under attack, an opposition that is decimated and dissents crushed, I'm prepared for the long haul.

No high concrete walls, barbed wires, or caged environment
can silence me. I remain free in spirit and unbroken. I'm not
giving up on my causes for truth, justice, and human rights.
To the world, keep watching the Philippines.[13]

A year later, de Lima was still in jail in what Amnesty International
called a 'blatant attempt to silence her courageous voice'.[14]

In February 2019, Maria Ressa, head of the Rappler news
website, was arrested and charged with criminal libel. The case
concerned a 2012 article – updated in 2014 – that accused a businessman of involvement in murder, drug deals and human traffick-
ing. Ressa denied the charge and was released on bail. Amnesty
International branded the case 'brazenly politically motivated'.[15] It
appeared to be part of an expanding crackdown on Rappler after
the authorities scrapped the company's operating licence and
accused it of tax evasion and violating rules on foreign ownership
– both of which the media organisation denied.

Days later, I met a group of senior Filipino government officials
visiting Brussels. They were touring Europe in an attempt to cut
off funding sources to development projects that they alleged were
being tapped by communist rebels. They were also there to mount
a defence of Duterte and his drugs war against what they branded
unfair criticism.

Lorraine Marie Badoy, undersecretary at the presidential
communications office, admitted that Duterte's rhetoric had made
her 'cringe' when he first took office. But she said she was now
unfazed by his talk of murder.

'He says: "I'm going to kill you" and what did that achieve?
Hundreds of thousands of drug surrenders,' she said. 'That's just his
mouth! He speaks the language of these people. They understand
him and they cower. We have never had anything like that before.'

Alex Paul Monteagudo, chief of the National Intelligence
Coordinating Agency, went still further. He compared the

anti-drugs crackdown to a war of national survival. 'Would Europe not defend itself if your countries are destroyed?' he asked, extending the metaphor to cast Russians in the role of Filipino drug dealers. 'Would you not kill Russians if the Russians invaded the EU? That's defence of your country.'

I asked how they personally viewed their leader. Badoy described him guardedly as a 'singular, singular president'. Monteagudo praised him in more intimate terms that also suggested how much Duterte had profited from the sense of imminent apocalypse he had conjured.

'He looks like a father who protects his children,' Monteagudo said. 'He says he's willing to lose his presidency, his honour and even his life protecting his family. If I am a father and my children are going to be put at risk, who wouldn't put his life on the line?'

II

THE WORLD AS IT IS

4

We Are Not a Lie

Syria's war had lasted so many years that even the UN had long ago stopped counting the dead. But Professor Debarati Guha-Sapir had not.

The Brussels-based public health researcher and her team had used body counts from the ground to demonstrate the devastating impact of a mid-conflict change in tactics by President Bashar al-Assad's regime. By 2016, the intensification of government air raids meant children made up almost a quarter of civilian deaths in opposition areas, according to the research published in *The Lancet Global Health* journal. That number had climbed sharply since the uprising began in 2011, as the Syrian military launched more air strikes and barrel bombs – improvised devices packed with high explosives and often shrapnel. In all, ninety-seven percent of deaths caused by barrel bombs were civilians – and twenty-seven percent of those were children. This contradicted regime claims that its offensive was a proportionate response to what it had characterised as a terrorist-led uprising. Instead, the numbers suggested 'indiscriminate or targeted warfare contrary to international humanitarian law and possibly constituting a war crime', the paper by Guha-Sapir's team concluded.[1]

When I went to see her in person, Guha-Sapir was no Syria polemicist. She was interested in the conflict and asked keen questions about it, but she did not pretend to be an expert on its politics and history. She saw her primary duty as to bring what evidence she could marshal to bear on a situation clouded by a miasma of online propaganda. 'What we are saying is not "You stop bombing",' she said. 'But what we are saying is . . . '"Don't give this story of 'this is an anti-rebel thing'" – you have a five times higher risk of killing children. That's what the data shows – and after that it is up to you and your conscience as to whether you bomb or not.'

Guha-Sapir was trying to do something unusual. She wanted to bring a little bit of statistical truth to a conflict being swarmed over by propagandists and armchair ideologues. The battle for Syria had – as with other modern wars, such as the Russian annex-ation of Crimea – triggered an electronic bombardment of claim and counterclaim. All sides had their disingenuous advocates. But those who sought to play down or even excuse the Assad regime's crimes loomed particularly large.

Assad had fought against an armed rebellion that had lasted longer than either of the two world wars. He claimed he was battling for the security of his country and even of Europe. He found many in the West, across the political spectrum, prepared to indulge his version of events. That required a rewriting of history in real time on a scale rarely before attempted – and perhaps only possible in an age of digital disinformation and distraction.

By contrast, Guha-Sapir wanted – however imperfectly – to build a picture of what actually happened to those targeted by war. While others preferred to grandstand on social media with tendentious theories, she sifted through the numbers. She was an empiricist in an age of exhibitionists.

'Whenever we see a conflict situation that has a lot of water vapour coming out, we are attracted to that,' she said of her team's ethos. 'And we want to see what the boiling pot really is.'

★   ★   ★

Syria's terrible conflict had made a deep impression on me. I visited periodically over eighteen months during the early part of the war and then followed it from a distance. I was struck – and, in one sense, horrified – by how international perceptions of it changed over that time. What started as a story of a dictatorship's savage brutality against peaceful protests morphed into a tale of the fanatical threat of ISIS and jihadism. The Assad regime, tacitly and sometimes openly, became normalised. The enemy of the West's enemy became, if not a friend, then at least a grudgingly accepted neighbour.

I had a small perspective of the pre-war Syria that added to the sense of tragedy. I'd visited the country to do an Arabic course in 2007. I found it an intoxicating place – who could not? I socialised in grand hidden courtyards in Damascus's old city, broke the Ramadan fast with worshippers at a mosque in Aleppo, and marvelled at the Roman city of Palmyra and the Crusader vain-glory of the Crac des Chevaliers. I acquired tastes that would stay with me long after: astringent pomegranate juice, sugared fruits from the Damascus hinterland's abundant orchards, the meze that Syrians insist makes their cooking even better than the cuisine of their more self-promotion-savvy neighbours in Lebanon. My photos of that time seemed supernaturally vivid, enriched by Armenian inscriptions, impossibly intense sunsets and Technicolor sprays of market spices. I felt the weight of palaeontological layers of history and civilisations – and, in the background, the control of the decades-old modern Assad dynasty.

I returned to Syria early in 2012 for my first reporting trip in a landscape at once familiar and alien. I would make five visits over eight months to the country as it slipped deeper into war. Demonstrations brutally suppressed by the regime during the early months of the 2011 Arab uprisings had quickly escalated into armed conflict. Although I entered each time officially on a government visa, I found I had a surprising amount of freedom to move around between regime and opposition areas. I assumed I was heavily monitored but I was rarely accompanied by an official minder – and never when I visited anti-regime enclaves. However nervous I was at times, my little surges of stress were just a small hint of the terror of people who lived in the war zones. My engagement with the country was also fleeting compared with that of many more courageous journalistic colleagues – some of whom did not survive.

The scale and speed of Syria's fall delivered a grim lesson in the impermanence of so many certainties we consider fixed. I had seen countries descend into conflict before, notably in West Africa. But these places were often blighted by a postcolonial history of instability: the suffering was no less traumatic, but it was less remarkable. The closest analogy to Syria I could think of from my own experience was the West African nation of Ivory Coast. Foreigners had once dubbed its biggest city, Abidjan, the 'Paris of West Africa', but the death of its post-independence strongman president, Félix Houphouët-Boigny, marked the start of an era of conflict and coups. I remembered a former government official explaining to me that 'after Houphouët died, the cement broke'. He meant it as praise, albeit double-edged, for the former leader's role in holding the country together. Years later, I read it most as a lesson for the implosion that often seemed to follow dictatorial rule.

The turbulent initial phase of Syria's war was the prelude to a wider crisis that would rock the region and the wider world for many years. Over time, more and more headlines focused on radical Islamist groups and the savagery of ISIS – particularly when it started filming its beheadings of Westerners in 2014, and then claimed authorship of terrorist attacks in Europe. The Syrian uprising triggered by the torture of children who had written anti-regime graffiti in the southern city of Dera'a increasingly seemed like a footnote. The nihilism of ISIS also began to obscure how, all the way through the conflict, the Assad regime bore responsibility for the vast majority of killings by far. It sometimes seemed the story of the battle for Syria was changing before my eyes.

I'd come across Guha-Sapir's Syria death toll work after I'd arrived in Brussels to become a *Financial Times* correspondent there. I saw she worked at Belgium's Catholic University of Louvain. It turned out her office was just a few metro stops from my house. Now and again, in journalism, the story really did come to you.

I visited the professor on a damp afternoon in April 2018 that did little to dispel the aftershock of my first north European winter for many years. I was glad to enter the warmth of the nondescript office block where she was based. I found her in excellent spirits, saying goodbye to some colleagues after throwing a small leaving party for one of them. She offered me tea and a leftover slice of a baked sugar tart, served winningly with fresh strawberries.

Guha-Sapir, who wore a large scarf thrown dashingly round her neck, had become an internationally recognised specialist in disaster and conflict. It was a focus of her work as director of the Centre for Research on the Epidemiology of Disasters. The centre's emblem was slightly disturbing: a large splotch radiating chaotically in all directions, bringing to mind the spatter of blood.

Guha-Sapir was born in the Indian city of Calcutta and went to university there. She did further study at Johns Hopkins University in the US and at the University of Louvain, before working for the World Health Organization. Her professional honours included membership of Belgium's Royal Academy of Medicine, and her authorial credits included a book with the forbidding title of *Thirty Years of National Disasters 1974–2003*.

Guha-Sapir's first work after her studies looked at how the pulp and paper industry in the US state of Wisconsin's Fox River Valley affected child health in the area. Since then, she had worked in many disaster zones, such as Indonesia's Aceh province and India's Tamil Nadu after the 2004 Asian tsunami. She had also done a project in famine-hit Chad in Central Africa, as well as building disaster health information systems in countries including Mozambique, Ethiopia and Sudan.

She had carved out a particular niche in estimating conflict death tolls. She described her specialism as a 'really important' idea, uniting ethics and empiricism. It also had potentially big implications for international policy and could inform efforts to try to protect people from lethal threats. 'It's a moral concept in terms of not forgetting the people who have died in these wars and having some kind of credible amplitude put on it,' Guha-Sapir said of her work. 'But, on the other hand, it's also important to have evidence-based conclusions, not just emotion-based conclusions.'

Researchers have long grappled with the difficulties of establishing the numbers of casualties of great atrocities. Often basic information, let alone documentation, is scarce. One example is the 1975–79 Khmer Rouge genocide in Cambodia. A thoughtful 2005 article compared attempts to gauge its scale to the old story of the group of blind men encountering an elephant:

> The first man feels the side of the elephant, and announces that it is a wall. The second man feels the trunk, and declares that it is a snake. The third man feels the leg and insists that it is a tree. The fourth man feels the tail, and says that it is a rope.
>
> We describe things on the basis of what we know ... but what we know is often incomplete. Grappling in the dark, we try to determine the size, the shape, the nature of the unknown.[2]

The piece goes on to note that even some otherwise excellent work on the Cambodian genocide is underpinned by dubious statistical estimates. It talks about the 'snowball effect: arbitrary figures become widely repeated, and soon become part of the conventional wisdom.' It adds: 'It is precisely *because* these works are thoughtful and articulate that they serve as good examples. Numbers are unforgiving: small errors can become big errors, but even faulty statistics are still imbued with authority by virtue of their source.'

Guha-Sapir's first big battle was over casualty rates in the conflict in west Sudan's Darfur region that began in the early 2000s, where the government in Khartoum was fighting a rebel movement. She described how she became increasingly uncomfortable with 'well-meaning colleagues in the US, who are close colleagues of mine still', whom she felt had quoted ever higher death toll numbers without sufficient evidence. Activist pressure for US action grew steadily, including from high-profile figures such as the actor George Clooney. In September 2004, the US declared that the killings in Darfur constituted genocide. The Coalition for International Justice, a now defunct non-profit organisation based in Washington and The Hague, estimated in April 2005 that as many as 400,000 people might have died.

Guha-Sapir said she and her colleagues started looking at the data and were bothered by what they saw as 'a kind of one-upmanship of the numbers of people who had died'. They felt that the campaigners' urge to poke US authorities into action had taken over. 'Different sources and the media would, depending on their political proclivities, cite a source of how many people have died and then somebody else would say it was even higher,' she said. 'And this went on and on, rising.'

Guha-Sapir and her team put out their take in May 2005. Their headline conclusion was that 120,000 deaths between September 2003 and January 2005 – less than a third of some estimates – were directly attributable to the conflict, 35,000 of them violent killings. They were careful to acknowledge that – however many people had died – the death toll was 'far too many' and the exact number would 'probably never be known', as there were so many uncertainties. 'Malnutrition, epidemics and violence occur sporadically, claiming many lives in some areas and none in others,' they wrote.[3]

In 2010, Guha-Sapir and a colleague published another study that argued for an updated number of about 300,000 conflict-related deaths in the Darfur region, with almost four fifths of those due to diseases such as diarrhoea.[4] This provoked a reaction from those who insisted the numbers were higher still. The Guha-Sapir work was criticised by one author for allegedly omitting a peak period for violent deaths.[5] He argued the numbers of dead should have been 500,000 by 2010 and 600,000 by 2018. Guha-Sapir told me that the mortality rates estimates underpinning those figures sounded too high; she also pointed me to a 2006 US Government Accountability Office survey of Darfur death estimates that rated her organisation's numbers best in terms of data, methods, objectivity and reporting of limitations.[6]

On Darfur, the UN had – as in Syria – stopped counting. UNICEF's website quoted an estimate of between 200,000 and 300,000 people killed since the start of the conflict in 2004. The tally appeared not to have been updated since 2008, according to a date given at the bottom of the page.

Disputes over the death toll from the Iraq War would prove even more bitter.

At their heart was a 2006 study in the *Lancet* that estimated 655,000 people had been killed because of the conflict, with more than 600,000 of them violent deaths.[7] Guha-Sapir and colleagues calculated a huge discrepancy, putting the toll at more like 125,000. Along with other critics, Guha-Sapir questioned whether the *Lancet* article researchers had oversampled areas where there were discrete very deadly events such as car-bombings. The Iraq paper authors made some limited admissions of error in the labelling and presentation of their data, but otherwise stood by their conclusions.[8]

Once Syria lapsed into a long-term conflict, it became an obvious subject for Guha-Sapir's investigations. The UN stopped issuing regular updates on the death toll in 2014. UN special envoy Staffan de Mistura estimated the figure at 400,000 in early 2016, although he acknowledged this was only a rough number. Various groups, some more independent than others, continued to count.

'Why do we count the dead? Why do we want to know how many people have died in Syria?' Guha-Sapir asked me rhetorically.

She listed some obvious reasons and other more subtle justifications. One motivation was to establish severity: understanding roughly where an event stood in the hierarchy of historical abominations had an impact on public opinion and how politicians responded to it. Second, looking at death tolls over time might also reveal if a conflict was becoming more or less severe – which could have implications for both humanitarian assistance and wider international policy. A third driver – 'which is not very appealing at all but is important' – was to see how the demographics of the population had changed, for instance if many young men have been killed. 'So suddenly in a population pyramid you will get dips on the male side say between twenty and forty – and that has implications for the future,' she said.

I mentioned how hard I'd found it when working on a book about Nigeria to find an agreed-on figure for casualties in the 1967–70 civil war over the breakaway self-declared state of Biafra. It was a particularly tough one to work out because so few of the fatalities were from fighting: many were from disease and starvation. Estimates of the toll ranged from several hundred thousand people to three million. It had disturbed me that we literally didn't know the fate of millions of people: were they dead or alive?

Guha-Sapir acknowledged that she and her colleagues took a relatively conservative approach to counting. Not everyone agreed with that. 'Our estimates tend to be lower than anybody else's – and we have been attacked on that,' she said. 'Indirect deaths are very, very difficult to estimate. Probably the only reasonable way of doing it is the demographers would look at the counterfactual: how many people you would have expected to die in those eight years if nothing had happened.'

The main source Guha-Sapir's team had used for its Syria work adopted a similarly cautious perspective. The Violations Documentation Center in Syria was linked to the peaceful opposition but had won credibility for its rigorous approach to confirming casualties, making full use of the proliferation of photo and video in modern conflict. 'They report strictly what they have seen and not what they have heard,' Guha-Sapir said.

The centre's work had made it enemies across the conflict spectrum. In December 2013, armed men stormed its office in the opposition Damascus suburb of Douma and abducted the lawyer Razan Zaitouneh, the organisation's head, and three colleagues, one of whom was also Zaitouneh's husband. As of February 2019, there was still no news of what had happened to them. Islamist militants were suspected of being responsible for their disappearance.

The VDC now worked from Switzerland, releasing monthly bulletins of estimated casualty numbers. Between the start of the uprising in mid-March 2011 and December 2018, the centre recorded 191,219 battle-related deaths, of which almost two thirds were civilians. Those figures were significantly lower than other estimates, including even the old UN figures. On the seventh anniversary of the start of the war, in March 2018, the Syrian Observatory for Human Rights, another opposition-linked group, put the number of deaths at about 511,000, of which it said it had identified more than 350,000 people.

The VDC said the Syrian government military and allied militias were responsible for the overwhelming majority – almost 85 percent – of the 123,279 civilian deaths recorded. Russian forces backing the Assad regime accounted for another 4.8% of the casualties, ISIS for 3.2%, armed opposition factions for 2.4% and the US-led international coalition for 2%.[9]

The first important message was: all sides had blood on their hands. The second: by far the bloodiest, accounting for almost ninety percent of civilian deaths, were those of Syrian government-aligned forces. Both those assertions are consistent with other credible analyses of the conflict death tolls. Many more deaths and abuses sat in the penumbra of this battlefield killing, including people who had died of starvation, disease and execution in custody. As much as half Syria's pre-war population of about 23 million had fled their homes: as of August 2018, the United Nations High Commissioner for Refugees (UNHCR) said 5.6 million people had escaped the country with another 6.6 million displaced internally.[10]

Guha-Sapir pointed to an 'extremely clear signal' of a shift in government war strategy in 2013, when Russia had yet to intervene officially on Assad's side and the regime's survival was still in doubt. Deaths from ground weapons – such as single-target guns, hand grenades and ground-launched missiles – were 'completely overshadowed' by killings by air-launched missiles and barrel-bombing raids. 'So just by looking at the deaths you can see how the war has changed,' she said.

Fast-forward five years and the regime's scorched earth approach seemed to be working – at terrible human cost. The Assad government had steadily taken back opposition-held territory with little but pro forma protests from Western powers, which had been preoccupied with driving ISIS from its self-proclaimed caliphate. 'It's a survival mode they're in and in which they're doing quite well,' Guha-Sapir noted of the regime's strategy. 'The international community has come to heel very nicely.'

A common allegation by the Syrian regime's defenders was that critics of Assad closed their eyes to rebel abuses. That was undoubtedly true in some cases, for reasons of political expediency. But the argument was deeply problematic as a generalisation. At its heart was often an effort to exculpate the Syrian government or, at best, suggest a false equivalence in scale between regime and anti-regime violence. Most of all, it could not explain away why a government supposedly fighting a war to defend its people had killed so many of them.

One of the many ghastly side effects of ISIS's brutality had been the way its horrors, widely disseminated on the Internet, obscured Syrian regime violence. Each ISIS execution or ISIS-inspired terror attack in Europe probably had more impact in the West than tens of thousands of unseen deaths at the hands of Assad's forces and the Iranian militias that helped prop them up. For many in Europe and the US, the battle for Syria became synonymous with the fight against ISIS.

I saw a different type of war. It was one I stumbled into by accident, on a cold morning in the Eastern Ghouta suburbs of Damascus in January 2012.

The sprawling Ghouta – noted for their orchards – marked the point where the streets of Syria's historic capital began to bleed into the countryside. Many craftspeople lived there, including a large community of carpenters known for their hand-built furniture. Ever the *Financial Times* reporter, I thought their business troubles might be a good way to tell the story of the social and economic impact of a conflict then already almost a year old.

I was barely twenty minutes' drive from central Damascus when the surroundings began to change. Daubed on the wall were flags that looked a bit like Syrian flags, but were not: they had three stars instead of two and the top bar of the horizontal tricolour was green instead of red. Up ahead was a checkpoint manned by youths dressed in a ragbag of military fatigues – but they were not from the Syrian military.

'Free Army!' cried one. 'We are independent. We are with the people,' he continued. A half-dozen of his comrades quickly gathered, one with a rocket-propelled grenade launcher over his shoulder.

I had not expected to find rebels operating so openly this close to the centre of the capital. They were skittish and clearly not in full control of the situation. But they moved freely around quiet streets lined by apartment blocks and largely deserted artisans' workshops of the kind I'd come to see.

Some of the young rebel fighters claimed to be among the mass defections from the army that had followed the initial regime crackdown. The most senior officer was a twenty-four-year-old university student who gave his name as Mohammed. He rolled up his sleeve to reveal what he said was a scar from a bullet wound suffered during the first anti-government protests back in March 2011. He sought a society that was 'not racist, balanced, with equal opportunity for everybody', he said, in an apparent reference to the tensions between the country's Sunni Muslim majority and the Alawite minority from which the Assads hailed. He added that he wanted to 'feel secure when I would like to sleep'.

The atmosphere hummed with both fear and possibility. In one of the few shops that was still open, I chatted to a group of four men, two brothers and a pair of their cousins. They soon launched into an extraordinarily candid political argument: three were for the regime and one for the opposition. All spoke movingly of the need for the right to differ peacefully after the stifling decades of dictatorship. One of the government supporters, a man named Abdulmohsin, gestured to his pro-opposition relative and pointed his fingers to his own head as if cocking a gun. 'I will kill myself before killing my cousin,' he declared.

★   ★   ★

Despite that briefly uplifting moment, several visits to Syria over the following months showed me I was on the edge of something very dark. As conflict spread to various parts of the country, central Damascus remained mostly peaceful – but the sound of mortar fire from the Ghouta and sometimes closer sporadically boomed all around. It was disturbingly easy to slip between worlds, from streets of quotidian normality to districts thick with the smell of death.

In July 2012, rebels rattled the regime with a series of attacks around Damascus. Those were nerve-racking days when it was not clear what would happen next – or where. Against a backing soundtrack of shelling elsewhere in the capital, my fixer and I drove around the city and ended up in a district named Qaboun.

Burned-out and bullet-riddled buildings bore the evidence of the battle that had taken place there. In a cemetery nearby we found people wearing disposable face masks, surrounded by seventeen white body bags. They zipped one open and gazed at the neatly bearded man with a bloody wound in his throat who lay inside. 'It's Ahmed,' said one. 'I heard he is a barber,' said a second, before resealing the body bag. A man turned away from the corpses to batter his hands against a pillar in sorrow and rage. 'This is what Bashar wants,' said one onlooker. 'An animal is better than Bashar,' spat another.

Residents said the regime had attacked with shelling and a helicopter after rebel Free Syrian Army (FSA) soldiers had appeared in the area. Some – though by no means all – Damascus residents were angered by such opposition tactics, since they knew the regime's response would be brutal. I asked one man, who gave his name as Ahmad, whether he thought the rebels had endangered the civilian population. He retorted that the government had already killed dozens of people, including his brother-in-law, through firing on peaceful demonstrations.

'The government is shooting, whether the FSA is here or not,' he said.

Those overseeing the perfunctory funerals in Qaboun did not want to linger and neither did we. We didn't have to drive far before we were back into the domain of coffee shops, boutiques, and business as usual. The famed Naranj restaurant in the old city was still open for sumptuous meals with business and diplomatic contacts. At the Dama Rose hotel, where the emasculated UN mission was holed up, the sound system was cranked up for weekend pool parties where a gilded Syrian elite of buff young men and women in swimsuits fought with water guns.

It was a time of different universes collapsing into each other like some warped quantum thought experiment. Once, when I greeted a government functionary and asked how he was, he replied with a question: 'Have you read the book *1984*?'

'Yes, why?' I replied.

'I am Winston Smith,' he confided, referring to the novel's main character, a small-time bureaucrat who rebels against the totalitarian state he works for.

The tension was pervasive. I woke in the early hours of each morning worried about what the day would bring. I probably didn't help myself by choosing as my literary distraction the detective thrillers of Ian Rankin. These tales of murder, corruption and the dismal side of the human spirit were not exactly an uplifting counterpoint to my environment. But they seemed in some sense appropriate.

Set against that were the many moments spent with those who dispelled pessimism like wind blowing through a bank of cloud. Many conversations were inevitably snatched, with people who did not want to be seen talking to me – or indeed be in a public place for long. I always made sure I arrived in Syria thick-haired and stubbly, so I had an excuse to go to the barbers and mingle while I had a cut and shave.

Other times I saw clandestine evening anti-regime protests and chatted at length with activists and artists who were either well hidden or enjoyed a status that gave them at least a measure of protection. The novelist Khaled Khalifa scorned the intellectuals and artists whom he saw as having sacrificed political integrity to keep favour with the regime. When we met, his left arm was still in plaster because of injuries sustained during the attack on the funeral of the musician Rabie al-Ghazzi, who was shot in a suspected assassination by regime loyalists. Khalifa described how mourners were set upon by pro-government agents armed with batons. Syrians who were against the regime could not even bury their dead in peace.

'The Syrian dream was to be a civil society,' he said, as we chatted at his small flat that clung to Mount Qasioun, the mountain overlooking central Damascus. 'But now the dream of the Syrian is just to live.'

It was a refrain I heard often elsewhere. Anti-regime activists were painfully aware that their calls for peaceful change were being obliterated as the conflict deepened and the pro-regime smears that they were a gang of terrorists grew ever louder. It drove one pro-democracy campaigner I met to a memorable declaration: 'We are not a lie!' she cried in frustration.

Over those nine months relatively early in the war, it was clear the horror would get far worse. Each time I visited Aleppo, the country's mercantile centre, people spoke of ever greater foreboding that the conflict in the surrounding countryside would eventually engulf it. By the time I returned in July 2012, that bleak forecast was about to be fulfilled.

Rebels had taken the city's Salaheddin area and were braced for the inevitable regime reaction. I could feel the disintegration and the desperation as I scurried from street to sketchy street of one of the world's oldest continuously inhabited cities.

'If I hear shooting now, I don't care,' an activist known as Tammouz told me, after we had dashed across a road to avoid gunfire audible not far away. He added: 'People are not worried, because they already lost everything that makes life beautiful.'

Regime helicopter gunship fire boomed around the city the next day. At the beautiful boutique courtyard hotel where I was staying – which I was later told had been destroyed by rocket fire – staff told my fixer and me that security agents had been looking for us. We decided not to return.

We drove just before nightfall out to the airport, along the highway where we'd seen several corpses dumped. Someone had set up a makeshift roadblock with concrete blocks and sticks. It was still unmanned and we were able to swerve around it.

We arrived back in Damascus after midnight. We drove through a succession of checkpoints guarded mostly by plain-clothes militia men, toting machine guns and clad in body armour. They had a wildness about them that seemed to mix aggression and terror.

It was the night of the opening ceremony of the London Olympics, which added an extra layer of the surreal. As we tried to allay the pro-Assad fighters' considerable suspicions about me, my phone beeped with text messages about stoic Brits blubbing with pride in their nation. Worlds collide in the electronic age in ways never before possible. In hindsight, the strange juxtaposition of events seemed another small sign of how international attention would forever be distracted from Syria's war.

When I returned to the country in June 2013, much had changed. It had been nine months since my last visit, because I was no longer being granted visas. I was told by the information ministry official who dealt with foreign journalists that something I'd written had upset the government. She didn't tell me what, but I suspected it was a piece about an alleged massacre in Daraya, a southern suburb of Damascus.

I read my readmittance as a sign of growing government confidence. I reckoned it had a story it wanted to tell. So it turned out.

I went to the city of Homs, which had once been a linchpin of the uprising. It was where the veteran US war correspondent Marie Colvin and the French photojournalist Rémi Ochlik had been killed by regime rocket fire in 2012. Government forces had been pounding the rebellion into submission since.

I visited a small detachment of government soldiers near the front line at an intersection of two roads strewn with wreckage. They told me they were safe where they were, but could not move past the side streets to the left or right of them for fear of a bullet in the head from rebel sniper vantage points there. They had made the most of their enforced immobility by setting up an ersatz open-air lounge formed from a couch and two baroque-style armchairs taken from abandoned houses nearby. A table bore a salver of under-ripe grapes.

'We have not been ordered to advance, so we are sitting here enjoying our tea,' said one young sergeant named Safwan, over *mate* tea served decorously in tiny cups with metal drinking straws. 'When we get the order to move, we are ready.'

He and his men showed me round the devastated streets. At one point, I stepped on a hard plastic sheet of the kind used to roof a shed or shack. I heard a cracking sound and then, suddenly, I was falling through space. Next I knew, I was waist-deep in foul water at the bottom of a drain hole more than two metres deep. I had been very lucky and landed with both feet on a muddy surface, rather than being impaled by an obtruding piece of metal. The water, rancid as it was, had also helped cushion my fall. The soldiers pulled me out, to some hilarity.

Afterwards, I reflected darkly on what might have happened had I died. The regime would have reported how I had suffered a bizarre accident – an explanation that would doubtless have aroused suspicion and ridicule, even though it would have been true. Who would believe such a story of apparent haplessness (except, perhaps, those who know me well)? It was a reminder that the apparently implausible can, sometimes, still be real.

The signs of the regime's greater feelings of security were everywhere. In Damascus, back roads that I'd travelled on during past visits to opposition areas had been sealed off. Previously inaccessible officials suddenly wanted to talk. The economy minister boasted to me about how Western attempts to cut off finance to the regime had failed because of its access to funds from Russia, China and Iran.

The deputy foreign minister Faisal Mekdad articulated this new regime swagger most bluntly. As salvos of government shells boomed in the background outside his office, he warned how the West would regret its opposition to Assad. Extremists in the opposition would soon be attacking countries in Europe, he predicted. Western countries were 'working for chaos not only in Syria, but in their region', he declared.[11]

My first thought was of the cynicism of the regime's attempts to distract the world from its crimes. My second was that its strategy would probably work.

The rise, fall and partial rehabilitation of President Bashar al-Assad in the Western imagination is instructive. When he took over on his father Hafez's death in 2000 after thirty years in power, many outsiders – including some who should have known better – hailed the change as a sign of modernisation and political loosening in Syria. It was even dubbed the 'Damascus Spring'. Debate in *muntadayat* (salons) began over possible reforms including the end of martial law, the release of political prisoners and the legalisation of political rivals to the ruling Ba'ath party. A prisoner release programme in late 2000 appeared to offer some hope of change.

But the etymological echo of the Prague Spring proved all too appropriate. Where the prospect of change in the Czech capital in 1968 was crushed by Soviet tanks, a clampdown and fresh round of imprisonments in Damascus snuffed out reform there. By the end of 2001, Bashar's rule was moving towards the authoritarianism of his father's notoriously repressive state.

Yet Bashar was able to continue to promote the fiction of significantly greater openness. While Hafez – a former air force officer – was the epitome of the thuggish and secretive autocrat, Bashar was a British-educated eye doctor. His wife, Asma, had grown up in the UK and worked for an investment bank. An analyst who had once worked for a charity sponsored by Asma al-Assad succinctly summarised the secret of Bashar's international charm offensive: 'He speaks English and his wife is hot.'[12]

Some Western countries also gave the Assad regime credibility. Tony Blair, Britain's prime minister, had visited Damascus in October 2001 – though the trip proved rocky as Assad attacked him over the war in Afghanistan. As late as 2008, French president Nicolas Sarkozy hosted his Syrian counterpart in Paris. France even awarded Assad its prestigious Légion d'honneur in 2001, moving to revoke it only in 2018.

In February 2011, just weeks before the uprising in Syria began, *Vogue* magazine ran an infamous profile of Asma al-Assad that married the personal and political propaganda of the Damascus regime. Headlined 'A Rose in the Desert', the piece cooed over the 'freshest and most magnetic of first ladies', a 'thin, long-limbed beauty with a trained analytic mind who dresses with cunning understatement'. While it did not entirely airbrush Syria's repressive security state, it was breathless about the supposed social liberalism of the 'safest country in the Middle East' where 'women earn as much as men and the Muslim veil is forbidden in universities.' Syria was a 'place without bombings, unrest, or kidnappings', the article observed, although it did offer one harbinger of trouble ahead by noting how the country's apparatus of control was 'deep and dark'.[13]

Even the regime's brutal crackdown once the revolt began in March didn't deter some leftist commentators who still seemed to see its supposed 'anti-Western' stance as more important than anything else. Years into the war, Syrian government defenders were still running the argument that Assad was 'democratically elected', even though the polls he contested were not worthy of the name. In 2000, after his father Hafez died, he was the only candidate and officially won more than 97 percent of the vote. He repeated the exercise in 2007, with the same result.

Another election – this time nominally multiparty – was held in June 2014, more than three years into the war. Ban Ki-moon, then UN secretary-general, had warned that holding the poll 'amid the ongoing conflict and massive displacement' would 'damage the political process and hamper the prospects for a political solution'. The regime went ahead anyway. This time Assad scored 88.7%, his nearest 'rival' coming in with less than 5%.

Another argument advanced by regime sympathisers was that the support for the uprising constituted only a minority of Syrians. They knew that this statement was impossible to disprove (or indeed prove). But it also ignored the deeper question, which needs to be asked in all authoritarian societies, of the reasons why people express support for dictatorship. Some Syrian Assad advocates were beneficiaries of the regime, or despised the revolution (or both). Others feared the consequences if they did not offer their backing. This was a regime whose followers chanted 'Assad or we burn the country'. Can a leader who rules by such intimidation ever be said to command 'support' in any meaningful or moral sense?

Yet, as the wheels of war ground mercilessly on, the 'Assad as the lesser evil' argument began to gain strength in the West. ISIS's destruction of parts of the Roman ruins of Palmyra was emblematic of how the regime was able to begin to turn the tables of outside opinion. ISIS fighters reportedly beheaded Khaled al-Asaad, an eighty-two-year-old scholar of the site, and hung his body on a column there, because he would not tell the militants where valuable artefacts were stored.[14]

The story could hardly have been more sickening. It was an obscene contrast to the magic I recalled from before the war of watching the sun set on Palmyra, bathing the Temple of Bel and the surrounding ruins in an orange glow. To imagine it deliberately flattened was indeed a kind of tragedy: but to move from that observation to support for a bloody dictatorship and its allies seemed a perverse non sequitur.

Advocates of detente with Assad, or even some kind of co-operation, included prominent Western politicians such as Boris Johnson, who would later become the UK's foreign secretary. In December 2015, he called for Britain to work with Presidents Assad and Vladimir Putin to defeat ISIS, as 'everything else is secondary'. He pointed out how Syrian government forces, with Russian air support, were close to recapturing Palmyra.

'Am I backing the Assad regime, and the Russians, in their joint enterprise to recapture that amazing site?' Britain's soon to be top diplomat wrote in his *Telegraph* column. 'You bet I am.'[15]

By the time I arrived in Brussels in late 2017, the Syrian regime was close to suffocating the rebellion. In April the following year, it was about to capture the Damascus suburb of Douma, the biggest rebel enclave in the vicinity of the capital. It was also a place I knew a bit.

I'd first visited Douma with a UN peace monitor mission in early 2012. The atmosphere was intense. Huge crowds chanted anti-regime slogans and pleaded for protection from what they said were regime snipers perched in nearby tall buildings. 'This is

Douma!' they yelled defiantly, like a football crowd. One man clutched a placard telling the UN Security Council that Syrians were tired of the 'lies, illusions, hypocrisy and silliness' they heard from the wider world.

At the imposing main mosque I met a fresh-faced student who called himself Abu Adel. It was hard to talk much because of the chaos, but I gave him my business card and we got in touch on Skype. I next saw him when I visited Douma later that year. He was standing outside an abandoned local school where a shell had punched a hole more than a metre long in the roof of the head teacher's office. He was full of urgency again, telling me stories of atrocities including the massacre of a family by regime militiamen – the notorious *shabiha* loyal to the Assad family and drawn largely from their Alawite minority sect. 'I saw blood that was unbeliev-able,' Abu Adel said.

We exchanged messages intermittently in the years after. He said he had started working for opposition media. I spoke to him in April 2018, as the regime prepared to take Douma. The area was under the control of a rebel group known as Jaysh al-Islam, or Army of Islam, which had been responsible for plenty of abuses of its own. The group held thousands of prisoners and hostages. It had also shelled Damascus neighbourhoods almost daily.

Abu Adel said his activism had always been peaceful. He told me he'd never fought, only filmed the battles. But he clearly had some sympathy for Jaysh al-Islam and was sufficiently trusted by the militia to be there. When I asked him about criticism of the group's record, he said it did 'good ... and bad' but declared it overall 'the best faction in Syria' in its ability to take on the regime.

There was much I did not know about Abu Adel. But whatever the gaps, there were things I did know that made his testimony valuable. He was a real person, for one thing. I also knew he had lived in Douma. What he told me would also turn out to be consistent with the broader reported story of siege and hardship in

the rebellious suburb – and the imminent regime assault on this
centre of Syria's uprising.

When I talked to Abu Adel on the eve of the attack by government forces on Douma, he was composed, open and trenchant. He
and other residents were awaiting the outcome of talks on a deal
to evacuate the area. He said he thought it would be agreed, but
would be difficult and would probably involve 'another military
campaign'. Jaysh al-Islam was 'preparing for the worst' as if 'the
war would start tomorrow'.

Abu Adel recognised the odds were stacked against him and his
fellow residents being able to stay. The regime and its allies were
determined to flush out this opposition heartland on the fringes of
the capital. It wouldn't be easy to come back. 'This is hard,' he said.
'But if we leave our land and our country, we will become like the
Palestinians. We will never see our homeland again.'

Ever the optimist, he pointed to silver linings brought by the
intensification of the conflict. Merchants whom he said had been
hoarding supplies of staple foods such as rice, flour and sugar had
fled, bringing prices down to their lowest levels for some time.
Shortages that had for so long been a feature of life in Douma had
eased.

I said it was shocking how long Syria's conflict had been going
on. The seven-year anniversary had fallen the previous month. 'It's
really unbelievable,' he agreed. 'The children that were born in
that year are now in school.'

I asked him how he was feeling. Like millions of his compatriots, he had seen tragedy. His younger brother had been killed in an
air strike in 2014. 'War changed me a lot,' he said. 'I think the
young man that was in me died, and was replaced by a man who
suffered in war and knew what it was to lose friends and family –
and knows happy times are precious, family are precious, and you

have to value this time. Bad times keep you in the mind of people who love you. Men leave – but love stays.'

He said he remembered me from our first meeting at Douma's grand mosque. 'I am very happy to communicate with you,' he said, adding: 'I know the action here makes you tired sometimes.' It seemed to me a generous way of saying that he had noticed how scared I had been during my visits. He continued: 'But you know that if a man wants freedom, he has to take it. Freedom is not given.'

We talked about my move to Brussels. I reflected to myself on the bizarreness of our exchange. I was sitting in my office across the road from the institutions at the heart of the European Union, whose pronouncements on Syria sounded ever more impotent. Weeks before, the bloc had said it was 'running out of words to describe the horror being experienced by the people of Eastern Ghouta'.

'I really wish to visit you,' Abu Adel said, before immediately anticipating how a return to stability could bring its own psychological discomforts. 'But it's very hard to blend with safety now. Living as a civilian in a place where there are no shells, no fires, no fighting will be very difficult now. It will be very strange.'

Friends of his who had made it to Europe said they had a 'real problem dealing with this situation', he said. 'It's a really funny thing to say.'

He said he would try to stay in Douma as long as he could, although it wasn't clear what would happen to him. He said he was wanted not just for his opposition support but for the military service that is compulsory for all young Syrian men. Authorities had arrested his mother earlier in the conflict as she tried to re-enter Douma from Damascus, detaining her for six months. He thought that was because they had been looking for him.

'The last thing I want now is to make a settlement with the authorities and fight with them against my people,' he said.

He noted Moscow's increasing influence over events in Syria since Russia had officially joined the war in 2015, purportedly to fight ISIS. 'I think we are under Russian invasion now, like Afghanistan,' he said, referring to the country's occupation by the Soviets between 1979 and 1989. 'We don't count on American support. We have to count on ourselves. So we have to find a way to save the rest of our country and fight the Russian invasion.'

I asked if he thought the world had let Syrians down. 'Of course,' he said. 'They let us down. And we as the Syrian people let ourselves down, because we counted on the countries outside – Saudi Arabia, France. All of them did nothing for us. We let ourselves down by counting on them. They were supporting us to kill us, to finish us – not to help us.'

I asked what he meant. Abu Adel explained how he saw foreign countries' behaviour as part of a plan to once again divide and rule his nation, which had seen conquering powers from the Romans to the Ottomans come and go over millennia. He also referenced the US hunger for petroleum, Russia's strategic Mediterranean foothold at the Tartus naval base, and Turkey's incursions into the Afrin area near Aleppo. 'America takes the oil, Russia takes the coast, Turkey takes the north,' he said. 'They give us money to destroy our land. We keep fighting and destroying so they have what they want – a destroyed country they can control. That thing that first happened in Iraq now happens here.'

We spoke of how the Syrian story had morphed in the mind of international audiences into a struggle to stop ISIS. Abu Adel picked up on the role of the regime in fuelling the extremist group, by freeing prisoners from May 2011 onwards. Some in the first batch released from Saydnaya military jail in Damascus were prominent terror convicts who then joined extremist groups, including ISIS. The Syrian government has claimed those freed were ordinary criminals, let out under an amnesty programme launched to prove the authorities' goodwill. 'They made them radical in prison and let them out early in the revolution,' Abu Adel said. 'They made ISIS by themselves.'

He continued: 'As a journalist, my job is to give the real picture. My job is to make people understand ISIS and the regime are on the same side, fighting the real revolution.'

The war looked very different now from the days in 2012 when the regime seemed to be under pressure and its future was in the balance. The international assault on ISIS had given ideal cover for Assad and his allies to crack down on all rebel groups, both Islamist and non-Islamist, which had now been driven out of much of the territory they once held. 'One day we were Ghouta,' Abu Adel said, referring to the extent of the vast Damascus suburbs the uprising once held. 'Now we are Douma – and we are not sure what will happen tomorrow. A lot of people got out, some people died. We don't know what will happen next.'

Hope was keeping those left alive, he said. He recalled a celebration for his twenty-fifth birthday a couple of months previously, when 'very hard bombing' made it unwise to be outside. 'A friend made a very dangerous move to get me some biscuits,' he recalled. 'We celebrated with biscuits and Nescafé. It was a very funny thing to do. Dangerous – but funny. I am very thankful to him.'

He added: 'We have a very hard time. But we are survivors. So we will get out of it, al-hamdu lillah [praise be to God].'

Abu Adel spoke of the disorientation of war, including not being able to use his real name. It seemed another small sign of how the conflict had stripped people of their identities and smashed anchoring ideas about what their country was – and perhaps even who their neighbours were. 'I think when I get out of Syria I will go back to my real name,' Abu Adel said. 'I don't like to use nicknames and hide. I want to use my real name, like anyone in journalism. And if I have a real job with a big media [group], I will use it and be proud.'

His parting shot gave something for the let-Assad-win-for-stability 'realists' to reflect on. 'We stayed in the basement for months,' he recalled of life in Douma during the years of war. 'It was very difficult to have water, to have food and medicine. But it was a good time. Because with all this difficulty, we succeeded to live. We didn't surrender to what happened. We didn't give the regime the opportunity to say they broke us.'

Then, without missing a beat, he switched back to the absurdities and small victories of life under siege.

'I will send you also a post on how to make a cup of Nescafé,' he said. 'You will find it very funny.'

The conversation with Abu Adel kindled something in me, years after my Douma visits. I was alone in the office and, recalling those times, I sat tearfully for a while at my desk, a stone's throw from the European Commission's hulking Berlaymont head-quarters. As the late-afternoon spring sunshine streamed around the blinds, four soldiers in combat fatigues walked down the hill on patrol in the street outside. For Brussels – as for several other European cities – events in Syria and the surrounding region were understandably most likely to be associated with terrorist atrocities. Two years earlier, ISIS had claimed responsibility for attacks on the Belgian capital's airport and metro network that had killed thirty-two victims and the three suicide bombers themselves.

My own experiences of Syria were separate from the atrocities of ISIS. I recalled the desperation of Douma and Dera'a and other places battered by the Assad regime. I felt the alarm in Aleppo as the storm that had gathered around it for months finally began to break. I also thought of the fears, often genuine and justifiable, of the people who spoke against the uprising and said they just wanted peace.

Most of all, I reflected on how the tyrannical status quo that Assad was attempting to reimpose was no kind of solution, either morally or practically. I saw in the words of Abu Adel a sign that a regime victory would not be the end of anything. The Assads' authoritarianism might harden once more, but – like reformed melted plastic – it would be more brittle than before.

I received a brief message from Abu Adel on the night of 6 April. Douma was being targeted by incendiary bombs, he said. The next day, reports began to emerge of a poison gas attack on the area. Soon the Internet was filled with hideous footage of corpses and people gasping for life from an apparent chemical weapons strike. I exchanged messages with Abu Adel, who said he was OK.

Immediately a meme began to spread across social media that this was a 'false flag' attempt by rebels to incriminate the regime and provoke US military intervention. Others fired off tweets saying that it couldn't be the regime because Russia had warned that there would be a chemical attack and people would blame it on Damascus. It seemed a bizarre leap of logic to suggest that if you said a crime was about to take place, it meant you should not fall under suspicion. Surely, if anything, the opposite should apply.

But there was something still more troubling about these outbursts than their flimsy intellectual moorings. They lacked a basic sense of decency. This went far beyond any question of pro- or anti-Western ideology. There were people out there who were prepared, with zero evidence, to exonerate the Syrian government of mass murder. Some even claimed an attack never happened. The willingness to scorn the victims and abandon even the pretence of a search for the truth was nauseating. The hypocrisy was also breathtaking, since some of these people would be among the first to attack critics of the Syrian regime and Russia for getting ahead of the established facts.

A superficially more reasonable-sounding response was to wait for the results of independent investigations of the chemical attack. This was the tenor of the British Labour Party's response. It called for 'concrete steps on all sides to re-start meaningful talks on a political solution and lasting peace' in Syria. 'The Syrian people have suffered too long from the atrocities and brutality of this war, whether committed by the Assad regime, by Jihadist militias, or by their respective international supporters, and it is time for that suffering to stop,' it concluded.[16]

But that statement did not bear much scrutiny either. Its call for a 'safe exit for the militias occupying Douma and any civilians who want to leave' risked looking like a green light for forced displacement – a war crime. The call for an end to the violence on all sides sounded like the equivalence narrative at work again. The push for an independent probe ignored how difficult this would be without the regime's cooperation, which experience showed was unlikely to happen. The Syrian government has consistently rejected UN investigations that found it has carried out more than thirty chemical attacks since 2013.

Self-styled sceptics often fall back on the idea that something needs to be proved 'beyond reasonable doubt' for it to be accepted as probably true. It might sound scrupulously fair: this is, after all, the standard English criminal court's demand for a jury to find a defendant guilty. But the comparison is false. A guilty finding in criminal court could lead to someone losing their liberty. It is right, given such consequences, that the standard should be stringent.

Politics is much more the realm of the balance of probabilities. There are plenty of Western crimes for which death tolls, or indeed the exact circumstances of what happened, remain uncertain. But they are rightly accepted as atrocities nonetheless. At its worst, the 'beyond reasonable doubt' standard becomes an excuse to almost never draw any conclusions about anything – which is, of course, what some of these pro-regime armchair proselytisers want.

In March 2019, the Hague-based Organisation for the Prohibition of Chemical Weapons (OPCW) said it was likely chlorine was used in the Douma attack.[17] The agency – whose 193 member states include Russia and Syria – did not assign blame for the assault, as that was not part of its mandate.[18] It found no evidence to support claims by Damascus that rebels had used buildings in the area to make and store chemical weapons.

Moscow's embassy to the Netherlands tweeted criticism of the OPCW for drawing its conclusion 'in spite of all the evidence presented by Russia, Syria, and even British journalists' that the Douma incident was a 'staged provocation'.[19] The diplomatic mission's complaint drew some waspish replies. 'Is that the same OPCW your [secret service] officers tried to hack into, failed, and got kicked out of the Netherlands?' read one, referring to claims made by Western governments in October 2018 of a cybercrime spree by Russian hackers to target the OPCW and other organisations probing alleged Kremlin wrongdoing. Moscow has denied any such plot.[20]

On the morning of Monday, 9 April, I messaged Abu Adel again. He wrote back to say a ceasefire had started and he and his family would soon leave Douma to travel north. I asked what had happened in the chemical attack.

He replied with a twenty-four-second audio clip.

'We are still searching for dead bodies and we are still finding some. A lot of people now are trying to prepare themselves to leave,' he said. 'Some are trying to' – he paused, his voice seeming to crack a little – 'prepare themselves to stay.'

'And' – he paused again to gather himself – 'it's not obvious how the future is.'

Our contact was sporadic over the following days. On Wednesday evening he sent me another brief audio message. I could hear a siren in the background. He was on a bus on his way to an area in the north of the country. 'Hi Mr Michael. Thanks to God we are now in . . . liberated area territories under the control of the Free Syrian Army. We are safe now.'

The next day, when I checked in with him mid-morning Brussels time, he sent back a longer message of just over a minute. He sounded sleepy and said he was happy. He said he'd mainly been resting and eating, a 'lot of things that we didn't have in the siege'.

He stifled a yawn, and paused for a moment. 'So I'm sort of lost these days because I don't know what to do, I don't know where to go . . . I want to settle, to have a job, a home for my own. This kind of stuff.'

After the Douma chemical attack, attention turned to the Western reaction. The US, UK and France soon threatened missile strikes. As they loomed, I went to a conference on Syria that happened to be on in Paris while I was in the city. It was a glorious spring day and a long queue of tourists snaked from the door of the Berthillon ice-cream shop on the Île Saint-Louis.

On the left bank of the Seine beyond, Syrian opposition activists were mingling with tourists on a sunny terrace of the Arab World Institute. I spoke to Bassma Kodmani, an opposition negotiator at the UN-backed Geneva peace talks on Syria and a regular lobbyist in Brussels. I asked her whether Syrians found it strange that there was so much international focus on chemical weapons but not 'normal' killings in Syria. She shrugged and said it was nothing new.

'I find it remarkable the apathy at an international level,' she said. 'It's remarkable how little attention this conflict has attracted, given the humanitarian and the security stakes.'

Not everyone had forgotten about Syria. Shortly after my meeting with Professor Guha-Sapir, she and colleagues put out a paper on chemical attacks in the country. It used Violations Documentation Center data to look at 1,206 deaths directly attributed to chemical weapons in non-government-controlled areas between March 2011 and April 2017. In all cases, the researchers had 'complete information on the victim's date and place of death, cause and demographic group'.[21]

The study found that in major attacks – defined as causing ten or more direct deaths – 97.6% of the victims were civilian. The researchers also found that the casualty rate for children in big chemical weapons attacks had risen. In the first three major attacks – in 2013 – between about thirteen and fourteen percent of the victims were children. That climbed to twenty-one percent in the major attack of 2016 and thirty-five percent in the assault at Khan Sheikhoun in Idlib in 2017.

The findings provided evidence that 'chemical weapons attacks were indiscriminate or targeted civilians directly,' the paper said. It also pointed out how high the child death toll was. Children were more at risk than adults, not just because their small bodies were more vulnerable, but because they were nearer to the ground where the heavy gases sank.

Guha-Sapir told me that in her future death toll work she planned to stick by her generally cautious approach. She spoke of the need to avoid having a 'kind of an auction of numbers of people dead'.

'There is no end to that,' she said. 'Don't invent numbers and don't inflate them – because somebody is going to shoot them down.'

I asked Guha-Sapir about the sheer quantity of false data swill-
ing around about the Syria conflict and how widely accepted it
had become. I wondered if she sometimes found it dispiriting how
those spreading disinformation created such effective smoke-
screens, by exaggerating the inevitable uncertainties in conflict
data. 'No, it's not dispiriting, Michael, it's not,' she chided, as bells
began pealing at a church somewhere nearby. 'Since we have been
working on this for ten to fifteen years on these kind of civil
conflicts, I've been gratified at the amount of attention we get
from the world at large. I have been gratified and somewhat
surprised by the influence seriousness can have on public
thinking.'

Guha-Sapir said she didn't think disinformation was in its
fundamental nature any worse now than in the past, even if there
are more channels to spread it. It was in the 'nature of our lives –
today they've done it, twenty years ago they've done it, fifty years
ago', she said. '[It] is part of the game and that is what the fight is
about ... People have always come out with just random stuff.'

She said there might even be an upside to the weight of outrageous claims. The flood of false data was perhaps making people
who retained a capacity for open-mindedness 'more wary' and
discerning. They would perhaps be 'more careful' what they
believed.

I asked if she wasn't afraid of simply being drowned out by the
sheer quantity of noise. She laughed at the sustained negative tilt
of my questioning. 'The drowning out is in fact a challenge for us,'
she said.

I asked if she felt people were more ideologically entrenched in
their views of conflicts now than they had been earlier in her
career. No, she said, citing her experience at college in Calcutta
during the Vietnam War – 'to put a date on me'. That was a 'hotbed
of Marxist–Leninist movements', she said. 'It's a fight over political
space, that's the essence of these problems,' she continued. 'The

modern communication configuration has changed some things but not fundamental things. It's the same kind of fights, the same kind of combat, the same kind of strategies.'

She paused for a moment. 'I'm probably wrong,' she added with a laugh.

I asked her what she thought could help people navigate the oceans of online propaganda. I wondered if experience of the scientific method helped to strip the mind of some of its illusions: experiments that you thought should work didn't; data that you hypothesised should prove something simply didn't stack up.

'I think what you have described prepares you to keep an open mind,' she said. 'You may want your work to . . . go this way but it doesn't. And then you have to deal with it.'

I asked Guha-Sapir finally what her dream project would be. She laughed and said it was what she was doing at the moment. I pressed her for a more compelling answer. She paused to think.

'You know, it's something very different from Syrian casualty tolls, very different,' she said. 'If I had the money and the time I would go in to look at why we're not doing better at vaccination. Something I would like to spend a lot more time on is measles – a disease which has a [near] 100 percent effective vaccine which doesn't cost anything any more because the patent has run out. And yet there are still hundreds of children dying a day of measles.'

Just like Syria's war, vaccination programmes had been compromised by sustained campaigns of disinformation questioning their safety. A few months after Guha-Sapir spoke those words, Italy's Senate voted to scrap a mandatory vaccination law, in line with a pledge by the country's new self-styled populist government. Italy had already emerged as a disease black spot: it accounted for almost one fifth of the measles cases in the thirty countries of the European Economic Area between April 2018 and March 2019.

In August 2018, the World Health Organization reported a sharp rise in the number of measles cases in Europe. It said at least thirty-seven people had died of the disease in the first half of 2018 as the number of cases jumped to more than 41,000 – almost eight times the total for the whole of 2016.[22]

Guha-Sapir noted how the limitations on measles vaccination were not technical. The inoculation was effective and cheap, yet it wasn't rigorously applied in many middle-income countries – and even, as Italy showed, some high-income states. The obstacles were logistical – and political.

Guha-Sapir and her team were making a model for how many children had died from or were likely to die from measles as a result of Yemen's war. Saudi and Emirati forces were in a destructive struggle with the Houthi militant movement. 'We have a website which gives us the number of air raids by governorate in Yemen,' she said. 'We have a very nice map that we've done. Essentially, in those governorates, there's been no vaccination at all.'

Guha-Sapir said it was not only Yemen that was a 'powder keg of disease'. She pointed to a 2017 outbreak of polio in eastern Syria caused by the war's disruption of vaccination programmes. 'In war-affected regions, we are making whole countries into susceptible populations,' she said. 'Populations who can be infected, be carriers and have a high transmission.'

Guha-Sapir described how the diseases of war in the Middle East were coming closer and closer to Europe, yet too few people were taking the threat seriously. The West could ignore the disease statistics, as it was more or less shrugging off Syria's conflict. But eventually there would be a price. In the end this refusal to engage was, as Guha-Sapir put it, 'something that we're going to have to pay for'.

5

From Criminal to VIP

Xavier Justo loved life on Koh Samui. The Swiss ex-banker had left behind his hard-partying days in Geneva and moved to the Thai holiday island with Laura, his fiancée. The couple had married and had a son. Now they were developing a hotel complex for the tourists who flocked to the archipelago beach resort by ferry, speedboat and numerous daily flights from Bangkok.

Justo's main task on Monday, 22 June 2015 was to renew his annual work permit. Nothing suggested this would be anything other than the formality of previous years. An immigration official who was supposed to come to his house the previous Friday to do the paperwork had called to postpone the visit until Monday afternoon instead. The forty-eight-year-old Justo, who had started to compete in triathlons as part of his healthier lifestyle, took advantage of the free morning to train and to call Laura.

At around 2 p.m., Justo's maid told him that people were arriving at the compound. It was the first sign of something unusual. 'I saw six cars, like fifteen people,' he recalled. 'I said: "Wow, I knew they were becoming more serious with the work permit – but, OK, everything is possible."'

He went out to greet the larger than expected party. He didn't recognise the man who seemed to be the group's leader. 'I went to shake his hand and the guy beside him, in two seconds went "schut schut schut",' Justo said, mimicking the action of handcuffs being clapped on him. 'We go inside the house and they show me some papers in Thai, a search warrant and whatever.'

The cuffs had been fastened so tight they made Justo's wrists bleed. He watched as officers grabbed papers and electronic devices for evidence. They took him to a local jail cell, where his maid held up a phone to the bars so he could talk to Laura. 'I was shouting at the phone through the window,' he remembered. 'Laura said: "What's happening?" And I said, "Don't worry, I have to go to Bangkok but I'll come back tomorrow." I was sure I was going to come back tomorrow.'

He didn't. He was charged with attempting to blackmail and extort money from his former employer, an oil company named PetroSaudi International, over an email trove he took when he left. Justo has insisted he did not steal it and has said it was given to him.

That data had become the basis for the first big story about what would grow into one of the world's most notorious financial scandals: the alleged misappropriation of billions of dollars from Malaysia's 1MDB state investment fund. PetroSaudi has consistently denied any wrongdoing. It has never been accused of any offence.

The 1MDB case would make big trouble for Justo and rock Malaysian prime minister Najib Razak's government. It would also trigger a barrage of claims and counterclaims in relation to the fund's dealings, a battle over the narrative of the scandal that would rage for years. For a long time, the Najib administration presented the affair as a fuss about nothing stoked by the premier's enemies. It was a strategy that seemed to be cynically effective – until events took an unexpected and transformative turn. As Najib's political position unravelled, the emerging 1MDB story revealed not only a sickness in Malaysia's governance but in an international financial system that had failed to live up to its pledge to reform after the financial crisis.

After Justo's arrest, Thai police paraded him before the media, as they habitually do with suspects in high-profile cases. A picture released by authorities at the time showed armed officers in black uniforms and shades looming behind the seated and bearded Swiss, who wore shorts, a Hugo Boss T-shirt and flip-flops. He peered over his glasses and looked surprisingly calm, appearing perhaps a man who had not yet fully come to terms with the gravity of his situation.

Justo later said he was taken to a grim prison cell crowded by dozens of other inmates. He said Thai officials and PetroSaudi representatives urged him to confess to receive a light sentence. (Thai authorities and PetroSaudi deny any improper behaviour.)

As Justo described it, he was gradually worn down as he saw no prospect to secure his freedom. In the absence of a better option, he caved in. 'They said: "So, Justo, you want to cooperate with us? Or you want to spend ten years there?",' he recalled. 'I said: "Whatever you want me to write, I will write. Whatever." And that's what I did.'

He confessed to the attempted blackmail and extortion. At the root of the case was a dispute over severance money when he left the company by mutual consent in 2011. PetroSaudi maintains Justo was paid a generous sum, but stole the data and then threatened to leak it unless he was paid more money. It has said the evidence against him in the attempted blackmail case was 'overwhelming and incontrovertible'. PetroSaudi denies Justo was pressured into pleading guilty, adding that one of its executives wrote to the Thai Court of Appeal after he was sentenced asking for his jail term to be reduced because he had shown remorse.

Justo now maintains he did nothing wrong. Despite his confession in his Thai trial, he claims he was not a blackmailer but was only trying to pursue the company for money he believed he was owed.

'I didn't do any crime. I didn't steal the data. I didn't blackmail them,' he said. 'I just told them: pay me my fucking money.'

After his admission of wrongdoing to Thai authorities, Justo prepared to serve what he thought would be a short jail term of a few months. He was confident he would be 'out by Christmas'. He pleaded guilty at a short court hearing almost two months after his arrest. Then the judge pronounced sentence.

'The translator wrote for me on a piece of paper: six-slash-three. When you plead guilty in Thailand your sentence is cut by half,' Justo said. 'So I said, "Ah, that's six months and three months. Oh Jesus, in three months I'm home!" And then she wrote: "six *years*".'

Justo's jailing marked a crucial moment in the 1MDB case. His incarceration boosted a growing campaign by supporters of Najib Razak, Malaysia's premier, to portray allegations of wrongdoing at the fund as malicious propaganda cooked up by his enemies. They focused on attacking Justo's character and his admitted behaviour, rather than on the serious questions about the fund raised in the documents he had disclosed. In legal and political terms, they played the man rather than the ball. 'I was the bad guy,' Justo recalled. 'Stealing, downloading, manipulating, working with the opposition, greedy, tattooed – they were nice! Because their goal was to make me . . . be seen officially as the bad guy.'

As the scandal over 1MDB grew and spread internationally after Justo's arrest, Najib and his allies simply insisted there was no cause to investigate. This would be a standard tactic for a tyranny that stifled its people. But Najib, who has always denied any wrongdoing in relation to 1MDB, was an elected leader ostensibly accountable at the ballot box for his actions – or inaction. His behaviour highlighted a disturbing trend among leaders in nominally democratic states, in the West as well as outside. Growing numbers are sufficiently brazen to simply shrug off corruption allegations that it would self-evidently be in the public interest to probe. In the 1MDB case, the fabulists were the officials of Najib's government who said there was nothing to scrutinise.

At the heart of the affair were two overlapping failures of governance. One was local: the deterioration of already shaky democratic norms in Malaysia. Najib's government was able to exploit a system in which political power had long been centralised and exercised autocratically. And it could sideline the matter for so long because there was nothing to stop it doing so, at home or abroad. For a long time, the strategy seemed to work.

The second problem was global. The web of dealings in the 1MDB scandal took full advantage of the privacy and cross-border complexity available in the international financial system. Despite limited improvements, the pattern had some echoes of a case I'd reported on a decade and a half previously. Then, the pursuit of billions of dollars allegedly looted by the late Nigerian dictator General Sani Abacha had embroiled financial institutions in the West over many years.

The same questions hung now over whether there would be full accountability in the 1MDB case. As of early 2019, it remained an open question how much money proven to have been misappropriated, if any, would ever be returned. In a 2018 report, the campaign group Global Witness had already branded the 1MDB case a 'failure' by international financial institutions. It said they had 'ignored the rules, turned a blind eye, kept profitable clients and continued handling billions of dollars of dirty money despite clear warning signs'.[1]

★　　★　　★

The story of 1MDB had begun way back in 2008. The fund grew out of an investment authority set up for the region of Terengganu on the eastern side of the Malay peninsula. By 2009, the Terengganu investment fund had been converted into a national financial institution: 1Malaysia Development Berhad, or 1MDB.

Najib became prime minister in April 2009 after his predecessor stepped down. The dapper former lawyer was an Anglophile who had studied in the UK at Nottingham University. He was a career politician and a political blue blood: he was the son of Malaysia's second post-independence premier and the nephew of the third. He was also finance minister and chairman of 1MDB's advisory board.

The official aim was for 1MDB to make investments that promoted economic growth, but with a difference. Unlike most sovereign wealth funds, it did not start with a big pile of cash. Instead it would take on debt to acquire assets, ranging from power generation interests to land, with some of the property sold to it at low prices by the government. This model perhaps helps explain why 1MDB escaped proper scrutiny for so long. There was not the obvious money trail of billions being paid directly from the country's oil and gas earnings, as there would be for a Norway-style wealth fund.

1MDB launched its first big venture months after Najib became prime minister. In September 2009, the fund announced a $2.5 billion joint venture with a little-known oil company named PetroSaudi. The Malaysians agreed to invest $1 billion in exchange for PetroSaudi bringing in mineral extraction concessions in Turkmenistan and Argentina that had been valued at $2.7 billion, according to a later US investigation.

PetroSaudi was created in 2005 with high-level connections in Riyadh. One of its co-founders was Prince Turki bin Abdullah bin Abdel Aziz, a son of King Abdullah, although the company said he ceased to be a shareholder in 2013. His business partner was Tarek

Obaid, a former banker. The company began in drilling and oilfield management before it expanded into oil trading. It had a UK corporate presence and offices in London's Mayfair district, complete with pictures of Saudi royalty and national flags. In 2016, the company's website listed projects in Ghana, Indonesia, Venezuela and Tunisia.

PetroSaudi also worked with high-profile individuals from Western politics and business. Tony Blair Associates, the consultancy set up by the former UK prime minister, has said it did a few months of advisory work for PetroSaudi, on business unconnected with Malaysia. Neither the consultancy nor Blair have been accused of any wrongdoing.

The 1MDB–PetroSaudi joint venture carried on with a low profile until it was wound up in 2012. 1MDB claimed it had been highly profitable. It said it used its share of the proceeds to buy offshore investments worth more than $2.3 billion in a Cayman Islands-registered fund.

But behind the scenes, the first questions were soon being asked. KPMG was sacked as 1MDB's auditor at the end of 2013 in a dispute over the Cayman money, according to a later report by Malaysia's auditor general. The accounting firm was unhappy because 1MDB would not share documents KPMG wanted to see in relation to the investment in the Caribbean islands. The disagreement did not become public at the time, so the controversy was contained. KPMG has not commented on the matter.

Queries about 1MDB did nevertheless begin to surface publicly. Not the least of them was how what was supposed to be a fund to generate wealth for the country had managed to slip $11 billion into debt. But the mutterings were manageable for the government, and might have remained so, had it not been for the falling-out between Justo and PetroSaudi.

★   ★   ★

When Justo failed in his efforts to obtain more money from PetroSaudi, he decided to do something with his precious electronic information hoard. He entered discussions with the website Sarawak Report's Clare Rewcastle Brown and Tong Kooi Ong, chairman of Malaysia's The Edge Media Group. Rewcastle Brown had a lifelong link with Malaysia: she was born in Sarawak to a colonial intelligence officer and had focused on corruption in the timber-rich state. She was well connected in Britain, too: she happened to be married to the brother of Gordon Brown, the former UK prime minister. All parties to Justo's talks over the data say Tong agreed to pay him $2 million but the money never changed hands, partly because the transfers were logistically hard to arrange. (In January 2019, Tong gave Justo $2 million for 'his contribution to Malaysia in helping to expose the kleptocracy of the past government'.[2])

'I never received the money so it's very good for my image,' Justo said of the original deal for him to disclose the emails. 'It could have changed if I had received the money so [people] could have said: "He's not a whistle-blower, he's a money guy."'

Justo said he had not fully analysed the emails before handing them over. He claimed he was as surprised as anyone when he saw the subsequent Sarawak Report story on the alleged misappropriation of $700 million of 1MDB money meant for the PetroSaudi joint venture.

Sarawak Report – and the *Wall Street Journal* – followed up those claims with a separate and still more explosive story. The two alleged that $681 million of money linked to 1MDB had been paid just before the 2013 election into Najib's personal bank account in Kuala Lumpur. Najib did not deny the payments, but said he had done nothing wrong and had received no personal gain.

The direct payment to Najib's account and the simplicity of the transaction meant the affair caught fire both in Malaysia and globally. In many stories of questionable deals, complex webs of payments can confuse and anaesthetise even the sharpest reader – and provide means to obfuscate for those with an interest in hiding the truth. Here, by contrast, the money flow could not have been more straightforward.

For a while, Najib looked to be teetering politically. He denounced the criticism of him over the payment as 'a concerted campaign of political sabotage to topple a democratically elected prime minister'.

One thing he and his representatives chose not to do was offer an alternative account of events. Instead, Malaysian authorities circled the wagons. The police chief announced a new 1MDB investigation – but into how bank transfer records and other papers at the heart of the new claims came to be leaked. The communications regulator stepped in to warn that people commenting on the affair online could end up in jail under harsh computer crime laws. This was a response in part to viral memes such as #1MDBMovies, which featured satirical mock-ups of Najib at the centre of film posters such as *Saving Private Account* and *Lord of the Ringgits* – a reference to the country's ailing currency.

The denial tactics appeared to be working. Tony Pua, an opposition MP and indefatigable investigator of 1MDB, put it pithily at the time. 'If there is no one shouting "I have been robbed," why would anyone think there has been a robbery?' said Pua, whom Najib's government would later hit with a foreign travel ban.

Najib tightened his grip over the following months. He replaced the country's attorney general and sacked his deputy prime minister, who had been critical. His administration detained opponents, imposed travel bans on others, temporarily suspended two of the Edge's publications and rushed through legislation described by Malaysia's bar council as a 'lurch towards an authoritarian government'.

The new attorney general appointed by the premier then ruled Najib had no case to answer over the funds transferred into his bank account. The law officer said they were a gift from the Saudi royal family. Several months later, in April 2016, the Saudi foreign minister Adel al-Jubeir said the funds were a 'genuine donation' from his country with 'nothing expected in return', according to Malaysian state media. The minister gave no further details.[3]

During my visits to Malaysia around that time, the atmosphere felt strained and conspiratorial. Everyone was trying to judge how much it was safe to say – and which way the political wind was blowing. The tension had a darkly absurd edge. Quite a few contacts wanted to meet in the vast Bangsar Shopping Centre in Kuala Lumpur. I would shuttle between various coffee shops and restaurants during back-to-back meetings with people who were sometimes mortal enemies. It sometimes seemed as if the Malaysian scandal was bubbling away in microcosm in that one mall.

There were also some strange characters whose agendas were not entirely clear. Among them was Khairuddin Abu Hassan, a former official in Najib's ruling United Malays National Organisation. He had been expelled from the party after he went bankrupt. Now he was pushing for international investigations into the 1MDB case.

Khairuddin was remarkably open about his sensitive mission, even offering a running social media commentary on his efforts. He divulged that he had reported his concerns to authorities in the UK, Switzerland and Hong Kong. These revelations risked jeopardising his security, given the political climate. When I met him in September 2015 at his suggested rendezvous of the Mandarin Oriental Hotel cigar lounge, he spoke openly about how he would leave shortly for the US to brief the Federal Bureau of Investigation.

As I was waiting for my flight home at Kuala Lumpur airport days later, I heard that he had been arrested. The news made me queasy, though I was sure it was his Facebook posts that had attracted official attention rather than any dealings with me. He was released some weeks later – but it was a sharp reminder of the stakes being played for.

The government targeted others who allegedly insulted Najib, such as the artist Fahmi Reza. He was jailed in February 2018 for depicting the premier as a clown. In the run-up to the 2018 election, parliament passed a law threatening jail sentences of up to six years for people deemed guilty of disseminating false information.

Ghastlier still was the September 2015 murder of Kevin Morais, a state prosecutor and former Malaysian Anti-Corruption Commission official. His body was found encased in cement in an oil drum. Authorities denied speculation that he was involved in the 1MDB case. Seven people without any apparent political connections were charged with his murder. Their trial was still to conclude as of June 2019.

The Morais murder brought back memories of other unexplained killings that had provided a dark backdrop to the country's recent history. Most notorious of all was the 2006 murder of Altantuya Shaariibuu, a young Mongolian woman whose body was blown apart with high explosives. Two police officers from a unit that provides protection for government officials and visiting foreign dignitaries were convicted of the killing in 2009. The verdict was overturned on appeal in 2013 and then reinstated by Malaysia's highest court in 2015. Questions over the case have lingered because of a perceived lack of motive of those convicted and because of Altantuya's social connections to the government at the time.

By the end of 2015, Najib and his allies seemed full of confidence that the controversy over 1MDB had been extinguished.

In a triumphant New Year message for 2016, the premier claimed it was 'clear that 1MDB's major challenges are now behind it' as the fund was being successfully restructured. He accused his critics of prejudging the results of the investigations into 1MDB and harming Malaysia's economy and 'our good name abroad'. A few weeks later the attorney general closed all probes into Najib. The premier then declared them an 'unnecessary distraction'.[4]

Najib may have overplayed his hand. Within days, Swiss authorities fired back, saying they had launched their own investigation into suspected bribery involving former 1MDB officials. The authorities reported that they had found 'serious indications' that $4 billion – earmarked for development projects – had been misappropriated from Malaysian state companies.[5] The announcement appeared to be a direct response to fears that the Malaysian government was trying to bury the case. But the Swiss gave few details and Najib's administration was able to ride that little storm out, too. As of June 2019, the Swiss investigations were continuing.

Six months after the Swiss statement, a real thunderbolt hit. The US Department of Justice unveiled a court claim[6] to recover assets allegedly bought with looted 1MDB money. The filing – which was amended and expanded in 2017[7] – was not a criminal case and Najib was not its target, nor even named. But, for the first time, a state authority gave a detailed account of an alleged 'international conspiracy' over several years to 'fraudulently divert billions of dollars from 1MDB through various means' for 'the personal benefit of the co-conspirators and their relatives and associates'.

The US government papers claimed the money was used to buy luxury real estate in the United States and overseas, pay gambling expenses at Las Vegas casinos and purchase more than $200 million in artwork, including works by Van Gogh, Monet and Rothko. Other tranches of money were allegedly used to invest in a big New York real estate development project and fund the production of major Hollywood films. The US authorities asserted that tens of millions of dollars diverted from 1MDB were used to fund the film production company Red Granite Pictures and its 2013 movie *The Wolf of Wall Street*, a dark comedy about corruption in the world of international finance. Red Granite has consistently denied any wrongdoing.

The Justice Department lawsuit alleged that 'multiple individuals, including public officials and their associates' were involved in the plot to misappropriate more than $3.5 billion from three big 1MDB international deals. One strand allegedly involved $1.367 billion from more than $3 billion raised by 1MDB through two separate bond issues arranged and underwritten by Goldman Sachs; another was said to have diverted more than $1.26 billion from a further $3 billion Goldman bond issue. Goldman has denied any wrongdoing.

The third part – and the first chronologically – is where the jailed Justo came in. The Justice Department claimed that under the pretence of investing in a joint venture between 1MDB and PetroSaudi, Malaysian fund officials and others arranged for the fraudulent transfer of more than $1 billion to an RBS Coutts Swiss bank account in the name of Good Star Limited, a Seychelles company. The Justice Department alleged that the Good Star account was beneficially owned by Low Taek Jho, a Malaysian businessman better known as Jho Low. The US government claimed Low laundered more than $400 million of the funds misappropriated from 1MDB through the Good Star account into the US, after which they were used for the 'personal gratification' of himself and his associates.

Low has consistently and vehemently denied any wrongdoing. His representatives have pointed to the fact that – as the US Justice Department acknowledged – Low held no formal position at 1MDB. They also note that, as of early 2019, none of the allegations made in relation to their client had been tested in court.

In a rare interview after the first 1MDB–PetroSaudi allegations came out in 2015, Low had blamed prejudices against him because he was part of Malaysia's ethnic Chinese minority. 'There are all these guys with their arrows out on me,' he said, in a *Euromoney* piece headlined 'Jho Low says it ain't so'. 'There seems to be a very, very coordinated attempt to say: "This young Chinaman, it's all his fault, he caused the failure of 1MDB and apparently he advised the PM and everything is screwed up now,"' the article cited Low as saying.[8]

The US Justice Department sought to paint a very different picture of Low's activities. In its 2017 filing, it asserted that he was involved in 1MDB's creation and 'exercised significant control over its dealings'. It claimed he was an adviser to the original Terengganu Investment Authority and its founders. It alleged he then played a role at 1MDB – including attending a special board meeting on 26 September 2009 to agree the fund's $1 billion payment to the PetroSaudi joint venture.

In its filings, the US government claimed Low used 1MDB money to buy L'Ermitage hotel in Beverly Hills and a stake in New York's Park Lane Hotel. He allegedly used other 1MDB funds to purchase an interest in EMI Music Publishing, a $35.4 million Bombardier private jet, and other properties in New York and California totalling more than $100 million.

The US Justice Department claimed that money traceable to the proceeds of sales of 1MDB bonds were used for other 'interests unrelated to the business of [the fund]'. These allegedly included gambling in Las Vegas by Low and others. One session was said to have involved Leonardo DiCaprio, who starred in *The Wolf of Wall Street* (and won a Golden Globe for it). DiCaprio has not been accused of any wrongdoing.

The US government's expansion of its claim in 2017 brought the total assets targeted to $1.7 billion. The new items identified included a $3.2 million Picasso painting given to DiCaprio. The actor later transferred the artwork to the US government as part of what his spokesperson said was a wider return of gifts given him by financiers linked to the 1MDB case. He had already given back an Oscar won by Marlon Brando that was gifted to him by Red Granite (at the time he was given the present, DiCaprio had yet to win a best actor Oscar himself). Separately, the Australian actress and model Miranda Kerr handed over jewellery that was alleged by US authorities to have been bought for her by Low with 1MDB funds. Kerr has not been accused of any wrongdoing.

In March 2018, Red Granite Films agreed to pay the US government $60 million over the claims against *The Wolf of Wall Street* and two other films: *Daddy's Home* and *Dumb and Dumber To*. The settlement agreement said the deal should not be considered 'an admission of wrongdoing or liability on the part of Red Granite'.[9]

Asked for comment on the US Justice Department allegations, legal representatives of Low reiterated his strong denials of any wrongdoing. They said suggestions in the media that he had played a central role in the 1MDB affair were 'utterly preposterous and disingenuous' and 'not fair, accurate or truthful'. They declined to address the detail of the claims.

The US Justice Department case also raised significant questions for Malaysian prime minister Najib. Although not named in the documents, he appeared under the thin anonymising cloak of 'Malaysian Official 1'. The biographical details made clear it was him.

The court filings described Najib as assuming a 'position of authority' with 1MDB on its formation. He had the power to approve appointments to – and removals from – both the fund's board and its senior management team, the US Justice Department claimed. Any 1MDB financial commitments likely to affect the Malaysian government's policies or guarantees for the fund also needed his sign-off.

The US government claim detailed the alleged transactions to send $681 million to Najib's personal bank account. It said the sum was transferred in two parts in March 2013 from another bank account that had shortly before received proceeds diverted from a sale of 1MDB bonds earlier in the year. About $620 million of the money was later returned from Najib's account, of which $27.3 million was used to buy a 22-carat pink diamond pendant and necklace for Najib's wife Rosmah Mansor, the court filings asserted. Both Najib and Rosmah have denied any wrongdoing.

Other authorities launched their own probes into the 1MDB affair. In October 2016, Mark Branson, chief executive of FINMA, the Swiss financial regulator, said the global financial system had been 'blatantly misused' in the 1MDB case and 'warning signals ignored'.[10] In December 2017, US Attorney General Jeff Sessions described the Malaysia case as 'kleptocracy at its worst'. 'In total, 1MDB officials allegedly laundered more than $4.5 billion in funds through a complex web of opaque transactions and fraudulent shell companies with bank accounts in countries ranging from Switzerland and Singapore to Luxembourg and the United States,' he told a conference in Washington.[11]

Further dominoes began to fall. Singapore authorities shuttered the local operation of Switzerland's BSI bank over its alleged failing in the scandal.[12] They fined more than half a dozen other banks, including UBS and DBS, for 1MDB-linked rule breaches. Several individual bankers were convicted.

Najib tightened his grip on power even as the allegations around 1MDB grew. He seemed to take encouragement from Donald Trump's election victory in 2016. A Malaysian government representative proclaimed that the two leaders were golfing buddies: Najib even had a photo of the pair on his desk with a dedication from Trump 'to my favorite prime minister'. (Najib had also golfed with Barack Obama in December 2014, shortly before the 1MDB affair blew up.) It is not hard to see why Najib might have felt he had found a kindred spirit in a new US president who had disclosed little about his financial affairs in the face of growing questions about them. Trump became the first US commander-in-chief in more than four decades to decline to release his tax returns.

Najib also retained the appearance of respectability on the world stage. In September 2017, he travelled to meet Trump in Washington and Britain's prime minister Theresa May in London. The UK government kept the meeting low-profile, but it seemed consistent with its urgent efforts to deepen relationships outside Europe after its decision to pull out of the EU. London could not afford to be choosy.

Even with the battle damage of the international investigations, Najib ploughed on. As Malaysia's 2018 election loomed, his strategy seemed still to be effective. His government had dismissed the scandal and stifled those at home who raised questions about it. It was hard to see who would challenge the status quo.

While Najib dug in, Xavier Justo's luck began to change. His first piece of good news came when his jail sentence was cut from three years to two in August 2016 in a royal prisoner amnesty ordered by Thailand's King Bhumibol Adulyadej, who had just marked seventy years on the throne.

A setback followed shortly after: in September, a request by Swiss authorities for Justo to serve the rest of his term at home was refused. The denial aroused suspicion, as it closely followed an official visit to Thailand by Najib. Both Malaysia and Thailand insisted the two events were not connected; the government in Bangkok said Justo had fallen foul of a rule that prisoners with less than one year of their sentence remaining could not be transferred to their home countries. The refusal surprised Swiss authorities and distressed Laura, Justo's wife, who had also been expecting it to go through. 'I am shocked by the decision,' she said. 'I don't know what interest Thailand has in keeping my husband.'[13]

But another unforeseen turn of events would soon work in Justo's favour. As we saw in chapter 2, King Bhumibol died in October 2016 and his son, Maha Vajiralongkorn, took the throne. In line with tradition, the new monarch issued a slew of royal prisoner pardons. Justo was one of those to benefit. His release date was set for December.

After the disappointment of just a few months previously, Justo worried he would again be thwarted. On the morning he was due to be released, his anxiety rose when he was called away from the rest of the prisoners due to be freed. An agent from the Thai secret service wanted to talk to him about what had happened in prison and the various visits he received, he said. Once that was done, the Swiss ambassador accompanied him in a trip in an armoured van to Bangkok's Suvarnabhumi airport and walked him to the door of a flight to Zurich.

Justo still wasn't quite sure it was over. He wondered if there might be a 'technical problem with the plane – maybe we had to land in Malaysia'. There wasn't. He had his first glass of wine for a year and a half and quickly felt drunk.

When he landed in Switzerland, he heard some police officers talking about him and his obviously unusual status. 'They were talking in German, which I understand a bit,' he recalled. 'One said: "criminal?" The other said: "No, VIP."'

On the connecting flight to Geneva, he marvelled 'like a kid' as he looked at the familiar lakes and mountains. Laura and his son were there to meet him, as was his lawyer, who arranged for the family to leave by a back entrance to avoid the waiting media. Justo knew the pressure on his family had been enormous and felt bad about that. 'In a way I have got a part of responsibility of this, what they did to my wife and my son,' he said.

Finally Justo was free, almost eighteen months after his Thai island paradise fantasy turned into a nightmare. He was not cowed, but angry. He wanted those whom he saw as behind his troubles to be held to account.

Back at home, Justo stayed out of the limelight and focused on his wife and son after their traumatic parting. He also started to work quietly on preparing a complaint to the Swiss authorities alleging he was pressured by Tarek Obaid, PetroSaudi's co-founder, and Patrick Mahony, a senior executive at the company, into pleading guilty in Thailand. The Swiss attorney general's office began a review of Justo's claims when he filed them in 2018. A legal representative for PetroSaudi, Mahony and Obaid denied his clients had taken any steps to force Justo to make a confession. Justo's complaints were a 'hollow' attempt to deflect attention from his own wrongdoing and admissions, the lawyer said.

In April 2018, Swiss authorities disclosed that – separately from Justo's complaint – they had launched their own investigation into two unnamed PetroSaudi officials. The pair were suspected of criminal mismanagement, bribery of foreign public officials, aggravated money laundering and misconduct in public office, the Swiss prosecutor said. One of the two was also suspected of document forgery.

A spokesperson for PetroSaudi said at the time that the company was 'aware of an ongoing investigation by the Swiss authorities related to 1MDB' but was not the subject of the probe. The company rejected any claims that it or any of its officials were involved in misappropriation from the Malaysian fund. PetroSaudi would cooperate fully with any investigating authorities, the spokesperson added. The company later declined through a legal

representative to name the two officials targeted in the Swiss investigation, saying that it did not want to comment on an ongoing
inquiry.

In November 2018, Swiss prosecutors opened criminal proceedings against Justo on suspicion of industrial espionage. The investigation followed a complaint by an unnamed suspect in a
1MDB-related probe, the prosecutors said. Justo has denied any
wrongdoing.

As the Swiss legal tit for tat escalated, the political ground was shift-
ing in Malaysia. Najib's re-election had been taken as a foregone
conclusion by many analysts. His party, the United Malays National
Organisation, had ruled since independence from Britain in 1963. He
had all the vast power of UMNO's network and patronage to rally
Malays, who account for more than two thirds of the population.

Najib's most formidable electoral opponent to date, Anwar
Ibrahim, was in jail for the second time on a sodomy charge widely
seen as politically motivated. Anwar's opposition coalition had
almost beaten Najib in the previous election in 2013, winning the
popular vote but losing the parliamentary seats tally because of
Malaysia's gerrymandered constituencies. Since Anwar had been
jailed for the second time in 2014, the coalition had fragmented
and the opposition threat seemed greatly diminished.

But then an unlikely political alliance upended the situation.
Mahathir Mohamad, the nonagenarian former prime minister of
twenty-two years and formerly Najib's mentor, joined forces with
Anwar. Mahathir had criticised Najib trenchantly after the 1MDB
affair erupted, but his pact with the jailed opposition leader, who
used to be his finance minister, was still eye-catching. After all, it
was under Mahathir that Anwar had been jailed for corruption in
1999 and sodomy in 2000. The sodomy verdict was overturned
only in 2004, after Mahathir had left office.

Najib's expected election cakewalk had turned into a dogfight.
Mahathir played on the claims of sleaze around the government,

alleging the prime minister was corrupt – which Najib always denied. Mahathir talked about the 1MDB scandal in his stump speeches, saying it was a scandal that affected everybody in Malaysia.

The results stunned everybody as they came through on election night in May 2018. Mahathir's coalition and allies won handsomely, picking up 121 seats to Najib's 79. Najib's defeat triggered an emotional reaction from Malaysians who had begun to despair of the prospect of change. 'Crying tbh!!!!' a friend WhatsApped me. 'I can't sleep!' messaged another. 'I guess there is justice in this world after all.'

Xavier Justo said he was also in tears as he and his wife followed the results online from Geneva. Within a few weeks, he was on his way to Kuala Lumpur, where he met Mahathir and received a hero's welcome. 'For the first time in my life I was a celebrity,' he recalled. 'You go to a restaurant you have people taking pictures of you. You say your name to book a table and there's silence … it was fun!'

I met Justo for the first time at Geneva's Cornavin train station in June 2018. An imposing 1.9-metre-tall figure, his face was fuller than in his pinched post-arrest state and he was dressed sharply in smart dark jeans and a striped shirt with cufflinks. His circle beard was neatly clipped and he seemed buoyant. I asked if it was good to be back. 'Good to be back in a normal country, with rules and regulations and trust,' he replied.

We rode together in a taxi to his office. He immediately began to reflect on the nature of wealth and its disparities. His parents had come to Geneva from Spain in the 1960s, his father working as a bus driver and his mother as a maid. It was, as he said, a 'different world' from the one he inhabited as a fast-living financier. Now imprisonment had shaken the kaleidoscope again, sharpening his appreciation for the emotional core of his life. 'Out of the bad you have to find good things,' he said. 'Before I was maybe a little bit less of a family man. Now, I just want to be with my wife, my son, my in-laws, a couple of friends.'

He talked about how he had coped with imprisonment. He was proud of the fact that – unlike most of his fellow inmates – he was 'never sick'. He put that down to his workouts for iron man triathlon events. He loved the pain of the long bike ride. 'Because if you are burning, you are losing fat.' he said. 'And if you are burning, everyone is burning.'

His Geneva office, which was owned by a friend, was decorated with faux-classical busts and murals of historical European pastorals. Justo said he was now working in real estate and earning enough, though not the money he was on before. He had owned a Ferrari previously; now he had a second-hand Audi Q3.

He was also still dealing with fallout from his Thai misadventure. He had struggled to open a bank account because his conviction in the South-East Asian kingdom was recorded on a private database used by financial institutions to check out potential clients. He was petitioning to have it removed. 'What can I do not to be classified as a criminal?' he demanded.

Justo had a dramatic way of speaking and a habit of exclaiming 'eh!' to indicate something surprising or shocking. His hands seemed to be constantly on the move and he was fidgety, crossing the office for an occasional cigarette. He also had a twinkling charm that you could imagine served him well in the old days, when he part-owned a Geneva nightclub and was a self-confessed 'hunter' who loved the 'game of seduction'.

Justo said he had been successful in the finance industry in Geneva in the boom years before the days of Western economic crisis. He recalled those times as being 'easy for the people with the will to do it – and I always had the will to succeed'. He was able to ride out some less successful ventures, including owning a wood factory in Romania in the 1990s. He had his own investment company at thirty-two and 'whatever you want in life as material pretty much I had. I had Porsches, I travelled first [class], I went to all the best places.'

There was much less international competition in the banking world at that time, Justo said. Switzerland's secrecy regime – including numbered bank accounts – was attractive to both legal and illicit money. 'It was good and bad: good for the moneymaking in Switzerland, bad for the reputation,' he said, although he insisted his clients were clean. 'Any kind of drug dealer or whatever could come there. Every dictator could come to Switzerland and open bank accounts.'

Justo said he met Tarek Obaid, the PetroSaudi co-founder, through basketball. The young Saudi was about ten years his junior and his high-status family background contrasted with Justo's humbler origins, but the two men hit it off straight away. Justo said he looked on Obaid as his friend and even his 'little brother'. 'We had a lot of fun because he was very funny, very smart, very quick – and I was the same,' Justo said. 'He wasn't afraid of saying to a guy "you're wrong" or "you should stop doing that." He was very direct and I liked this.'

He later met Mahony, an old schoolmate of Obaid's who also became a senior PetroSaudi executive, and was immediately impressed. Mahony was working in finance and Justo described him as 'one of the smartest guys I ever met' – and very persuasive.

'He's the perfect guy, Mr Nice – you would love your daughter to marry him if you don't know him,' he said. 'He's brilliant. I think he has a gift to know what you're expecting, the exact words. He has the ability to tell you what you want to hear at the precise moment.'

Until 1MDB came along, PetroSaudi was a relatively small operation, Justo claimed. He said the royal connection – with Prince Turki as the co-founder – was its 'main asset' because it impressed potential partners and clients. 'That was opening all the doors,' he said, although big deals were still thin on the ground: 'Until the Malaysian money, PetroSaudi was nothing.'

PetroSaudi has contested this characterisation of its work. It has said through its legal representative that it entered into business contracts worth billions of dollars, employing more than four hundred people and holding oil and gas interests around the world.

In 2017, Prince Turki was detained in Riyadh's Ritz-Carlton hotel along with more than a hundred other high-profile individuals, as part of the purported anti-corruption crackdown launched under Saudi Crown Prince Mohammed bin Salman and described in chapter 1. No reason was given for Prince Turki's imprisonment. He has not been charged with any offence in Saudi Arabia or elsewhere.

Xavier Justo does not present himself as some kind of saint or ascetic. He is honest about his desire to be rich and live well. 'We all love money,' he told me. 'You love money: it's better to travel in first than with EasyJet. If you have the choice, it's better to put the family in a five-star hotel on vacation than camping.'

He was also unromantic about his own role in drawing attention to the 1MDB affair. He pointed out how – like many other allegations of financial scandal – it came to light initially not because of some great moral imperative, but because of a falling-out. 'Nobody is born a whistle-blower,' he said, perhaps a little too dismissive of those whose actions do stem from a sense of integrity. 'The whole whistle-blower story ... at one stage it's a fight. There's an argument that starts whistle-blowing. It's either financial conditions, the way you are treated – it's always like this.'

Justo added that this meant it was wrong for people in Malaysia to portray him as a hero. 'The people who are suffering are the heroes,' he said. 'You see me as the hero because I'm the only stupid guy that for the time being went to jail.'

He said he ran into trouble in Thailand because of overconfidence. He was not a 'totally innocent and naive guy'. He knew the oil business could be rough. But he assumed that any legal action over his falling-out with PetroSaudi would be launched in Switzerland and would be a civil matter, with no chance of him going to jail.

'I didn't steal anything. I discovered something big,' he said. 'I had a normal life. Now going back in time I should have said, "Oh fuck, it's a lot. Let's go back to Geneva and we're safe."'

Justo remembered his prison experience as being, above all, exhausting. It was impossible to sleep properly on the cell floor with no mattress. 'You sleep for an hour, thirty minutes,' he said. 'There are four lights up to your face at night. It's 40 degrees and there is one fan.'

The prisoners were kicked out of the cell at six in the morning and then idled for most of the day. 'From six o'clock to three you have nothing to do,' he said. 'There's no TV so what do you do? You read, you smoke, and you think ... You have time to think about a lot of things. You enter as a man; you exit as another man.'

I said that he made it sound almost like a religious conversion.

'Eh! In eighteen months you have a lot of time for thinking,' he replied. 'I'm not a religious guy, whatever. There was a small section of English library books, 132 books. I read all of them. I kept a count – 132 – and it was from, like, the discovery of black holes through to how the young ladies were dressed in schools in the sixteenth century in the UK.'

Justo acknowledged that the past few turbulent years had taught him some hard lessons. He certainly felt less cavalier. 'When you are making a decision, think about the consequences,' he said. 'And if you are involving your family, your loved ones, better think three times, or however many times you want. So I was smart – but not smart enough.'

Justo thinks he was far from the only one in the 1MDB affair to have underestimated the threats to him. He sees Najib as having fallen prey to a similar kind of arrogance. 'You have to understand that these kind of dictators, after so many years they think that they are untouchable and the country is theirs,' he said. 'He was convinced he would be re-elected.'

Yet Justo also acknowledges how close the toppled premier's strategy of simply arguing there was no problem with 1MDB came to succeeding. If Mahathir had not intervened, Najib 'would have had another five years and the story would have been, like, disappearing slowly, slowly'.

'You cannot fight ten years, fifteen years with the same subject,' Justo said. 'You know journalists would have been fed up with this story. Writing every three months and nothing was happening.'

Instead, the tables had turned. The Mahathir government said it was pursuing the 1MDB case strongly. It offered the cooperation with overseas authorities that Najib's administration had denied. Malaysian police conducted raids on properties linked to Najib's family in which they seized almost three hundred boxes of designer handbags, as well as cash and jewellery.

The news prompted a fresh wave of criticism of the opulent lifestyle of Rosmah Mansor, the ousted first lady. In late 2018, Malaysian authorities charged her with money laundering and soliciting and receiving bribes. She pleaded not guilty.

Najib said most of the handbags were gifts to Rosmah and their daughter. These were offered by various people including his son-in-law Daniyar Nazarbayev, nephew of Kazakhstan strongman president Nursultan Nazarbayev.

In the second half of 2018, Najib was charged in Malaysia with more than three dozen counts of money laundering, graft and breach of trust. Many related to the 1MDB case. The ex-premier pleaded not guilty.

★　★　★

The long search for the truth about what happened at 1MDB is as much a tale of institutional failure as individual actions. In Malaysia, a whole system of supposedly independent scrutiny collapsed. It was a sobering reminder of how easy it is for investigations to be derailed even in ostensibly democratic countries.

Mohamed Apandi Ali, the attorney general Najib appointed in 2015, ended or refused to launch investigations into both the premier himself and the wider 1MDB affair. Malaysia's central bank had recommended the attorney general press criminal charges against the fund for allegedly making inaccurate or incomplete disclosures between 2009 and 2011 in relation to its Cayman investments. Apandi Ali said 1MDB had no case to answer.

Once 1MDB ran into financial trouble, the government had brought in Arul Kanda, a respected banker, to sort out the fund's finances. There was no suggestion Kanda was involved in the alleged misappropriation himself: he arrived in 2015, after the contentious deals had been done. But his continued insistence that the fund's own investigations had found no evidence of wrongdoing neutralised pressure to properly probe the historic transactions. In the light of what has emerged, his stance raised questions about whether those internal inquiries were adequate.

There was also little enlightenment from some of the other countries caught up in the transactions, even where they appeared to be potential victims. Abu Dhabi loomed particularly large. The emirate had formed a strategic partnership with Malaysia in 2013, backed by Abu Dhabi's Crown Prince Mohammed bin Zayed and Najib. US investigators alleged $1.26 billion from a bond sale linked to the international partnership was misappropriated in a plot involving finance officials from 1MDB and Abu Dhabi.

I was not surprised to see that the tightly controlled Gulf emirate pursued the case discreetly and released almost no information about it. In November 2018, Abu Dhabi's IPIC sovereign wealth fund finally broke cover. It filed a US lawsuit against Goldman Sachs and others in an effort to recover losses allegedly suffered in the 1MDB affair. Goldman said it expected to contest the case.

Saudi Arabia also kept a low profile over 1MDB, even as Najib was claiming that the royal family there were the source of the $681 million of payments to him. It seemed clear that more publicity would not be welcomed by Riyadh. 'We got most of our money back,' said one person familiar with the matter, referring to the return of about $620 million. 'There is nothing for us to investigate.'

In other countries, there were few signs of inquiries where some might have been expected. One was the UK. There were numerous alleged links between the 1MDB case and UK entities including property, companies and bank accounts.

The lack of action in London contrasted with the political rhetoric there. In a speech by UK prime minister David Cameron to an anti-corruption conference he convened in London in May 2016, just two months before the US published its comprehensive allegations about the 1MDB case, he said the UK wanted to 'clean up our property market and show that there is no home for the corrupt in Britain'. He spoke in general terms and said this was part of a wider effort aimed at 'stopping the corrupt hiding their loot from the authorities'. 'It means that when people steal money from your country and hide it in mine – we can expose them and return the money to you,' Cameron said.[14]

Barely a month later, Cameron was announcing his resignation outside 10 Downing Street after UK voters backed Brexit in a referendum. His anti-corruption agenda seemed to disappear with him. In 2018, only the prospect of a rebellion of Conservative MPs forced Theresa May's government to reverse its opposition to an amendment to make British Overseas Territories establish publicly accessible registers of the true owners of companies. Britain's Overseas Territories include tax havens that loomed large in the 1MDB case, such as the Cayman Islands and British Virgin Islands.

The change belatedly accepted by the government was welcome but limited. The measures would not apply to the UK's Crown Dependencies, the Channel Islands and the Isle of Man. Even more pertinently, onshore jurisdictions such as the US state of Delaware – the home state of both Barack Obama's vice president Joe Biden and more than a million companies – maintain high levels of secrecy. The world remains full of corporate black boxes, which hinder exposure of even relatively crude schemes such as the one US authorities allege was used to misappropriate money from 1MDB.

In the end, one of the most striking points about the pan-continental hunt for Malaysia's money is the international breadth of cynicism it has exposed. Away from the central allegations of criminality, there was a whole supporting cast of lawyers, bankers and public relations people who in one way or another helped enable or defend the enterprise. I asked a tough lawyer friend why she thought people were able to set aside their consciences in the face of such red flags and the possibility of reputational damage.

'It's a nihilistic view of the world,' she shrugged. '"Mankind is unimprovable and what I do won't make a difference either way, so I might as well get what I can."'

There was a revealing coda to Najib's fall from grace. Before the election, the premier's allies would often say that corruption and cronyism had flourished under his nemesis, Mahathir. It was shameless whataboutery, intended to distract from Najib's troubles. It was also true. While nothing on the scale of 1MDB had been exposed during Mahathir's time, his more than two decades in office had entrenched the kind of failures of accountability seen under Najib's rule.

It was chastening to look back at a 'Lunch with the *FT*' Mahathir did in 2017, before the election. He met my colleague in a Japanese-style bakery that was part of a chain he founded. He dismissed his past suppression of dissent, saying all that mattered now was how he and the people he once cracked down on were united in the 'same objective – overthrowing the government'.

Mahathir also declined to distance himself from racially stereotyping remarks he had made in the past. He has written that there is 'no reason to believe understanding and sympathy are strong Chinese traits', and that Jews 'understand money instinctively'. During the 1997 South-East Asian financial crisis, he said he suspected a Jewish 'agenda' behind the currency market speculation against the Malaysian ringgit, as 'Jews are not happy to see Muslims progress.'[15] Twenty years later, he told his FT interviewer that he had no problem with being described as anti-Semitic. He also endorsed the conspiracy theory that the September 11 terrorist attacks were a 'false flag' operation by the US itself, or maybe Israel.[16]

Some of Mahathir's early actions on regaining the premiership did not inspire confidence either. In June 2018, he enthused in an interview that investigators had 'an almost perfect case' against the 1MDB suspects, adding that his predecessor was 'totally responsible' for the fund.[17] These seemed potentially prejudicial remarks ahead of a trial of Najib that needed to be both fair and perceived to be so.

Mahathir said shortly after the election that he would redefine rather than revoke the Najib government's contentious law against 'fake news', although his administration later moved to scrap it. He also said during a live TV broadcast that freedom of speech and the press had limits. He pledged to hand over power within two years to his former foe Anwar, who was released from jail shortly after the election. But he added that he would 'play a role in the background even when I step down'.

In the end, Najib was outmanoeuvred and outmuscled. He proved the weaker of two strongmen. His opponent Mahathir, having ruled for twenty-two years as the representative of the dominant UMNO movement, was able to co-opt political machinery the party had built up during its long unbroken rule for his own purposes. Mahathir's victory over Najib was more like a palace coup, endorsed by the people: the toppling of an individual, like the fall of Egypt's President Hosni Mubarak, rather than the overthrow of a system.

Even as Malaysians I knew celebrated change, I worried about the potential for the delight to turn to dismay. Like many others, I had been inspired by the elation in Cairo's Tahrir Square the day after the fall of Mubarak in February 2011. Protestors cleaned up the debris with signs pinned to their jumpers that read 'Sorry for the disturbance, we are building Egypt.' But a darker thought also flashed across my mind: enjoy the moment, because it might not get better than this. Mubarak's near-three-decade rule was over, but he seemed like a strategic sacrifice by the military to purge public anger and maintain its deeper grip on the country. Almost a decade later, after the brief interlude of an Islamist government toppled by a 2013 coup, many people said the general turned president Abdel Fattah el-Sisi was clamping down on dissent even more harshly than Mubarak's regime.

The long unravelling of 1MDB continued through late 2018, almost a decade after the fund's original joint venture with PetroSaudi. In November, the US Justice Department unveiled a guilty plea by Tim Leissner, the former head of Goldman Sachs' South-East Asia operation, to conspiring to launder money and pay bribes. Leissner was ordered to forfeit $43.7 million as a result of his crimes. Goldman has denied wrongdoing.

On the same day, the US Justice Department issued a criminal indictment of Jho Low and Ng Chong Hwa, a former Goldman

Sachs banker better known as Roger Ng, over the alleged misappropriation of more than $2.7 billion from 1MDB by them and others.[18] Both Low and Ng denied any wrongdoing through their legal representatives. A spokesperson for Low said the bond issues at the centre of the allegations 'were undertaken openly and lawfully between experienced, well-regulated financial institutions and government entities'. The spokesperson added: 'Mr Low simply asks that the public keep an open mind regarding this case until all of the evidence comes to light, which he believes will vindicate him.'

In December 2018, Malaysian authorities charged Low and four others with money-laundering and breach of trust offences linked to 1MDB.[19] A spokesperson for Low said he maintained his innocence and branded the charges part of a 'trial by media and political reprisals' by the government. 'It is clear that Mr. Low cannot get a fair trial in Malaysia, where the regime has proven numerous times that they have no interest in the rule of law,' the spokesperson said.

As the claims against Low built, so did the intensity of his denials. He or his representatives set up a website in 2018 to rebut the allegations against him, describing him as a 'global philanthropist, investor, and entrepreneur'. The public relations material included a personal letter ostensibly signed by Low himself. 'Let me be clear: I am innocent,' Low's online plea read in part. 'With hindsight I may have done things differently, like any young person, but any mistakes I made do not amount to the sweepingly broad and destructive allegations being made against me. There are so many fundamental facts that those seeking to lay blame at my door find convenient to ignore.'[20]

He and the US investigators of 1MDB had constructed two different realities. As of June 2019, the test of which was right awaited.

★   ★   ★

For Xavier Justo, vindication felt closer at hand. He was sanguine about his reputation and shrugged off the efforts to discredit him. 'Eh, my friends they know me, my family know me, all the colleagues I've had in life know me,' he said. 'The people that don't know me, they may still be thinking that 1MDB and PetroSaudi are good, and I'm bad. I don't know, I don't care.'

Justo said all that was needed was for the facts about 1MDB to be allowed to speak for themselves. The ex-Swiss banker had gone from Thai jailbird to hero of Malaysia's new era. He felt relaxed enough now to deliver a sardonic final message to those involved in the fund dealings now under such high-profile scrutiny. 'Good luck for them to explain the numbers,' he said.

6

Small Americas

Richard Bowyer ran for cover as rain lashed the jungles of southern Laos, a fresh deluge from skies where US bombs once teemed. Decades ago, B-52s pulverised this supply route to the communist regime in neighbouring North Vietnam. Now Bowyer, a former British army officer, was part of efforts to clear up the unexploded American ordnance still scattered along the Laotian side of the border.

'The Vietnam War is still going on,' Bowyer, a whip-thin old Etonian who recalled watching the fall of Saigon on television as a teenager, told me. 'In some ways, I feel as if I am playing a part in the last act.'

The US air offensive in Laos, which spanned the administrations of Presidents Lyndon Johnson and Richard Nixon, is reckoned to be the heaviest per capita bombing of a country in history. Washington dropped more tonnage than it unleashed on Germany and Japan combined during the Second World War. One Laotian official survey has claimed 270 million bombs fell on the country between 1964 and 1973, as many as a third of which did not explode. They are still killing and maiming people today.

The search for US bombs that still plague a faraway country two generations after they were let loose is a stark illustration of the damage done by great power militarism. It is also a cautionary tale for anyone who believes in the basic high-mindedness of Western interactions with the rest of the world.

That point was underlined just two months after my Laos trip, when Donald Trump was elected president. His rule would have many baleful effects, but he also unintentionally illuminated some of US foreign policy's darker secrets. In particular, his naked power games and his enthusiasm for autocratic regimes whom he thought could offer something lifted a curtain on the logic of how Washington and other Western capitals behaved. As his presidency unfolded, Trump torpedoed the comforting myth of the US as an international bulwark against dictatorship.

In Laos, Bowyer was part of a substantial operation to clean up after a long-ago conflict mostly forgotten stateside. He was the country operations manager for the HALO Trust, a non-profit group working to clear war debris in various countries. He told me he liked his job because it had 'many of the elements of being a soldier without actually killing people'.

As Bowyer and I shared a beer in the courtyard of my hotel on the night of my arrival, I had stopped mid-sentence, having noticed several large bombs standing like ornaments behind the table. The ex-officer commented in a seemingly mordant aside that they were like 'upmarket garden gnomes'. I realised over the following days that his remark was in fact literal: householders around the area used the UXBs as decorations and fence posts.

Bowyer explained the uniqueness of Laos's problem. In other conflict zones from Afghanistan to Angola, HALO and similar organisations were cleaning up landmines mostly set methodically in identifiable fields. In Laos, by contrast, the unexploded ordnance had come from the heavens and was now scattered over wide and unpredictable areas. The ravages of time and weathering added to HALO's task. Devices had lost their markings and become corroded, making them more difficult to handle. In the rainy season, conditions could make work impossible. In the dry season, they could make it more dangerous, because the searchers had to use more force with machetes to dig the explosives out of the hard ground.

One day I drove with Bowyer and his team from HALO's regional headquarters in Xepon, through well-watered rice paddies that had flourished into a lush cover of brilliant green. Fisherwomen in the region's distinctive conical hats cast large nets into a stream, their faces and necks wrapped in bandanas. We passed through a small village where buffalo waded through the flooded roadside and rooted in the damp undergrowth. A school-girl in a traditional *sinh* tube skirt hared excitedly towards a large puddle as if to leap into it, veering away at the last moment. Life went on, even as potential disaster lurked. 'There will always be residual danger,' Bowyer said, pointing to a pool by the roadside and close to a school. 'That's a crater. Now, it looks like a duck pond.'

HALO staff in blue overalls ran painstaking area-by-area clearances in the lee of mist-shrouded hills. Dragonflies buzzed us constantly, occasionally catching glancing blows on my bare arms before correcting course. Bomb-clearers in goggles and body armour pegged out zones to vet, first with blue-framed metal detectors and then with classic upright models for closer investigation. Much of their time was spent dealing with false alarms: most of their discoveries were shrapnel from bombs that had already gone off.

The detectors wore US flags Velcroed to their flak vests, in a nod to funding belatedly offered by Washington for the clearance efforts. Some of HALO's Laotian staff have suffered directly from the deadly US legacy. One told how his father had lost a hand. Another, Laphoukham Vilayvieng, said her brother-in-law had been killed. Asked what she felt about the US now, she was diplomatic. 'I am sad about it, but it's in the past. Now it's different and Laos is developing.'

We arrived in a hamlet of wooden houses raised on stilts, some edged by balconies with walls of bamboo weave. A sagging blue-and-yellow curtain added a dash of colour to one family home. In the open common area between the upper floor and the ground, a man sat with his wife, four children and a dog.

His name was Ing and he had two stumps for arms and a blinded eye. He told how he had gone out one day the previous year to clear land for farming and found a metal object lying on the ground. When he tried to open it up, it detonated. 'Before I had my accident, I had my two arms, good eyes and was strong,' he said. 'But after the accident, my life was changed. I can't do anything, including eating for myself.'

Now he couldn't plant rice or use the husking machine next to him. A life he once rated comfortable had been upended. His wife watched silently, flanked by their fifteen-year-old son and daughters of thirteen, four and two. 'My wife now does everything for the family and it's hard for her because we don't have enough food,' Ing said, his eyes filling with tears. 'In the future, it will be difficult for my family to live.'

Hundreds of kilometres away, in the Laotian capital, Vientiane, President Barack Obama had touched down. It was the first visit to the country by a sitting US president. He would come face to face with the consequences of this early prototype of what was to become a favoured US model of dealing death from the sky. One of Obama's legacies had been his expansion of drone warfare in places like Yemen and Somalia.

During his visit, Obama acknowledged that Laos's people 'continued to live under the shadow of war'. He met bomb victims and visited a centre that provides artificial limbs to them. He also admitted the US 'did not acknowledge' at the time what it was doing to Laos. He announced an extra $90 million of funding over three years for ordnance clearance and help for the maimed.

Obama concluded his trip with a press conference at a hotel on the banks of the Mekong River. The last question went to the point. Given what the president had learned about the bombing campaign and witnessed during what he'd described as an 'at times moving' visit to Laos, should he apologise fully to the country?

Obama, who was born in 1961, began by reflecting that at the time of the destruction he was too young to fully understand what was going on. Then he declared that the US 'was on the right side of history when it came to the Cold War'. He followed this with a convoluted explanation of Washington's actions that seemed more self-justification than apology.

> There may have been moments, particularly here in Southeast Asia, in which, in our singular focus on defeating an expansion-ist and very aggressive communism, that we didn't think through all the implications of what we did as policymakers. And certainly when you see the dropping of cluster bombs, trying to figure out how that was going to be effective – particularly since part of the job was to win over hearts and minds – how that was going to work, I think with the benefit of hindsight, we have to say that a lot of those consequences were not ones that necessarily served our interests.[1]

The lack of clear contrition came as no surprise. Leaders of power-ful countries don't generally go round saying sorry to small states, for all kinds of political reasons. But what was really striking was his attempt to play down US intent. Because Washington 'didn't think through all the implications' of what it was doing, 'a lot of those consequences were not ones that necessarily served our interests.' It was the familiar 'clumsy America' excuse: maybe we got it wrong, but that was mostly through excess zeal for a good cause – and certainly not in bad faith.

The way a speaker as gifted as Obama stumbled through this, including the hackneyed reference to 'hearts and minds', perhaps betrayed his awkwardness at making a bad argument. After all, it's not as if US officials could realistically have overlooked the implications of violence on the scale they visited on Laos. Indeed, the campaign's magnitude was the whole point: it is called carpet-bombing for a reason. It was self-evident that many of these bombs would not explode and would instead punch deadly roosts in the jungle where they would lurk for years to come.

Obama's triangulations by the Mekong made me think of how much time I had spent in countries that bore scars from encounters with Washington. I had passed a good part of my career observing the US as it was viewed from outside, in various parts of the world. I had seen a little of the countries where Washington had launched its most contentious and high-profile twenty-first century interventions, notably Iraq, Afghanistan and Yemen. I had experienced much more of the wide hinterland of places where the US imprint is less known – or, at least, less talked about.

What emerged from those travels was something that ought to be a commonplace, but to many in the US and elsewhere in the West is not. For all America's cultural attractions and its intermittent support for freedom, the idea of the country as a global force for good seems to some bizarre and even perverse. For this reason, I could not share the Western political establishment hand-wringing over the supposed threat posed by Trump to what many dubbed the 'US-led liberal order' and the 'international rules-based system'. The failings obscured by these phrases had long undercut efforts to combat the menacing authoritarianism of regimes in countries such as China, Russia and Iran.

In many parts of the world I'd visited, people cherished neither US leadership nor the power structures through which it operated. Sometimes Washington's actions flatly contradicted its supposed values of democracy and human rights. As for the 'rules-based international system', it seemed to me to exist only to the extent that those who controlled it found it helpful for themselves and others to obey. The US and its allies have been quite willing to flout laws and norms when it suits them, such as in launching the Iraq War.

In other multilateral spheres, such as the International Criminal Court, the US opted out because it did not want its hands tied. In the court's case, it didn't want to risk its soldiers and other US citizens being put on trial for war crimes. Washington wanted the kudos of moral leadership without the fetters.

The idea of the US as the leading progressive influence in the world is deeply rooted in postwar Western thinking. It is a view characterised by both naivety and a determined effort of propaganda and omission. Commentators might acknowledge Washington's shortcomings to various degrees, but the core idea of the US as an agent of betterment had been remarkably durable, at least until Trump showed up. As the Libyan author Hisham Matar has put it: 'Perhaps they are aware of the myth of themselves and have simply decided it is too useful a myth to give up.'[2]

Obama's words in Vientiane acquired even greater significance in hindsight. The press conference took place in September 2016, so he spoke about the imminent US election. He was dismissive of Trump, whom he said was not 'qualified' to be president. In an era when Western conservative movements were successfully – if misleadingly – branding themselves as anti-elitist, to disparage someone in this way sounded to me condescending and electorally dangerous.

Obama also showed misplaced confidence in the capacity for Trump's rhetoric to drive voters away. He said: 'I think the most important thing for the public and the press is to just listen to what he says and follow up and ask questions about what appear to be either contradictory or uninformed or outright wacky ideas.'

In one sense, Obama was of course not wrong about the unique oddness of his successor. Once he became president, Trump exhibited plenty of contradictory, uninformed and even 'outright wacky' behaviour. Demonstrable untruths did issue from his mouth at an extraordinary rate.

But, in a more fundamental way, the othering of Trump by Obama and most of the rest of the political establishment was off the mark. Trump's open embrace of raw power and realpolitik in world affairs provoked horror among both liberals and some traditional Republicans, as if this was something the US had never done before. The similar reactions to his indulgence of authoritarian leaders also suggested this was a way of operating that had previously been beneath Washington.

One incident in the first weeks of Trump's presidency highlighted this revealing trend. Replying to an interviewer's assertion that Russia's President Vladimir Putin was a 'killer', Trump fired back that there were a 'lot of killers' around. He added: 'You think our country's so innocent?'[3]

His remarks provoked condemnation across the political spectrum. High-profile commentators from the conservative Charles Krauthammer to CNN's Anderson Cooper deplored the 'equivalence' of Trump's statement. Michael McFaul, a former US ambassador to Russia, even defended Washington by citing its supposed distaste for heavy bombing campaigns. 'Mr. President, our soldiers dont [sic] carpet bomb cities. We dont [sic] assassinate government critics,' he tweeted.[4]

Trump could certainly be attacked for making an expedient and unmerited attempt to defend Putin against criticisms of serious rights abuses and military aggression under his rule. But the domestic criticism of what Trump said ran deeper than that. He was being attacked in part for questioning Washington's benign self-image. This has been woven through the truisms of both main parties, from Reagan's idea of the US as a 'shining city on a hill' to the Obama administration's declaration that Washington would be a 'force for good' internationally. It is also a foundational point for a good part of the Western commentariat.

Trump's arrival had the effect of inflaming his opponents' rhetoric about America's supposedly positive role in world affairs. In December 2017, Susan Rice, national security adviser under Obama, took the new White House to task for drawing up a national security strategy that embraced a 'self-serving, confrontational vision of the world'. She wrote stirringly of the power of US ideals and 'the value of promoting democracy and universal rights'.[5] 'Relinquishing the nation's moral authority in these difficult times will only embolden rivals and weaken ourselves,' she wrote.

Other critiques of the Trump administration made similar points. Typically, while these acknowledged past US 'mistakes', they would also seek to mitigate them. US interventions were 'misjudged' or had 'unintended consequences'. Or it was said that Washington had 'not always lived up to its ideals'. This would be contrasted with Trump's world, in which might was right. 'This is not who we are' became a signature lament from anti-Trumpists of both the left and right.

Yet Trump is no foreign policy iconoclast. A good deal of what his administration did in its first eighteen months ran with conventional US thinking. He further intensified the strategy of drone strikes already heavily used by Obama. Even as Trump showed personal deference to Putin, he surrounded himself with Russia hawks.

What seemed to make people especially uncomfortable was how Trump sometimes showed a savant's talent for getting to the uncomfortable heart of the matter. His questioning of the future of NATO – which as a presidential candidate he had declared 'obsolete' – brought howls from the foreign policy establishment. Yet it did not seem unreasonable to debate the role of a nearly seventy-year-old organisation that was a creature of the Second World War and a Cold War that had ended more than a quarter of a century previously. There was a legitimate argument to be had about NATO's purpose and relevance.

Some of Trump's more thoughtful critics acknowledged this. 'In some ways this is one of his strengths,' Rob Malley, president of the International Crisis Group and a former Obama administration official, said of Trump's often accidental illumination of the flaws in received wisdom. 'He asks the most basic questions people don't ask any more.'

Even Trump's praise for autocrats, while cringeworthy in its expression, is in one way no more than a guileless endorsement of long-standing US policy. Historically, it was not dictators per se who needed to worry about flak from the US over human rights, but rather those who lacked energy reserves, military strategic importance or some other asset that would make Washington reluctant to offend them. From Nicaragua to Egypt, dictators have often enjoyed US support for as long as they were useful. The defining, if perhaps apocryphal, maxim has been: 'He may be a son of a bitch, but he's our son of a bitch.'

Dick Cheney captured a similar sentiment during his days as chief executive of the oil services company Halliburton: 'The good Lord didn't see fit to put oil and gas only where there are democratically elected regimes friendly to the United States,' the future US vice president said in 1998. 'Occasionally we have to operate in places where, all things considered, one would not normally choose to go. But, we go where the business is.'[6]

Trump's offence in his open praise for dictators was less break-ing a US principle than laying bare an inconvenient truth. He had

broken what has been branded the 'norm against noticing'[7] the
discrepancies between the way Washington presents its foreign
policy and the way it acts. He might not even have been aware of
how he had challenged the central myth of the 'good US'. This
fable had long showed its contradictions in places far distant from
Washington, not least in a country conceived in America that I
had seen up close in West Africa.

I was gripped by a powerful sense that I wanted to stay alive as I
stood on the roof of a hotel in Monrovia, Liberia, listening to the
sound of mortar fire. The shots came from rebels fighting towards
the gates of the capital, where they hoped to oust President Charles
Taylor. The proximity of this sudden burst of fire showed they
were closer than anyone had guessed. That's why there were so
few journalists there to hear it.

At least I was in good company that night in 2003. One of the
handful atop the Mamba Point hotel was Sebastian Junger. His
book *The Perfect Storm*, about a fishing disaster off New England,
had already been made into a blockbuster movie starring George
Clooney. I marvelled at Junger's calmness on that trip, whether in
taking time out for a game of chess or musing on the nature of
conflict reporting: in the middle of a fast-moving and intense situation, was it better to focus on gathering impressions or detailed
granular observations? I, on the other hand, felt out of my depth.
Even the name of the small peninsula we were on, Mamba Point,
suggested deadly menace. With the sea flanking us on three sides,
on one of which the US embassy was strategically placed, it all felt
uncomfortably tight.

We were witnessing the latest violent spasm of a conflict that
had plagued Liberia since the 1980 military coup against President
William Tolbert. The filmed public execution of thirteen of his
top officials on a beach after his murder set the tone for a brutal

quarter-century for the West African country. The leader of that putsch, Samuel Doe, was himself ousted and killed in 1990. His torture became another grisly movie that did the rounds in the region on videotape and, later, on the Internet. The video showed the militia leader who captured him – Prince Yormie Johnson – sipping a Budweiser while his men cut off Doe's ears. (Prince Johnson would later stand in Liberia's 2011 presidential election, finishing third.)

Years of war followed before Charles Taylor, a civil servant turned warlord, emerged as the strongest armed group leader. In as much as they were noticed by the rest of the world, Liberia's internal battles became a byword for the ghastly. Marauding militias racked up atrocities, many of them carried out by child soldiers and fighters sometimes clad with incongruous accessories such as Mickey Mouse bags or women's wigs. In 1997, Taylor won an election in which a slogan favoured by some of his supporters captured the ghoulishness of those years: 'He killed my ma, he killed my pa, I'll vote for him,' the pro-Taylor chant went, echoing the fears of voters who backed the rebel leader mainly because they feared he would go back to war if he lost.

I'd visited Liberia for the first time the following year and glimpsed both a little of the wildness and the country's haunting underlay. It remains one of the most unsettling places I've ever been. Even the glowering skies of Monrovia, one of the world's rainiest capitals, felt loaded with a long history of suffering ready to unload in a deluge.

When I made that first trip in 1998, Taylor was firmly in charge. I saw how he ruled one day as I drove with staff from an aid agency on a road outside the north-central town of Gbarnga. A car with blacked-out windows suddenly veered in front of us and forced us to stop. Plain-clothes security agents swarmed out and dragged our driver from his seat, before bundling him into their vehicle and speeding off. We sat in shock on the highway: only moments before I had been preoccupied with trying to get BBC World Service coverage of the English FA Cup football final.

I went up the road to where the car had disappeared with the driver. I asked around and found him, apparently still in somewhat loose custody, outside an official building where a small crowd had gathered. He looked at me quizzically and said rather chillingly: 'What are you doing, Michael?' The message: I should have kept my head down.

We all ended up at the house of a government minister who gave us a long and threatening lecture. He accused the driver of overtaking recklessly and of kicking up a stone that had damaged his official car. He was also angry, he said, pointing across at me, that I had falsely accused his men of brutalising the driver. It was part of a bigger problem, he said, of journalists and other outsiders 'telling lies about Liberia'.

The aid agency worker handled it deftly, soaking up the minister's anger and promising this behaviour wouldn't be repeated. She and I had agreed on the short drive to the minister's house that I wouldn't reveal I was a journalist for fear of making a bad situation worse. I had stuffed my press card down the back of the seat. I sat there feeling afraid and stupid – and thanking God that the minister wasn't more curious about who I was.

Now Taylor himself was about to become the latest casualty of Liberia's bloody power struggles. The despot's days seemed numbered but no one was yet sure – and he continued to resist. I stayed in a resort hotel, not too far from where Samuel Doe's drunken troops had sprayed bullets on the ousted Tolbert government ministers stripped down to loincloths and tied to posts. The owner told me the usual occupant of my room was a diamond dealer who had fled.

I shared the lodging with a *Newsweek* correspondent and a rat. The rodent feasted on Pringles that – despite the war – Monrovia's savvy Lebanese traders were still able to supply. One night, I woke to the sound of gunfire nearby and cowered ready for escape, or the end. The shots died down and, next morning, the guards told us they had foiled an attempted robbery. The assailants had tried to scale the compound wall that gave on to the beach where the government officials had been killed.

For all the easy *Heart of Darkness* tropes that a lazy Western correspondent could reach for, the chaos was grimly logical rather than primal. It seemed almost inevitable that any country short of money and shorn of institutions – whether in Africa, Europe or elsewhere – would degenerate into a cruel power struggle. What was distinctive in Liberia was the American underpinnings of it all. My travels elsewhere in West Africa had exposed me to various British and French colonial hangovers. Monrovia offered something new and striking, especially given how the US has always prided itself on supposedly avoiding the European vice of empire.

Shiploads of liberated US slaves and freeborn blacks were sent to Liberia in the nineteenth century under the auspices of the American Colonization Society. The organisation was a meeting of strange bedfellows: anti-slavery Protestant reform groups and slaveholders. Both shared a contentious view that black people should be sent from the US to Africa, either to help better themselves (the religionists' idea) or to keep them from agitating in the US (the slaveholders' wish). The society established the colony in 1822 and installed the first African-American governor – who had been born free in Virginia – in 1841. He then proclaimed the country an independent republic in 1847.

While Washington did not formally occupy Liberia, it had a heavy influence on the modern state. The capital is named for President James Monroe. The country's flag is a lone star and stripes. At one point during the uprising against Taylor, the front line appeared to be a bridge that ran across Providence Island, where the first US settlers arrived. The warring parties each had a view of a monument telling them to 'Respect the civilians' and 'Respect human dignity'.

The nineteenth-century arrivals from stateside quickly installed themselves as rulers over the thickly forested country's indigenous people. They imported some customs of the slave-owning South that had abused them and their ancestors. The settlers acquired a taste for morning coats, despite the muggy West African coastal heat. They built antebellum-style mansions and an imposing Masonic lodge on a commanding height not far from where the US embassy now stands. Tolbert, the last Americo-Liberian president before the fall, had been the lodge's grand master. During Liberia's wars, the building was occupied by squatters and deteriorated to a blackened husk until attempts to revive it were launched after Taylor fell.

The Americo-Liberian elite even ran a system close to slavery. A League of Nations report in 1930 said the government had 'systematically fostered and encouraged' a 'policy of gross intimidation and suppression' towards the indigenous population, including forced labour. It said authorities oppressed 'the native' and acted to 'prevent him from realising his powers and his limitations and prevent him from asserting himself in any way whatever'. The ruling class constituted a 'dominant and colonizing race', even though they were also of African descent.[8] The report triggered the resignation of President Charles King who, as Liberian secretary of state, had signed the post-First World War Treaty of Versailles in 1919.

Liberian society remained starkly divided, with top jobs in government and business dominated by descendants of the US settlers. Various administrations made marginal improvements after the Second World War, but the power relationships in society remained in essence as they had been for more than a century. The oppressed had in a sense become the oppressors.

Many black Americans, including activists and musicians, were drawn to Liberia after the Second World War. The pull was understandable: there was great power in the idea of descendants of freed slaves running a country from the continent where their ancestors were kidnapped. One enthusiast was Nina Simone, who spent three years in Liberia in the 1970s. It was also, according to a brilliant account of her years there by Katherina Grace Thomas, 'among the most decadent places to party in Africa'. The Americo-Liberian elite and their guests would spend evenings 'eating carpaccio at Salvatore's Italian restaurant [and] sipping cocktails in the swim-up bar at the iconic Ducor Palace Hotel', whose elevated position later made it a perfect outpost for snipers during the war.

'Africa, half a world away from NewYork,' Simone wrote in her memoir before travelling to Monrovia. 'Maybe I could find some peace there, or a husband. Maybe it would be like going home.'[9]

President Tolbert had supposedly brought a fresh wave of liberalism after the long and increasingly stifling twenty-seven-year rule of his predecessor, William Tubman. But, if change was happening, it didn't come quickly enough. 'They'd believed they were breathing fresh political air into the country,' wrote Thomas. 'But perhaps it had flowed no further than the confines of their own circle, which swelled like an overblown balloon and then burst.'

The end of the Americo-Liberian hegemony was horrific. But there was a reason many Liberians cheered the immolation of the class who had taken control of their country. The gutting of President Tolbert in a corridor of the Executive Mansion was not just a power grab by a group of opportunistic young soldiers, but the culmination of more than a century of repression.

The US itself has also profited in modern times from its relationship with Liberia. In 1926, the Firestone company received a very favourable, million-acre, ninety-nine-year concession for a giant rubber plantation. The company remains active in the country today.

Liberia was also useful to Washington during the Cold War. It served as a site for strategic installations such as the Omega transmission station, which served as a navigation post for aircraft and ships in the Atlantic. The US gave the Doe regime hundreds of millions of dollars of aid in the 1980s despite mounting evidence of its abuses.

Now, during the death throes of the Taylor government, people showed the same ambiguity towards Washington that I'd seen formerly European-occupied countries display towards their ex-colonists. Liberians pleaded for help and some described the US as a big brother. People protested at the lack of American intervention by piling corpses outside the US embassy. As one man hunkering down with thousands of others in the main national sports stadium put it: 'Liberia is small America.'

A billboard near the Executive Mansion where Liberia's leaders lived highlighted the unhealthy blend of dominance and dependency. Entitled 'US–Liberia relations', it depicted a path dotted with significant dates in the West African country's history, including the 1847 foundation, the 1980 coup and Taylor's election in 1997. At the end of the route, a small figure in shorts, flip-flops and Liberian traditional top looked up at a tall Uncle Sam-style figure, who was dressed in a baggy blue suit and stars-and-stripes hat. 'We've come a long way, big brother, but it's still rough! We are suffering,' said the diminutive Liberian. 'For true?' his American counterpart incredulously replied.

As the rebels approached central Monrovia, people flocked naturally to the perceived sanctuary of the area around the American embassy. Greystone, a walled compound where US diplomats had once lived across the road from the main embassy premises, became home to a tarpaulin city of thousands of displaced people. I wandered round, marvelling at how many had

congregated near this wild Atlantic shoreline, like passengers
flocking to the still-afloat end of a capsizing ship.

A mortar blast hit Greystone one day as I walked with journalist colleagues past the entrance to the embassy. A short time later,
a second explosion sent the retreating crowd into a panic. I almost
ran into a vanful of armed youths; they barely noticed in their
hasty retreat. Dozens were killed in the attack. As so often in
Liberia, those responsible – loyalist or rebel – were never
identified.

Charles Taylor did not go down without a fight, even after
President George W. Bush demanded he step down. He dug in
against the rebel advance until fellow African leaders strong-armed
him into accepting a deal to go into exile. The US sent a company
of troops as a symbolic presence on the ground, with a shipload of
marines waiting offshore.

The Liberian President's relationship with the US, like his
country's, had always been equivocal. His father was Americo-
Liberian and Taylor studied in the US. He was a finance official
in the Doe government who fled to the US when the then
leader accused him of embezzlement. He was detained and held
in a Massachusetts jail on a Liberian government extradition
request, before escaping in mysterious circumstances in 1985.
He returned to West Africa and, in 1989, launched his rebellion
against Doe.

Taylor's links with Washington have never been fully explained.
He has denied longstanding speculation that he worked as an
informant for US intelligence agencies since the 1980s.

Taylor left the wreckage of his country with a vainglorious
flourish. At a special ceremony in a small auditorium in the presidential Executive Mansion, he delivered a valediction on his
destructive fifteen years at the heart of Liberian life. Flanked by

three other African presidents – South Africa's Thabo Mbeki, Joaquim Chissano of Mozambique, and Ghana's John Kufuor – he was dressed in his trademark white safari suit as if to project a messianic air. He described himself as both 'whipping boy' and 'sacrificial lamb'. He said he thought history would be kind to him. He thanked Bush, saying that the US president had been misled but 'God will reveal the truth to him.' Taylor's parting shot was even purer chutzpah. 'God willing, I will be back.'

The ousted president went into exile in Nigeria, where I made a futile attempt to interview him. He was forced out more than two years later after an international court set up to investigate war crimes in neighbouring Sierra Leone issued an extradition request for him. Taylor was arrested as he tried to flee across the Nigeria–Cameroon border.

The Special Court for Sierra Leone transferred Taylor for trial in the Netherlands, for fear that holding proceedings in Freetown would destabilise a country where he was also accused of stoking war. In 2012, he was convicted and sentenced to fifty years in jail for aiding and abetting war crimes, including delivering weapons, food, medical supplies, fuel and equipment to forces in Sierra Leone that were guilty of atrocities. He had compared his actions to those of George W. Bush in the 'war on terror'.

In 2013, Taylor was transferred to a jail in north-east England. He still meddled in Liberian politics. A phone conversation with allies in the country was leaked in 2017. He was still describing himself as a 'sacrificial lamb'.

Taylor left another legacy that resonates today. His regime was fond of branding its critics as sources of what would become known in the US years later as 'fake news'. During his time in office, visitors arriving in central Monrovia would pass two large billboards on the main road from the distant Robertsfield airport. One, headlined 'Unbalanced news is also a human rights abuse', showed a radio presenter broadcasting false messages that scared listeners and left one young man holding his head in despair.

The poster's even more vivid companion piece warned that 'Words can be more harmful than bullets.' It showed a speaker at a podium addressing a crowd and spitting rounds machine-gun style at two men in dark suits. One of the targets, who may have been foreign investors, dropped a briefcase from which bundles of banknotes cascaded. It was another version of the 'lies about Liberia' about which the minister had lectured me five years previously.

Now I look back at the photo a colleague took of me in front of one of those giant posters and think that Taylor was a man ahead of his time. I was intrigued by the sly tacit acknowledgement of wrongdoing in the statement that 'unbalanced news is also a human rights abuse.' In other words, the Liberian government appeared to be admitting it abused human rights, while accusing journalists of doing the same. It looked like the equivalence narrative favoured by some more knowing pro-Trump propagandists: 'Yeah, maybe we tell lies and do bad things, but so does the other side.' Truth was not just contested; it was irrelevant, because everybody bent it.

I thought back to the Taylor rhetorical style after I saw Trump for the first time in person. Superficially, the comparison might seem ridiculous: what could a warlord found guilty of crimes against humanity possibly have in common with a man who, for all the questions hanging over him, was an elected US president? But there was something in the nervous giggles from the assembled journalists at Trump's press conference at the 2018 NATO summit in Brussels that brought back reactions I'd seen to erratic autocrats like Taylor (and, more recently, Rodrigo Duterte). In the backs of people's minds was always the anxiety: would he turn on the charm, or turn on the media as 'enemies of the people'?

Like Taylor in his grandiose farewell, Trump had the charisma to hold an audience. In contrast to the Obama press conference in Laos two years previously, Trump also took questions spontaneously rather than by prearrangement. The clamour obviously pleased him – as did the chance for journalists from all over the world to ask questions.

Trump's answers were sometimes inadequate or nonsensical, giving the impression of accountability without the substance of it. But in the moment, the chaos looked democratic and equalising even to some of those present. As a fellow journalist put it: 'He owned the room and at the end of it we all felt good. He takes questions from anyone – he doesn't care. When did *Croatia Daily* and Kurdistan TV get a chance to ask a question of the American president?'

The quick-fire cacophony also helped dilute some sinister stuff, including his claim that immigration was 'taking over Europe'. It also hurried him past false assertions – including that his father was from Germany (it was his grandfather). He wrongly claimed that he had done better than Ronald Reagan by winning the state of Wisconsin (Reagan in fact won it during both his election victories). As the *Washington Post* later pointed out, it was at least the third time Trump had made this incorrect comparison.[10]

The next day, Trump repeated the false claim that he had predicted Brexit while opening his Turnberry golf course in Scotland the day before the 23 June 2016 referendum vote. In fact, he was at Turnberry the day after. As one European official wearily put it: 'It's the Goebbels argument – the difference between truth and lies is repetition.' (Perhaps aptly, the quote has never been definitively attributed to the Nazi propagandist, but has become associated with him by plausibility and years of recapitulation.)

Trump is much less a pioneer of playing fast and loose with the facts than some imagine, even if he does it with unprecedented frequency. As long ago as 2004, the *New York Times* famously reported an unidentified Bush administration aide's scorn for what he called 'the *reality-based community*' – people hamstrung by their belief that political solutions would emerge from a 'judicious study of discernible reality', while 'history's actors' got on with 'creating other new realities'. The adviser's declaration seems an apt summary summary of how Washington has always seen the value of flexibility in its principles, particularly when it comes to its attitudes to human rights and corruption. As the official put it then: 'We're an empire now, and when we act, we create our own reality.'[11]

Many years after my visits to Liberia, I saw how heavily US actions also weighed in South-East Asia. The record of Henry Kissinger, a key architect of US foreign policy during the 1970s as national security adviser and secretary of state, provoked particular anger in the region. The bombing of Cambodia that the US carried out until the early 1970s helped stoke the rise of the genocidal Khmer Rouge. When I asked Theary Seng, a lawyer who escaped Cambodia as a girl after the Khmer Rouge killed her parents, what she thought about the respect Kissinger continued to enjoy as a statesman, she said: 'It's no surprise to me that he thinks of himself that way. But it surprises me when informed individuals continue to come to his defence.'

Kissinger and President Gerald Ford later gave the green light to Indonesia's December 1975 annexation of East Timor, according to official documents released years afterwards. The two men met Suharto, the dictator in Jakarta, who wanted to crush a guerrilla movement in East Timor, the day before the invasion. Kissinger told Suharto: 'We understand your problem and the need to move quickly.' The then US secretary of state's main concern was about optics: he worried that 'the use of US-made arms could create problems', although he promised to try to 'influence the reaction in America'. Suharto pressed ahead with an invasion that led to the deaths of an estimated 150,000 or more people, or a fifth of the population, over the next quarter-century.

In subsequent years, Kissinger defended many of the Vietnam War-era policies he oversaw in South-East Asia. He has lamented how critiques of 'arguable' decisions have 'transmuted' into a debate over the 'moral adequacy of America in conducting any kind of traditional foreign policy'.[12] He added that the Vietnam conflict was 'America's first experience with limits in foreign policy, and it was something painful to accept'.

My circuitous journey from Liberia to Laos took me well over a decade. I have spent very little time in the US during my adult life, but I have often been in Washington's wider orbit. The places where I have spent time in Africa, the Middle East and Asia have their own agency and have written their own stories. But the US has played a formative – and quite often negative – role in many of them.

The line from Trump's approach to the world and that of his predecessors does not seem so hard to see. As long as he is portrayed as an aberration and *sui generis*, it is hard to see how there will be an honest accounting for US actions abroad. If there is no reckoning, there can be no remedy – and no occupation of the moral high ground.

In the forests of Laos, Bowyer and his colleagues pressed on with their endless search for US bombs. I watched as the disposal team hacked through the jungle with their machetes and used the tips to pick away cautiously at objects buried in the mud. Bowyer called across to show me a find. He pointed to a rocket-shaped device with a finned end: a Rockeye cluster bomb. Bowyer compared it to a small anti-tank weapon. 'It's very dangerous,' he said, peering at it through his goggles. 'It has a shaped charge and it effectively burns its way through metal.'

This former soldier was self-evidently no pacifist. But he said the enduring deadly impact of US handiwork in this wedge of South-East Asia that rarely makes the international news these days had taught him something about conflict. 'It hasn't exactly turned me anti-war,' he said. 'But it has made me realise what a waste of bloody time and resources it is – and how short-sighted people are when they wage it.'

III

FALSE PROPHETS

7

The Lady Vanishes

Aung San Suu Kyi had spent a quarter of a century campaigning for democracy in Myanmar. Now, on the threshold of a historic election, she refused to say whether she was the right person to lead the country.

'I don't think these questions can really be answered until years and years have passed,' she told me in her MP's office in Naypyidaw, the capital city built by the military junta. 'It's always history that decides, and history never decides sometimes – otherwise historians would be out of a job.'

Judgement day came sooner than Suu Kyi thought. Less than three years after those 2015 remarks, many observers in a Western world that once idolised her would condemn her stewardship of Myanmar. In 2017, after her National League for Democracy had swept to a landslide at the polls, the military launched pogroms that burned Muslim Rohingya villages and sent hundreds of thousands of people fleeing into neighbouring Bangladesh with stories of murder, rape and torture. Suu Kyi's response – or rather the lack of it – drew widespread condemnation.

The atrocity upended a generation of foreign idealisation of Suu Kyi. The Nobel laureate's estranged international backers branded her a hypocrite, given her previous rhetoric on human rights. Some former fans of the woman widely known as 'The Lady' bitterly contrasted her attitude towards the Rohingya with her previous calls for 'a world free from the displaced, the homeless and the hopeless, a world of which each and every corner is a true sanctuary'.[1]

The fall of Aung San Suu Kyi from her pedestal in the Western imagination is a lesson for the modern age. Not for the first time, Americans and Europeans built up a leader's stature and created a dangerous gap between expectation and likely reality. They also played down the scale of problems facing a nation at the crossroads of Asia that, by dint of a long history of repression, had never been in harmony – nor even, some would say, a nation at all.

I visited Myanmar over four tumultuous years between 2013 and 2017, while I was based in Bangkok for the *Financial Times*. These captivating travels took me from chilly trading towns near the Chinese border to beaches where young men played football as the sun set over the Indian Ocean behind them. My memories of the countryside are wreathed in woodsmoke and the sight of people lining roads at dawn to offer passing monks rice; in Yangon I saw how a digital revolution unleashed a suppressed generation of entrepreneurs.

My trips also spanned much of the arc in international percep-tions of Suu Kyi from excitement to disillusionment. Those who knew the history and habits of both the country and the woman also dubbed as Mother Suu could have seen something like this coming. Not only were the atrocities against the Rohingya unsur-prising; they were almost inevitable in a state ruled for half a century by a brutal military that was not about to retreat quietly into the background.

★　　★　　★

Suu Kyi was released from house arrest late in 2010, days after an ugly election rigged so the military-backed Union Solidarity and Development Party would win. The junta finally formally stepped down in March 2011, one year short of its fiftieth anniversary in power. The National League for Democracy had boycotted the 2010 polls but decided to fight dozens of by-elections scheduled for 2012. Suu Kyi herself was one of the victors as her party romped home, winning all but one of the seats contested.

My interview with her took me and an *FT* colleague to Naypyidaw, one of the world's more peculiar capitals. The story of how the seat of government shifted in the mid-2000s from estuarine Yangon to a remote site hundreds of kilometres inland encapsulated the strangeness of the junta era. The generals had given no explanation. Some observers speculated that it had been ordered for astrological reasons; others said it was a precaution against coup attempts from inside or outside the country. Naypyidaw had neither its predecessor's densely populated centre nor its potential vulnerability to waterborne invasion.

The new city's sprawling geography and lack of crowds certainly made it hard to do anything surreptitiously there. Passengers rattled around in its outsize airport, which ran precious few flights. Whenever I took the evening Bangkok Airways turboprop shuttle back to Thailand, it was the only departure listed on the screen.

The approach to the parliament was via a highway that had ten lanes in either direction – but often not a single vehicle. The rumour was that it had been designed to be big enough to allow aircraft to land, although the undulating surface might have tested the theory to destruction. So peaceful was it that we were able to record a piece to camera unmolested in the middle of the road. Later, I saw children happily playing football along another big highway nearby.

Even the government's official tourism and conference promotion literature for the capital acknowledged the surreal spectacle it

presented. 'The scenes it provides are often those of quaint juxta-
positions,' its website read. 'An ox-drawn cart rattling down the
shoulder of an eight-lane highway while a motorcade of black
government SUVs speeds past is not an unusual sight.'

The parliament occupied a vast site comprising thirty-one
buildings, apparently inspired by the number of planes of existence
in Buddhist cosmology. The construction borrowed heavily from
pagoda architecture, with multi-tiered eaves rising to a point. Suu
Kyi's office was in one of a cluster of identical offices whose white-
painted walls were fringed in the red, yellow and green of the
Myanmar flag and topped by roofs of brick red.

It was near the end of a hot dry-season day and Suu Kyi seemed
a little tired when she arrived. She wore a pink traditional dress,
her hair tied at the back and decorated with a small garland of red
flowers. The contrast between her slight elegance and the thuggish generals had done much to animate Myanmar's struggles in
the international mind – and to narrow them down to a straightforward battle between the two contrasting protagonists. It has also
tinged the Western view of Suu Kyi with orientalism.

Suu Kyi started off on a frustrated note. She was deep in a
last-ditch – and ultimately unsuccessful – pre-election effort by
her party to change the constitution to loosen the military's
grip a little. Myanmar had not really gone beyond a 'parody of
democracy', she said. She wasn't even sure the NLD would
compete in the polls. She was still looking for 'one brave soldier'
to go against orders and demand constitutional change. Asked if
such a person even existed, she said: 'I haven't seen one who was
prepared to vote against orders from above yet. But that doesn't
mean they don't exist. It may just mean that I haven't seen one
yet.'

This sardonic caveat set the tone. She batted aside a question on
corruption with similar terseness. The way to tackle corruption
was by employing people who were honest, she said. In a way, her

straightforwardness was refreshing: there were certainly no honeyed words or extravagant promises.

'I think one of the simplest but most necessary steps to take if you want to get rid of corruption is to make sure that your government is not corrupt, that you are able to set up a government whose members are not corrupt,' she said. 'If the members of the government are corrupt, how are they going to get rid of corruption in this country?'

She was more expansive on the question of vested interests who had profited under military rule. These so-called 'cronies' were notorious in Myanmar: they had earned huge sums and built up dominant positions in industries ranging from jade mining to banking. Some were darker and more extravagant figures than others. A good number were under Western sanctions, such as Tay Za, who made his fortune in industries ranging from fuel to airlines. In one interview in which he railed against the US action, the journalist watched as a pet bear cub shinned up his chair. Many 'cronies' were now scrambling to reinvent themselves through philanthropy, in an effort to position themselves for the new era and mitigate possible retribution. Debate raged both in Myanmar and in diplomatic circles over the culpability of these beneficiaries of junta rule – and what was the right way to deal with them.

Suu Kyi took the line that the country had to 'move on'. It was a clue that she was prepared to overlook some wrongdoing in the name of pragmatism. She was not wedded to the idea that there had to be accountability at all costs. The past was 'there for us to learn from, not for us to be shackled by', she said. Anyone who had done anything illegal could be taken to court, but those not proven guilty 'must be deemed innocent'. She referred pointedly – and accurately – to the way the monopolistic and profiteering robber barons of US industrial history had been able to reinvent themselves and even set up leading charitable foundations.

'I do want to give everybody a chance to redeem themselves, either economically or otherwise,' she said. 'A lot of so-called cronies are now engaged in good works, which is not a bad thing. Of course, in the West too, once upon a time those who are now very respectable and very rich did not get rich through the most respectable means.'

We moved on to talk about whether she had been idealised internationally. She bridled at the notion that she had once been spared scrutiny because of her status as a prisoner of conscience. 'I was criticised by many, many people, including in the West, who said that I was not flexible enough, that I should be nicer to the military government, that if I was more cooperative they would be nicer to me,' she said. 'This kind of criticism was there all the time. So what surprises me is not that people criticise me now, but that people have forgotten that they were criticising me then as well.'

On the long-running and sporadically deadly Rohingya crisis, she was still more defensive. The backdrop here was the systematic discrimination against the group in junta-ruled Myanmar. The military-backed Union Solidarity and Development Party had cynically milked Rohingya support in the 2010 election, only to later entrench hard-line policies against them. Rohingya were mostly denied citizenship and faced restrictions on their rights to work and travel. The government even proposed curbing the number of children Rohingya women could have. It was part of a narrative, familiar from the European far right, that the high birth rate of Muslim foreigners threatened to swamp Myanmar and the Buddhist faith.

In 2013, Suu Kyi had blamed a 'climate of fear' on both sides of the communal divide. It was a truth too little acknowledged that the Rakhine Buddhists had also suffered at the hands of the junta. But Suu Kyi's formulation appeared to go further and suggest an equivalence, even though the Rohingya were demonstrably at greater physical risk. 'Muslims have been targeted but Buddhists have also been subjected to violence,' Suu Kyi said. 'This fear is what is leading to all this trouble.'[2]

Suu Kyi rejected the idea that she had not spoken out sufficiently strongly. Even what to international observers looked like weak statements had earned her heavy criticism at home. Like just about every other politician in Myanmar, Suu Kyi refused to use the word 'Rohingya'. Nationalists called the group 'Bengalis' as part of an attempt to portray them as interlopers from Bangladesh. Naming them 'Rohingya' would give weight to their case that they should join the official list of more than 130 ethnic groups.

Suu Kyi returned to the broad theme that 'fear was at the root of a lot of the hatred between the two communities'. It echoed an idea central to her political thinking, as expressed in her book *Freedom from Fear* – a phrase that echoed the 1948 Universal Declaration of Human Rights.

'Among the basic freedoms to which men aspire that their lives might be full and uncramped, freedom from fear stands out as both a means and an end,' she had written. 'A people who would build a nation in which strong, democratic institutions are firmly established as a guarantee against state-induced power must first learn to liberate their own minds from apathy and fear.'

Now she said people should recognise that 'the [Buddhist] Rakhine are as frightened as the Muslims.' This ought to be understandable, she suggested, as the Rakhine were very poor, even if the Muslims were poorer. She then raised – but did not disavow – the quasi-medieval language used by some Rakhine Buddhist nationalists to portray the country as being under siege from Muslims.

'There is a genuine fear on the part of the Buddhists that the Muslim population is growing and it seems to be growing bigger for the simple reason that for years and years it was government policy not to allow the Muslims out of the Rakhine state,' Suu Kyi said. 'So they were in fact in a ghetto there and many Rakhine have said that they feel as though they were – they put it this way – that they were made to be keepers of the Western gate, that they have been made to take on the task of keeping the Muslims out of the rest of Burma. That's how they feel.'

A notorious nationalist monk named Ashin Wirathu had weeks earlier called Yanghee Lee, the UN special rapporteur on Myanmar, a 'bitch' and a 'whore' after she spoke of the discrimination Rohingya faced. The UN's human rights chief Zeid Ra'ad al-Hussein called on religious and political leaders to condemn the remarks. Wirathu had been jailed under the military junta for inciting anti-Muslim violence, almost certainly more out of a concern for public order than to protect a religious minority. He was released under a political prisoner amnesty in the early 2010s.

Suu Kyi stopped well short of a condemnation of Wirathu. She said she thought the remarks 'very sad because it's not how our Buddhists like us to be seen by the world. It's not how we would like us to be seen by the world.' She urged a study of what monks who had criticised Wirathu's statement had said for a 'better insight into what the Buddhist values are'.

We returned to the subject of Myanmar's stunted democratisation. Suu Kyi warned that some countries – including the US – were 'overly optimistic' about the country's direction. It was not easy to change the 'military dictatorship culture', she said. 'It's a question of the military coming to terms with the new situation,' she said. 'If they really want to move onto democracy then they must accept that civilian control, civilian authority should be supreme and it's the people's right to choose the government of their choice. If they believe in democracy, if they say that that's what they believe in then that's what they have to accept.'

She said she thought sanctions still had a 'role to play' and could 'help as political weapons' in the democratisation process, although she was 'not too devastated' that some had been lifted as it would help open up economic opportunities. She bristled at the suggestion that sanctions had been counterproductive, by throttling the military at a time when it was looking for an agreed exit.

But in her response she did not seek to defend the punitive measures: rather, she attempted to distance herself from them. She was not the one who asked for sanctions, she said. People 'seem to forget that I was under house arrest and had nothing to do with the outside world' when they were imposed, she said pointedly. But she acknowledged that she backed them, rather than repudiating them. 'I did support them once they were in place. I stood behind those who had asked for sanctions and managed to achieve them,' she added.

I asked what she made of criticism that her tight control of her party had stopped political talent – including potential successors – coming through. She denied this and said part of the problem was a generation gap in skills, because under the military the education system 'practically collapsed'. The NLD was the only party that had actually bothered instructing young people in subjects such as English or economics – as well as giving them vital practical information on subjects such as HIV/AIDS. 'We've been trying to train up people all the time and encouraging them to try to take over more responsibilities,' she said, before adding a revealing rider: 'But I have to confess that sometimes I feel that a lot of people are more interested in just getting into an important position rather than in accepting responsibility.'

Dictatorship had disempowered people to the degree that 'nobody really thinks that they have to take responsibility for anything,' she elaborated. It was something that 'cuts across society' and could only be dealt with, perhaps, by skipping a leadership generation.

'The answer is to persevere. They will come up. They have to,' she said, of the people who would take over the country after the present ageing generation of politicians on both the military and

NLD sides had moved on. 'I think they will come up because the younger people of course have more time in which to educate themselves and make themselves ready for the responsibilities they have to take on.'

I closed by asking what a Suu Kyi government would look like and what we would see five years after the election. What kind of programmes would it have enacted? The proposition was abstract and the country's transition still uncertain, to be sure. But Suu Kyi's refusal even to pay lip service to an answer was still remarkable.

'I don't know. It's a very big question. It's a very iffy question,' she said. 'We haven't even decided whether or not we're going to be contesting the elections. So how can I tell you what kind of government there will be?'

It is easy to forget now that Suu Kyi's career as a politician and freedom fighter started with an accident. She had grown up the peripatetic daughter of the murdered nationalist hero Aung San, living for some time in Delhi, where her mother was ambassador. A degree at Oxford and then a short-lived job at the UN – led by Burma's U Thant – gave way to married life in Oxford with the British academic Michael Aris. By the late 1980s, when Suu Kyi was already in her early forties, she was focused on bringing up the couple's two boys. Friends of the time have spoken since of how they sensed a frustration in Suu Kyi as she searched for a wider role.

Then, in 1988, came the call that changed everything. Suu Kyi learned that her mother was seriously ill in Myanmar. She flew to see her and walked into the most serious uprising in more than a quarter-century of military rule. The junta crackdown after the demonstrations launched on 8 August 1988 is thought to have killed thousands of people.

Suu Kyi's family pedigree made her an immediate focus of resistance to the generals. A speech she gave at Yangon's Shwedagon Pagoda, a vast gold-covered Buddhist shrine that rises to about 100 metres, drew huge crowds. Her popularity boomed and she started to tour the country to spread her message. She and others founded the National League for Democracy, with the aim of forcing the junta to hold elections.

'If democracy should fail the world cannot stand back and just look on, and therefore Burma would one day, like Japan and Germany, be despised,' she said that day at the Shwedagon. 'Democracy is the only ideology which is consistent with freedom. It is also an ideology that promotes and strengthens peace. It is therefore the only ideology we should aim for.'[3]

When the junta held polls in 1990, the NLD won a landslide victory. The generals responded with brutal repression. They rounded up party leaders and put Suu Kyi herself under house arrest. Her incarceration for three quarters of the next two decades in her lakeside home in Yangon turned her into an international symbol of resistance.

Suu Kyi tended to dwell little on her personal pain and sacrifice, but it was self-evident. Her sons had been about eleven and fifteen when she left. She would occasionally speak briefly – and even shed a tear – about missing them, but she was focused on a sense of duty to her country and her father's memory. She told an interviewer in 1989 how, when her mother was informed in the middle of a meeting that Suu Kyi's nine-year-old brother had drowned, she 'stayed and finished her work'.

In 1997, her husband, Aris, was diagnosed with terminal cancer. His repeated efforts to get a visa to pay a last visit to his wife were refused. He died on his birthday in 1999, half a world away from Suu Kyi.

Perhaps most difficult of all for Suu Kyi was that she always had a choice. The generals wanted rid of the threat her presence posed.

But even they must have baulked at the international outcry that killing her would cause, so their strategy was to force her into exile instead. They made clear that she could opt to leave to return to her family at any point – at the price of not being allowed to come back. So for all those years of separation from her growing children and dying husband, Suu Kyi always had the opportunity to reunite with them. She elected – with Aris's support – never to take it.

It was to be twenty years after the 1990 election crackdown before Suu Kyi was finally released from house arrest, to international acclaim. In 2012 she picked up the US Congress's highest civilian honour. A picture of her receiving the award showed how her cause united sworn political enemies: in the background are Hillary Clinton, then secretary of state, and Mitch McConnell, the Republican Senate leader. Clinton described the moment as 'almost too delicious to believe'. McConnell said Suu Kyi's peaceful campaign for change resembled the efforts of Martin Luther King and Mahatma Gandhi. 'It was impossible not to be moved by her quiet resolve, her hidden yet luminous heroism,' he said.[4]

When Suu Kyi's National League for Democracy finally won another crushing victory at the polls in late 2015, it was hailed around the world. Here, it seemed, was the ultimate feel-good story: a country that had suffered under a long eviscerating dictatorship, free at last. It was inspiring on election day to see the voting that started with long queues before dawn and continued through afternoon downpours.

The military-drafted constitution prevented Suu Kyi from becoming president, on account of her sons' foreign nationality. But she created the bespoke office of state counsellor amid overwhelming international goodwill, drawing parallels with Nelson Mandela's triumph in leading South Africa out of apartheid in the 1990s after long imprisonment.

Then, just six months after the new government took office, the rupture began. In October 2016, the army launched a brutal crackdown on Rohingya communities in Rakhine state after nine police officers were killed in attacks by militants close to the Bangladeshi border. Rohingya people said soldiers then went on a spree of murder, rape and arson, sending tens of thousands of people fleeing to Bangladesh. Myanmar security forces launched a 'calculated policy of terror' in Rohingya areas that killed hundreds of people, according to a report published in February 2017 by the Office of the UN High Commissioner for Human Rights.[5]

Suu Kyi drew opprobrium in the West for failing to act or speak out forcefully against the military's violence. Some government officials and state media even claimed allegations of abuses were fabricated. Suu Kyi opposed a planned UN Human Rights Council fact-finding mission, saying it would 'divide' communities in Rakhine.

Almost a dozen Nobel Peace Prize winners attacked the de facto Myanmar leader in an open letter to the UN Security Council in December 2016. They branded the action against the Rohingya a 'human tragedy amounting to ethnic cleansing', drawing parallels with Rwanda and Bosnia.[6]

Even worse followed. In August 2017, members of the Arakan Rohingya Salvation Army (ARSA) militia targeted about thirty police posts and an army base in Rakhine, killing several people in a deadly raid. The military clampdown that followed was still more savage than the previous one, triggering an exodus of a further 700,000 Rohingya to Bangladesh. The UN human rights chief called the clampdown a 'textbook example of ethnic cleansing'[7] and later said he strongly suspected 'acts of genocide may have taken place.'[8] The US followed suit and later announced sanctions against Myanmar military members deemed responsible, as did the EU. Judges at the International Criminal Court requested that they be allowed jurisdiction over alleged crimes in Rakhine.

Suu Kyi denied ethnic cleansing had taken place and suggested some of the claims were exaggerated. According to her office, in a call to Turkey's President Recep Tayyip Ergogan, she made a Trumpian commitment to defend 'all the people' in Rakhine. She seized on the misleading social media activity of some Rohingya advocates to dismiss a 'huge iceberg of misinformation' on the crisis aimed at 'promoting the interests of the terrorists'. She drew further international criticism for her response to the December 2017 arrest of two Reuters journalists, Wa Lone and Kyaw Soe Oo, who had exposed the killing of ten Rohingya men and boys, an atrocity for which seven soldiers were jailed. Suu Kyi insisted the reporters' case had nothing to do with freedom of expression.[9] (They were released in May 2019.)

The Western condemnation of Suu Kyi was as harsh as the praise had once been gushing. Bob Geldof, the singer turned activist, branded her an 'accomplice to murder' and a 'handmaiden to ethnic cleansing'. Suu Kyi's freedom of the city of Oxford was revoked. Her old college, St Hugh's, took down a portrait of its famous alumna. The US Holocaust Museum removed its top award from her, as did Amnesty International.[10] Others called for her Nobel Prize to be revoked.

Archbishop Desmond Tutu, the veteran anti-apartheid campaigner, caught the sense of anguish in an impassioned open letter to his fellow Nobel Laureate in September 2017. 'My dear sister: If the political price of your ascension to the highest office in Myanmar is your silence, the price is surely too steep,' he wrote. 'We pray for you to speak out for justice, human rights and the unity of your people. We pray for you to intervene.'[11]

Beyond the ghastly facts of the Rohingya massacres, there was the aggravation of a sense of betrayal. The world had certain ideas and dreams of Suu Kyi that she had now smashed. Cate Blanchett, the Australian actor who visited displaced Rohingya as a UN goodwill ambassador, summed up an international sense of dismay and disbelief. 'It is bewildering, is it not, that someone who has been such a fighter for even a fragile democracy, and who has been hailed as someone who upholds human rights, does not seem to be speaking out more clearly about the atrocities that are so very clearly happening under her watch,' she said.[12]

Westerners have long been prone to fantasies about Myanmar. The most famous poem in English about the country – Rudyard Kipling's 'Mandalay' – was an act of projection from a man who only paid one short visit to the country and never went to Mandalay. Kipling's conceit of a British soldier posted in Myanmar included the inevitable orientalist fantasy about a local woman, as well as a reference to the 'Great Gawd Budd'. Boris Johnson, then Britain's foreign secretary, began to recite lines from 'Mandalay' during a 2017 visit to the Shwedagon Pagoda, until the British ambassador Andrew Patrick wisely advised him it was 'not appropriate'.

Similar international wishful thinking seemed to underpin the idea that Myanmar would prosper under Suu Kyi despite the big obstacles to it being able to do so. It was a blunt fact that, whatever Suu Kyi's deepest feelings about the Rohingya, she could not control the country's military. This was not some bug of Myanmar's political transition. It was a feature of the junta-drafted constitution that Western countries had urged Suu Kyi to accept because they felt it was a compromise worth making for the sake of imperfect change.

The Myanmar generals had taken other steps to maintain the power they had built up during a near half-century in charge. They expanded on the example of Indonesia, where the military received guaranteed seats in the legislature after the dictator Suharto stepped down in 1998. In Myanmar, the armed forces awarded themselves a quarter of parliamentary seats. Further, any constitutional reform required a seventy-five percent plus one majority – meaning that the military had an effective veto if its MPs voted as a bloc.

Other measures entrenched military power deeper still into the future of the country. The armed forces would hold one of the vice presidencies and control key security posts, including the ministries of the interior and defence. Most strikingly of all, parliament could be overruled by a special committee on which the military had a majority. In other words, not only did the generals have the possibility to take over, but they also had the right to do so. In a legal sense, their authority was even more entrenched than it had been under full-blown dictatorship.

Western countries had their own political reasons for going along with this. After the Arab Spring dissolved into conflicts across the region, the US approach towards the Middle East came in for heavy criticism. A foreign policy 'win' in Myanmar became increasingly important to Washington and especially to Secretary of State Hillary Clinton, who was due to step down from the role in early 2013. Clinton visited Myanmar in November 2011 in the first high-level US trip there since before the years of dictatorship. Obama followed in 2012.

Clinton later dwelled on her role in Myanmar at length in her book *Hard Choices*. She said she had her 'eyes open about the risks' of engaging with the generals, but 'didn't see how we could pass up this opportunity'. She issued a statement just after Myanmar's November 2015 election that proved as over-optimistic about the country's trajectory as it was about her own personal prospects. 'When I was Secretary of State, President Obama and I worked with Aung San Suu Kyi and others on the ground in Burma to nurture flickers of progress into a real opening,' she said. 'As President, I will ensure that the United States continues to stand with them and with everyone around the world who seeks liberty and dignity.'[13]

Her enthusiasm was part of a wider pattern that went back to long before the Myanmar junta stepped down in 2011. Some of the most pertinent criticisms made of Suu Kyi are for acts supported – or even led – by Western countries. One was the imposition – with her backing – of tough sanctions against the generals, starting in the late 1990s. This resulted in Myanmar becoming largely isolated from the West and increasingly reliant on its giant neighbour China instead.

Some believe that this clampdown scotched emerging efforts by the junta for a soft formal exit from power. In a high-profile apparent overture for international détente, the generals had temporarily released Suu Kyi from house arrest in 1995. The question of whether military rule would have ended years sooner without the sanctions is a great counterfactual still argued over in Myanmar today. Thant Myint-U, a respected historian, author and analyst of the country, has been a vocal critic of the punishment measures the world enacted. 'In Burma they proved an unmitigated disaster, hurting the poorest, weakening public institutions, fuelling cronyism, entrenching xenophobia, doing nothing to dent elite lifestyles, and making any transition from tyranny less likely to succeed,' he tweeted in 2018. 'Yet no one has been held accountable.'[14]

This is not a position that has surfaced only in hindsight. In 1998, the writer Ma Thanegi, who had been Suu Kyi's personal assistant during the early years of the pro-democracy movement, publicly denounced her boss's pro-sanctions stance. In an article titled 'The Burmese Fairy Tale', she launched a stinging attack against international policy on Myanmar. 'For years, outsiders portrayed the troubles of my country as a morality play: good against evil, with no shade of gray in between – a simplistic picture, but one the world believes,' wrote Ma Thanegi, who had been jailed for almost three years for her anti-junta activism. 'The response of the West has been equally simplistic: It wages a moral crusade against evil, using such "magic wands" as sanctions and boycotts.'[15]

It was a powerful polemic, the more so because of the evident emotional pain weaved through it. Thanegi's was the raw howl of the former believer who wants to keep the faith but feels they cannot. 'In my time with Ma Suu, I came to love her deeply,' Thanegi declared. 'I still do.'

Suu Kyi's 'highly moral and uncompromising' position had caught the imagination of the world but came 'at a real price for the rest of us', Thanegi argued. Sanctions had increased tensions with the government, cost jobs and made it harder for an already impoverished people 'to put food on the table'. Thanegi was contemptuous of what she saw as the West playing with people's lives to test its own theories of political change.

'Two Westerners – one a prominent academic and the other a diplomat – once suggested to me that if sanctions and boycotts undermined the economy, people would have less to lose and would be willing to start a revolution,' she recounted. 'They seemed very pleased with this idea, a revolution to watch from the safety of their own country. This naive romanticism angers many of us here in Burma. You would deliberately make us poor to force us to fight a revolution?'

Another criticism that had dogged Suu Kyi for years but been played down by some of her international backers concerned her allegedly autocratic style. Most people who talked about this in the years before she took office were reluctant to go on the record: they all had a stake in the transition, one way or another, so open warfare with an internationally feted leader wouldn't have suited them. Her ruthlessness was clear enough, though. In 2015, the NLD – over which she had unchallenged control – blocked some former political prisoners who had wanted to stand for election as MPs.

The world also seemed too unwilling to recognise the extent to which Suu Kyi's apparent ambivalence about the Rohingya went with the grain of public opinion. This was a revealing failure of perception: if Western countries want to envision a society in which Muslim minorities are the targets of suspicion and hostility, they need only look inside their own borders. The road from incessant anti-minority rhetoric to pogroms is not such an unimaginable one.

Grotesque as it may seem, Suu Kyi was seen at home as a moderate on the Rohingya – or even as too sympathetic. This was a worry for her party ahead of the 2015 elections, so much so that she addressed it head-on in stump speeches. At a rally in Rakhine a few weeks before the polls, she warned it was unconstitutional for people to 'spread propaganda using religion and race'. She had repeatedly been targeted by nationalists as too soft on the Rohingya. During election year, the wife of a government minister posted a Photoshopped picture on social media of Suu Kyi in Muslim dress.

Perhaps the most fundamental international dereliction on Myanmar was the belief that change would be simpler and cleaner than it turned out to be. The focus – from Suu Kyi, her supporters outside and many in Myanmar – was naturally on the election and the degree of democratisation it would bring. But in the obsession with that undeniably important goal, many other vital matters were neglected.

I often felt this strange disjunction in my coverage. I would write news stories regularly about the prepoll game of cat and mouse between Suu Kyi and the military-backed government. But whenever I dived into longer pieces – about the illicit jade trade, drug-resistant malaria and, especially, land rights – I found seemingly intractable troubles that would confound any government anywhere. The starburst of techies, artists and restaurateurs that gave Yangon a beguiling sheen seemed far removed from a harshness elsewhere.

Unlike some countries in Europe and elsewhere that have recovered from war, Myanmar didn't have the luxury of a

previously functional model of state and institutions. It had gone
from being a nineteenth-century absolute monarchy with highly
autonomous regions to a British colony to a military dictatorship,
in almost unbroken succession. Even the precious few years
between independence in 1948 and the arrival of General Ne
Win's junta in 1962 were plagued by conflict and ever-weakening
government. In some ways, it resembled a patchwork of often
ethnically defined regions more than a unitary state.

Even naming the nation had been a choice between unappeal-
ing options. Burma, which was still used by Suu Kyi, the US and
Britain, was freighted with connotations of both colonialism and
the dominance of the Bamar ethnic group. Myanmar was also
unsatisfactory, as that was the choice of the military junta. The
best answer I settled on in interviews was to be led by the wishes
of my interlocutors, whatever they turned out to be. It seemed an
apt metaphor for a country that, in a way, had yet to be conjured.

Someone who knew Myanmar well once highlighted to me the
singular nature of Aung San Suu Kyi's focus. She wanted to bring
democracy to Myanmar to honour her father's legacy, this person
said – everything else was a detail. He pointed to the Suu Kyi
biography in which people she knew said she wanted to study
another subject such as English at Oxford University, but her strict
mother forced her to study politics, philosophy and economics
instead. She achieved only a third class degree, bottom of the four
classes of honours. This was not because of lack of ability, but
because she didn't find the subject as stimulating – at least not how
it was taught in a venerable Western university.

Her relationship with the Myanmar people and their aspirations
was also unusual for a folk hero. In some ways she had little in
common with most of those who idolised her. She was the daughter of a slain national idol but had spent many years overseas, even

marrying a foreigner. Her currency with her people stemmed more from difference than proximity.

When Suu Kyi had picked up an honorary degree from Oxford University in 2012, she had reminisced about punting on the River Cherwell, reading on the lawn at her college, or sitting in the library looking out of the windows. She segued rather surprisingly, even sentimentally, from those refined elite spaces to the privations of Myanmar under the military.

'But these were very precious memories – because I had lived a happy life,' she said. 'And this made me understand so much better the young people of Burma – who wanted to live a happy life and who had never been given an opportunity to lead one.'[16]

People admired Suu Kyi's considerable bravery, resilience and articulate defiance of the military. Now and again, though, the distance between their lives and hers would become apparent. One case was during her work for an inquiry that the transitional government craftily appointed her to lead into the contentious Chinese-run Letpadaung copper mine in central Myanmar. Residents of the area, including monks, had suffered violent military crackdowns after they protested against alleged land-grabbing, which the Chinese operators denied. Suu Kyi's commission recommended in March 2013 that the facility be allowed to expand, with provisions for compensation for local people and environmental protection. She looked unusually uncomfortable when she visited the area to justify the decision. Hundreds of people chanted, 'We don't want Aung San Suu Kyi. We don't want the copper project.'[17]

A contrasting encounter the previous year had delivered an even clearer warning of the troubles Suu Kyi would face. She had finally made it to Norway to collect her Nobel Peace Prize, more than two decades after it was awarded. Dressed in a traditional outfit of *longyi*, blouse and scarf in different shades of purple, she rose at Oslo City Hall to speak at a podium fronted by a representation of a gold medal bearing the image of Alfred Nobel.

The speech was vintage Suu Kyi. It blended stirring calls for universal democracy and human rights with demure asides that could have come from the Jane Austen novels she loved. She began with an anecdote about listening at home in Britain years ago to an episode of *Desert Island Discs*, a long-running BBC radio programme in which famous guests use favourite pieces of music as a framework to talk about their lives. She recalled joking afterwards with her young son Alexander that she might one day be invited on the show if she won a Nobel Prize – for Literature. 'We both laughed,' she said. 'The prospect seemed pleasant but hardly probable.'[18]

If that story captured the extraordinary bend of Suu Kyi's journey from bourgeois domestic life in Oxford to internationally lauded prisoner of conscience, then what followed foreshadowed her difficulties to come. She spoke of how, in western Myanmar, 'communal violence resulting in arson and murder was taking place just several days before I started out on the journey that has brought me here today.' She was referring to clashes in Rakhine state that would kill more than two hundred people and displace an estimated 140,000 Rohingya.

In a line buried midway through the address, she hinted at how the Rohingya crisis was part of a network of regional conflicts that had ebbed and flowed in Myanmar for more than six decades. Her rise to power would lay bare misapprehensions about what she could do about this, what she would do, and about the nature of the state she would finally govern.

'Since we achieved independence in 1948, there never has been a time when we could claim the whole country was at peace,' she warned the admiring crowd who had come to see an icon fulfil her destiny. 'We have not been able to develop the trust and understanding necessary to remove causes of conflict.'

★   ★   ★

The scale of the National League for Democracy's election victory surprised even its most optimistic operatives. It easily won an absolute majority in parliament, even with the handicap of the military's twenty-five percent contingent. Raucous celebrations ensued outside the NLD's ramshackle Yangon headquarters but a sense of restraint – and uncertainty – also lingered. Suu Kyi, once again channelling the British Victorian vernacular, warned her supporters not to 'make themselves obstreperous'. By the time the final result was confirmed, the NLD offices had once again fallen silent. The instruction had come down: 'there will be no party,' an activist said, when I asked about what celebrations were planned. We ended up going for a quiet drink to pick over the campaign instead.

The following years showed the scale of the task facing Suu Kyi's government – and not just in Rakhine. Fighting broke out in other ethnic minority areas. The military maintained its deep claw-hold on the economy, in industries ranging from banking to brewing. By 2017, a chronic electricity problem had become a crisis, with regular outages even in central Yangon.

A telling everyday illustration of the complexity – even uniqueness – of Myanmar's challenge was the traffic on the country's roads. The military had switched in the 1970s from driving on the left, like the British colonialists, to driving on the right. The problem was that almost all the second-hand cars imported in the years that followed were right-hand drive vehicles manufactured for fellow Asian countries that drive on the left, such as Japan and Thailand. This made any overtaking manoeuvre a heart-in-mouth affair, with the passenger having to play a crucial role in telling the unsighted driver when to move. It was, as a contact put it, a 'perfect example of policy incoherence'.

It was also one of many ways in which Myanmar seemed caught between two worlds, physically as well as politically, during those years. Even as change came, the fallout from the years of military rule continued. It had been half a century of national trauma, in which many brutalist memorials still stood as a reminder.

One was the Drug Elimination Museum, a hulking Yangon monument to the junta's pervasive propaganda. On the day I visited, its entrance door stood just ajar, as inviting as a haunted house, beneath a sky thick with the promise of rain. An eager stray dog followed me in, causing me to hurry through in case my companion decided to take advantage of any pauses to leave his mark.

The two of us edged through the gloom by the light of my mobile phone, past graphic dioramas. In one, British redcoats gunned down Chinese victims of the Opium Wars: a reminder of London's historical contribution to the thriving drugs trade in Asia today. The high poppy production in conflict areas of Myanmar during modern times had bought riches to various armed groups, not least the country's military. The museum, unsurprisingly, chose to represent the generals as warriors against narcotics.

I gave my canine sidekick the slip at the doors to a small enclosed section in the centre of the building. Inside, the almost complete darkness enhanced the creepiness of tableaux showing the successive stages of drug addiction. The display turned phantasmagorical, depicting wailing souls, skeletons and a giant red bony hand that reached out from a pond, a mansion looming from the darkness behind.

I fled upstairs, where a ceiling tile brought down by the weight of rain lay on the floor surrounded by shattered fragments. As I passed by the stairway to the administrative offices, a man emerged and called out to me sharply that the museum was closed today. I left quickly, past a painting of army officers striding heroically along a red carpet and waving at a grateful populace.

The museum's oddness has made it the periodic target of long mocking articles by Western visitors, but I took away a different message. I saw in the decaying and little-visited facility an epitaph for an era that was harsh and unsustainable. The junta's attempts to stamp timeless authority on an isolated country had already started to disintegrate.

Elsewhere a different city was starting to bud, one that revived past glories, raised ambitions and betrayed anxieties. The way people talked of the past, when Myanmar had once been an imperial power itself, recalled a visit I had made to Yemen some years previously. There was a similar sense of historical pride amid reduced modern-day circumstances. Having ruled and lost seemed to hurt more psychologically than never having ruled at all. It could also give rise to dangerous pathologies about restoring greatness and avenging past humiliations.

A restored house in Yangon was a reminder of a status Myanmar once had. The pleasant pale yellow colonial-era villa in a tree-lined compound was formerly the home of U Thant, the man who become the first non-European secretary-general of the UN. Displays of photographs in the house show its former occupant at the centre of great events of his 1961–71 tenure. There is correspondence between him and President John F. Kennedy and Russian leader Nikita Khrushchev in which he tries to reduce tensions in the Cuban Missile Crisis. A signed letter from the assassinated Kennedy's successor, Lyndon Johnson, is dedicated 'To U Thant, who works so hard in the cause of peace'.

U Thant appears with Emperor Haile Selassie of Ethiopia, France's Charles de Gaulle, King Faisal of Saudi Arabia, India's Indira Gandhi and, in Delhi, under a pink umbrella, with Aung San Suu Kyi's mother, Khin Kyi. He is pictured with the Apollo 11 moon landing astronauts, reflecting an interest in extra-terrestrial possibilities that led him to push UFOs on to the UN agenda.

On the ground floor of the house, a small animal lay curled up and shivering on a towel in the corner. Htet Myo Htut Aung, an assistant at the museum, explained that the creature was an injured

palm civet. She had found it on the roof yesterday, wounded apparently from a fight. Now she was feeding it milk and needed to take
it to the vet later. 'Half her face is swollen,' said the civet's saviour,
who told me she went by the nickname Pinky.

Pinky was fittingly dressed in a traditional *longyi* of that colour.
She had a long black fringe that seemed to merge with her big
round glasses. She was a part-time musician who played in a band
called Inappropriate Thoughts.

We chatted about the future of Myanmar. Pinky was worried
about the education system. She'd been to a government school
until the age of ten before switching to a French school. She characterised the change as from night to day. In the state school, 'I was
like a sheep and they were like shepherds. I didn't learn much,' she
said, but in the international school: 'They just taught us to ask
questions. They taught us to ask the question: why?'

Pinky said she admired Suu Kyi but did not worship her. She
recalled how the Lady had come to the French school once. 'She
came secretly at night,' Pinky said. 'She asked why we were learn-
ing French and what we could do for the country.'

A power cut briefly interrupted our conversation. Pinky rolled her
eyes and said it happened 'all the time'. Then she broke into French
to continue our discussion about Suu Kyi. 'The things people say: she's
going to change Myanmar into Singapore in six years!' She switched
back to English: 'That's the kind of thing that's unrealistic to me.'

Pinky pointed out how manifest infrastructural improvements
since the military stepped down had at times outpaced people's
abilities to take advantage of them. She gave the example of a new
fleet of Chinese-made buses in Yangon. 'Even though the buses are
good, the drivers are the same as before, so there have been some
terrible accidents,' she said.

Improving the education system was the most important thing,
she concluded. Suu Kyi was appointed education minister after
the transition, but then gave up the job after a week. Yet the

country's people desperately needed to be equipped to tackle the huge problems they faced.

'You can bring a lot of change from outside, but you cannot progress further without these kinds of thinking skills,' Pinky said, echoing Suu Kyi's comments to me.

That evening, I visited one of the many new cultural ventures that had sprung up around Yangon in a flaring of artistic freedom. Pamsuriya was an offshoot of a gallery set up in 2008 amid the rickety colonial-era architectural huddle of downtown. It was a popular place with artwork spilling from every corner, including the inevitable portrait of Aung San in a British military-issue greatcoat.[19] The garment was a gift from India's Jawaharlal Nehru ahead of the trip Suu Kyi's father made to chilly London for independence talks with Clement Attlee's government in January 1947.

The photos of Aung San outside Downing Street are the most enduring surviving images of him: six months later, he would be dead. He was gunned down along with six ministerial colleagues in the council chamber in Yangon, a conspiracy for which U Saw, a former prime minister and political rival of Aung San's, was executed. Suu Kyi was just two years old at the time, so the father she later venerated – and whose name stood at the start of her own – was a figure of her imagination rather than someone of whom she had clear memories.

I'd come to Pansuriya to meet one of the partners in the venture. Axiao Jiang, also known as Ngwe San Aung, wore a white collarless shirt and neat black hair clippered short at the sides. His thoughtful style immediately drew me in. It turned out he was a Suu Kyi sceptic. 'She doesn't represent the whole Myanmar,' he said. 'I always think that she's a very nationalistic Bamar leader. She's trying. But it's not good enough.'

Jiang's grandparents were from China and his stronger language was Chinese, so he felt the country's ethnic and linguistic differences sharply. He was not optimistic.

'Since we were young we grew up to be racist,' he told me
bleakly. 'When I was young, if I didn't behave, my parents would
say, "Hey, we are going to give you away to the Indians!" So even
from day one we saw Indians as different.' He feared it would take
a 'long, long time for people in this country to work together'. He
pointed to conflicts across society, including in the student union
movements, about the powers regional groups should have. He
himself felt somewhat alienated from mainstream Bamar culture.
He even found his Burmese name 'really too much': Ngwe San
Aung can be translated as 'Money Famous Success'.

'It's difficult for people like me to recognise this as a country,' he
said, in words familiar in this diverse land sandwiched between
China and India. 'What history do you want me to follow?'

Tensions in Myanmar's ethnic minority areas continued to
simmer after the election – and sometimes tipped over into
conflict. Efforts by the previous government to agree the country's
first nationwide ceasefire for more than sixty years had foundered.
Now there was sporadic fighting from Kachin state in the north to
Shan in the east. People also feared the Rohingya crisis was about
to blow up again.

That anxiety hung over an interview I did the next morning
with Wai Wai Nu, a Rohingya activist and former political prisoner. We talked on Skype, as she was studying in the US: a sign of
her rising international profile. Since her release under a transition
prison amnesty in 2012, this lawyer of barely thirty had campaigned
with maturity and boldness on the need for communal reconcili-
ation and justice. She had earned widespread international recognition, including a Hillary Clinton Award from Washington's
Georgetown University.

Wai Wai Nu was confident but also seemed a little uncomfortable with her growing celebrity status – and, no doubt, foreign
media demands that had been further inflated through her being
young, female and fluent in English. She spoke carefully and was

concerned about the impact of what she said, asking how her words would be used.

Her analysis – just weeks before the military's biggest anti-Rohingya rampage – proved all too accurate. She began by noting how the armed forces had faced no sanction in the eight months since their previous offensive in Rakhine. The danger was that it might have emboldened them to do the same again, but on an even larger scale.

'Obviously it shows that domestic mechanisms don't work. We don't have an independent and strong judiciary,' Wai Wai Nu said. 'Traditionally, when it comes to military crimes there are no channels to bring cases to court and ask for accountability and justice. So it has become a tradition.'

Wai Wai Nu had experienced the abusiveness of Myanmar's generals first hand. She was jailed in 2005 along with her father, Kyaw Win, and other family members over his political activities. He had been elected as a National League for Democracy MP in the 1990 Suu Kyi landslide that was overridden by the junta. After a secret trial, he received a forty-seven-year sentence and she, her mother, sister and brother seventeen years. It was part of a policy of collective punishment of families and communities that is among the most inhuman aspects of totalitarian states. Wai Wai Nu, an eighteen-year-old law student at the time, served her time along with her female relatives at the notorious Insein jail, where many other political prisoners were also incarcerated.

She had suffered terribly, but she also recognised that in an important sense she was a privileged exception. As a Rohingya from a successful family, she had access to the Myanmar citizenship – and a passport – denied to many. She had spoken of how her seven years in jail amounted to her 'University of Life'. It opened her eyes to how many of the poor women jailed alongside her were there because they lacked the money and influence to fight their cases properly. After her release, she finished her law degree and moved into activism including a 2015 initiative called 'My Friend', a social media campaign promoting tolerance and pluralism.

Now she criticised the Suu Kyi administration's lack of 'serious effort and willingness' to address past rights abuses, including those from the Rakhine violence in 2012. 'The government is saying it is trying to address it domestically but it's not working. This is very odious. This is why it's very important to have international investigations or independent bodies looking at the issues.'

But Wai Wai Nu also noted the lack of apparent appetite around the world for coming down too hard on Suu Kyi's government. That chimed with an anxiety felt among diplomats not to push too much, for fear of jeopardising the broader political transition. 'It's a very worrisome situation because the civilian government has a reputation and legitimacy internationally; that's why we are seeing more and more reluctance to respond to the situation in Rakhine state by international bodies,' Wai Wai Nu said. 'I think it's quite dangerous. More people will suffer and the side effects will get bigger – not only domestically, but across the region.'

She pointed out that this was not simply a case of the government being passive, but of officials and state institutions working 'to not only cover up but actively provide misinformation, confusing the public and international bodies'. In April 2017, Suu Kyi herself said that ethnic cleansing was 'too strong' a description for what was happening in Rakhine, adding that 'it is Muslims killing Muslims as well.'[20]

The English-language *Global New Light of Myanmar* – a government-owned paper that had turned from a promoter of the junta to an enthusiast for the NLD – decried the international criticism in ultra-patriotic terms. 'A strong sense of nationalism did not occur in the minds of the people without rhyme or reason,' read an opinion piece published a few months after my conversation with Wai Wai Nu. 'Based on the false allegations that ethnic cleansing was being committed in Rakhine State, nationalistic spirit welled up in the hearts of the Myanmar people as the said accusations affected the national dignity and image of the country.'[21]

Zaw Htay, a government spokesperson who was part of Suu Kyi's office of the state counsellor, made prominent efforts on social media to discredit the Rohingya allegations. In December 2016, he tweeted a picture apparently of a Rohingya woman telling a group of people how she had been abused. Zaw Htay added the comment 'Fake #Rape in the #Rakhine #State'.[22] He linked to a seven-minute video on the official Myanmar President's Office Facebook page detailing alleged fabricated stories from Rohingya.

Wai Wai Nu condemned the way government officials had echoed 'misinformation' put about by pro-military sources. 'The approach of the civilian government is dangerous,' she said. 'If the civilian government doesn't have authority they shouldn't take the approach of protecting military violations. They shouldn't stand on the side of the military.'

Wai Wai Nu's own family history suggested another ominous trend. While the NLD once put up Rohingya candidates like her father – and attracted support from many Muslims – the idea of a Rohingya MP now seemed far-fetched. In the 2015 election, neither the NLD nor its USDP rivals fielded a single Muslim candidate.

I asked Wai Wai Nu if Suu Kyi's tenure so far had proved she was not a good leader, whatever her other qualities. The young lawyer deflected the question but did not defend the Lady.

'I don't know,' she said. 'But in these days, her stands ... on minorities are really unclear and disappointing.'

Wai Wai Nu ended with a pessimistic assessment of the likely international response to further military outrages. She thought these would always be tempered by the idea that, whatever their faults, Suu Kyi and her government still deserved support, because another bout of full-blown military rule was the likely alternative.

'I think most of the countries these days are not prioritising human rights violations in Burma,' Wai Wai Nu said. 'They are trying to improve relations with the government, and economic opportunities. They are trying to celebrate the fact that there were elections and there is a civilian government.'

This left open the question of whether there came a point when the failures of a transition were so great that foreign support became indefensible. It seemed morally wrong to accept that groups of people could be sacrificed to terror and slaughter as long as freedoms appeared to improve for the majority.

As Wai Wai Nu put it: 'Democracy and human rights cannot be separated. They come together.'

My final encounter on my last trip to Myanmar was with another female former political prisoner – and one who saw Suu Kyi's problems earlier than most. Ma Thida had seen the process of idolisation close-up. In her days as a young medic, she had accompanied the Lady on travels around the country to campaign for greater freedoms after the military bloodily suppressed the 1988 uprising. Working as an assistant and doctor to Suu Kyi, Thida would later go to jail for six years.

Thida was a distinctive presence with her wavy black hair and tinted glasses that lent her a slightly brooding air. We met in a popular restaurant on the edge of a Yangon park opposite the Shwedagon Pagoda. The abandoned hulks of two Myanmar Airways aircraft lay nearby, part of the city's haunting backdrop. The ragged dusk chorus of crows always sounded particularly ominous to my ear. It made me think back to the repressions of the late 1980s and early 1990s that had disturbed me when I'd first read about them as a teenager in the UK.

In those early days of open dissent against the military, Thida saw the power of the Lady as she roamed the realm. She had been out of the country for many years and wanted – in Thida's words – to 'prove her passion' for it. She talked to citizens as she found them, mostly 'very grassroots' people, such as vegetable sellers, who were used to being ignored and oppressed.

'She tried to greet everybody and was trying to learn "what's going on in this area, what's the real problem, so-and-so?". She tried to listen to the people and then respond,' Thida recalled. 'People knew she genuinely wanted to deal with them. So, yes, people were so happy.'

Thida, a restless soul who was a writer as a well as a doctor and award-winning activist, noticed something else. In her book *The Sunflower*, drafted in the early 1990s but banned by the junta, Thida described Suu Kyi as a 'prisoner of applause'. It meant that already, hopes of what she would – and could – achieve had grown too big. She was destined to disappoint. 'No one could meet the expectation,' Thida told me, more than two decades after her initial judgement made during those heady, sketchy days of defiance. 'It was so high, you know.'

Thida was sent to Insein prison in 1993. Her health declined and she caught tuberculosis, but she says she kept together in part through marathon Vipassana Buddhist meditation sessions that sometimes stretched to twenty hours a day. She described refusing to sleep during one interrogation period, until her inquisitors begged her to do so to allow them to go home. They realised it was 'not easy' to deal with her, she says, speculating that this was maybe why she was set free after six years rather than serving her full twenty-year sentence. 'They released me because they really didn't want to keep me any more,' she said. 'One of the jailers told me, "Ma Thida, you are free, we are not."'

After her release, Thida shifted her attention from politics to medicine and literature. She worked in a Muslim women's hospital, giving her an inside view of how people were suffering during the late junta era. She later spent some time in the US, returning to the country to edit a news journal after the military stepped down in 2011.

Now Thida lived quietly with her ailing mother in a flat on the outskirts of central Yangon. The Shwedagon Pagoda, where Suu Kyi had given her landmark 1988 speech, glimmered in the distance through the heavy wet season air. Thida's front room was a microcosm of Myanmar's modern political history. On one side was a photo of her activist grandfather who'd been arrested during 1920 student strikes to protest against British rule; on another there were awards she'd received such as a key denoting the freedom of the city of Hazard, Kentucky.

Thida told me she was working on a novel on the new Myanmar. She planned to focus on the phenomenon Naypyidaw represented. Its empty streets and gargantuan architecture made it an ideal metaphor for out-of-touch governing elites. She noted how electricity supplies were more reliable in the capital than elsewhere – but that didn't mean its new NLD masters had a vision for the country. 'The darkness makes us blind,' she said. 'But if it is too light, it can still make us blind.'

She worried that Suu Kyi was stuck behind 'layers of barriers' of advisers and hangers-on and so had 'lost the chance to listen'. She did not expect the Lady to retire any time soon, as urged by some former supporters – including her biographer – who are aghast at how she has dealt with the Rohingya crisis. Thida took off her glasses and rubbed her eyes as she considered the Lady's future.

'She truly needs to get rest from her very long endeavour,' Thida said. 'She said she needs to work until she will no longer be needed. But in ten years' time, will people still need her or not? Her ambition is very high – and big.'

Thida was cautious on the Rohingya – as were so many in the NLD. Like some other observers, Thida felt Suu Kyi lacked full information about what was going on and appeared overly reliant on what the military told her. But people also needed to take account of the 'history and politics' behind the situation in Rahkine, Thida said. A lot of people, 'especially the international community', did not 'understand the whole picture', she added. (When I spoke to her some months later, after the August 2017 offensive, she described the Rohingya as oppressed, though she also raised concerns about Rohingya militant group activity.)

Ultimately, the troubles went to the heart of Suu Kyi's relationship with the military, Thida said. 'I have been a little bit surprised – why should she be the only person who has been blamed by the international community?' she asked. 'I won't do that, even though I am not a big fan of hers any more.'

Thida described how a kind of hierarchy of anguish inside Myanmar had also chafed with the international approach to the country. Because so many people had endured awful experiences that had not been acknowledged or addressed, they become hardened to the distress of others and even resentful of attempts by outsiders to help. 'A lot of people have been in despair already,' Thida said. 'They lost their life. They lost their land. They lost their living, livelihoods. They lost their everything. How can they have empathy for these [other] people? They think: "We are in a similar situation, but the whole world neglects our suffering. They don't care about our concerns."'

Thida said people were also still starved of information about the country. She told of a woman from upper Myanmar she'd met who said it was only when she read Thida's prison memoir that she realised the military was lying when it claimed student protests were responsible for her troubles. 'They just believed what the propaganda said, you know: "These students make that problem, that's why we cannot eat,"' she said.

A dark side of Myanmar's greater freedom has been the opportunity it has offered to propagandists who now have far greater potential reach than the military did when it ruled in analogue isolationism. Websites and social media accounts that spread false information and hatred – and not just about the Rohingya – have flourished. The arrival of foreign telecom companies made mobile phones ubiquitous and brought the price of SIM cards down from $150 as recently as 2013 to less than $2 today. By 2017, smartphone penetration rates had soared to seventy percent, according to industry figures. That was higher than both the Asia-Pacific average of fifty-three percent and the European level of sixty-eight percent.

Thida agreed that the country and the wider world needed to prepare themselves for life after Suu Kyi, who would be seventy-five by the time the next election, expected in 2020. She thought outsiders had focused too much on the Lady's battle with the generals, at the expense of Myanmar's wider troubles. Outsiders needed a neat story and the David versus Goliath struggle for democracy provided it. 'They tried to simplify our problems in order to fit their knowledge, their understanding,' she said. 'So because of that simplified knowledge, their concern has not matched our concern – and their way of looking at the solution is also not very constructive or effective.'

I asked Thida whether – both internationally and domestically – people had turned Suu Kyi into something that she was not and could never be. Had she, in a way, become more myth than reality? Thida's nuanced answer captured the conundrum of how Suu Kyi could be inspiring but also a source of unhealthy dependence.

'Even though she cannot be as capable as all people expected, the respect and the love for her will still remain, because of her big sacrifice and her commitment,' Thida said. 'So she's really playing a role still because the majority of people just cannot afford to lose her.'

Thida described Suu Kui as not sitting on a fence but walking uncomfortably on it. She was a heroine of the people, but she could not afford to alienate an army that still held huge power. That tension could be broken only by substantial and historic concessions by the military.

'If they do have a more visionary, not arrogant, leadership, the military can change, I hope,' she said.

What were the chances of the generals doing that? I asked.

'I don't know,' she admitted. 'Hopefully the younger generation will.'

Her observation echoed efforts by the UK to engage more junior Myanmar military officers, offering them training in the English language, democracy and leadership. That arrangement was scrapped in September 2017, in response to the worst phase yet of the Rohingya crisis. In October that year, the EU suspended invitations to top Myanmar commanders, including General Min Aung Hlaing, the armed forces chief, who had in the previous year visited several European countries and hosted a top EU military official in Myanmar. Both the US and EU later imposed sanctions on Myanmar military officers alleged to be responsible for atrocities against the Rohingya.

In August 2018, Suu Kyi's state counsellor office announced that Myanmar would not cooperate with the International Criminal Court's request for jurisdiction over the Rohingya crisis. The statement said Myanmar declined even to give the ICC a formal reply to its request, citing seven reasons including alleged bad faith, technical irregularities and lack of transparency. It criticised the court for allowing submissions 'consisting of mostly charged narratives of harrowing personal tragedies calculated to place emotional pressure on the Court'. It added that Myanmar's cooperation with the request might have set a 'dangerous precedent' that would encourage future cases on 'populist causes' to be mounted 'at the urging of biased stakeholders and non-governmental organizations'.[23]

The lights of democracy were at least half-lit in Myanmar again, but – as Thida would have it – people seemed increasingly dazzled.

Suu Kyi's aura had blinded everybody, possibly even including herself. More than a quarter of a century of devotion had obscured the flaws in both the person and the system she inherited.

Myanmar needed to do something it had never done before: conceptualise itself as a country. Repression by various internal and external powers had long denied it that chance. The question now was whether it was already too late.

In July 2018, Thant Myint-U, historian and grandson of U Thant, wrote that, in the absence of more innovative thinking, 'this country may, within people's lifetime, disappear.'[24] Thida, who was there near the creation of the Suu Kyi phenomenon, also feared that denial about the full weight of the nation's burdens ran wide and deep. 'After five decades of heavy censorship we are really intellectually blind,' she said. 'We live in a virtual world.'

8

A Question of Values

The commuters poured up from their morning ferries and buses into the old heart of Valletta, shirtsleeves and summer dresses still the order of the day in the southern European October sun. Most streamed downtown past the Auberge de Castille, an imposing baroque building that now serves as the prime minister's office in the Maltese capital. It used to be the lodgings of the Knights of St John, who centuries ago made the city their stronghold and fed a sense of historically layered mysteries that lingers in the Mediterranean island state today.

I took a taxi and headed north, along quiet roads where prickly pear cactuses tumbled over crumbling dry stone walls. We passed the ancient hilltop settlement of Mdina, the old capital known as the 'silent city' because cars are all but forbidden within its fortified walls where few people now live. Founded by the Phoenicians more than two and half millennia before, it had been under Roman, Arab, French and British occupation. Like the climate and the Maltese language, Mdina was a reminder of how the EU's smallest state is a cultural entrepôt that lies at a more southerly latitude than Tunis and only a few hundred kilometres from Tripoli.

A police officer standing in the road stopped us as we neared our destination. When I explained that I had an appointment, he let me walk on to a nearby house with a driveway. A young man arrived at the gate to greet me and warn me not to walk in the ruts made by the car wheels, for fear of disturbing potential evidence. We moved silently in single file along the centre of the gravel track, into a home in the grip of terrible mourning.

Less than forty-eight hours before, my host Matthew Caruana Galizia had rushed down the very same drive after the house was shaken by a large explosion nearby. His mother, the journalist Daphne Caruana Galizia, had left in her car moments before. Matthew sprinted down the road and saw Daphne's white Peugeot ablaze in a field by the side of the tarmac. It would quickly become clear that she had been killed by a bomb.

'I am never going to forget, running around the inferno in the field, trying to figure out a way to open the door, the horn of the car still blaring, screaming at two policemen who turned up with a single fire extinguisher to use it,' Matthew wrote in a Facebook post soon after the murder. 'They stared at me. "I'm sorry, there is nothing we can do," one of them said. I looked down and there were my mother's body parts all around me. I realised they were right, it was hopeless.'

Matthew's words soon turned into much more than a primal scream of pain. He made a direct link between his mother's assassination and what he branded a culture of corruption and incompetence that had turned Malta into a 'mafia state'. His mother had gone deeper and deeper into exposing that alleged wrongdoing – and now, it seemed, she had paid an unconscionable price.

'I am sorry for being graphic, but this is what war looks like, and you need to know,' Matthew wrote. 'We are a people at war against the state and organised crime, which have become indistinguishable.'

I had covered political murders during years spent reporting from many venal and autocratic states. But I hadn't expected that my first big assignment on returning to the EU in late 2017 after a long absence would be to write about the killing of a columnist and blogger whose family were convinced she had been targeted because of her work. It would only be a matter of months before the Malta murder was followed by the killing of another journalist in an EU country: Ján Kuciak along with his fiancée, Martina Kušnírová, in Slovakia. Days before the first anniversary of Caruana Galizia's murder, Bulgarian television presenter Viktoria Marinova was found dead in a park in the northern town of Ruse, having been raped and murdered, according to authorities. Like Kuciak, she had reported on corruption including alleged fraud related to EU funds. As of February 2019, a Bulgarian national was on trial over Marinova's murder in a case authorities insisted was unconnected to her work.[1] In March 2019, a Slovak businessman was charged with ordering the murders of Kuciak and Kusnirova.[2]

Daphne Caruana Galizia had seemed to foretell her own death. In the early afternoon of 16 October, she published a blog on offshore companies allegedly run by Maltese government officials. Within half an hour of it appearing, she was dead. Her last public words seemed horrifically prescient. 'There are crooks everywhere you look now,' the blog concluded. 'The situation is desperate.'[3]

The journalist murders and the suspicions around them brutally exposed a wider cause of alarm: the deterioration of the rule of law in the EU. The bloc spent a lot of time proclaiming its supposed values on human rights and democracy and urging others around the world to follow them. What, though, if the twenty-eight-member European club had rotted from within?

The EU's troubles were growing. People in many countries in all parts of Europe were increasingly drawn to demagogues who fuelled and thrived on hostility to outsiders. Some of these European leaders, including Hungary's Viktor Orbán, were former dissidents who had fought totalitarian states. Their rise had, along with a broader slide into lawlessness, changed the face of Europe – or, perhaps, it had simply torn away the mask.

There were serious problems across the union. The rise of authoritarianism in countries such as Hungary, Poland and Romania had rightly sparked criticism in Brussels and beyond. In Budapest, Orbán boasted of creating an 'illiberal democracy' as his government condemned immigration, demonised the financier George Soros and undermined the independence of the courts and the media. In Warsaw, Poland ousted two dozen supreme court justices as part of a sweeping judicial overhaul it claimed was needed to break the link with its repressive communist past. Both Poland and Hungary faced disciplinary proceedings in front of fellow member states for allegedly breaching fundamental EU values – but each could count on the other to stop any move towards serious sanctions, such as by suspending their voting rights at bloc meetings.

There was humbug, too, from the EU's longer-standing Western European member states. They were complicit in – and in some cases driving forces of – the bloc's increasingly harsh approach to migration. They were also rarely inclined to look too closely at their own problems with corruption, whether it was the action of British, French or German companies overseas, or the conflicts of interest that plagued politicians such as Silvio Berlusconi in Italy.

Then there was the problem of history. Western Europe's lectures on governance and ethics have long looked preachy and hypocritical to both their neighbours and the wider world, particularly the part of it that suffered imperial occupation by powers such as Britain, France, Spain, the Netherlands, Belgium and Italy. Just as the British often overlook their own history to present themselves as exemplars of certain desirable qualities, so other influential EU countries had their own flattering self-mythology. At a conference in Brussels, a French fellow attendee told me she was glad to be a European because only Europeans had the right values to project into the world. The remark seemed particularly perverse, as we had just been talking about Liberia – a country surrounded by states formerly occupied by European powers, including the ex-French colonies of Guinea and Ivory Coast.

EU enlargement has brought many of these old tensions to the surface. The conflicts are particularly obvious in the smaller countries, where the problems are concentrated and easier to see. One is Malta, with its electorate of just a few hundred thousand voters perched on the EU's southern frontier.

Inside Daphne Caruana Galizia's house, Matthew and his two brothers Andrew and Paul sat down with me round a large coffee table to talk about their mother. The house had been beautifully decorated by Daphne. One of her last acts had been to buy saplings for her already abundant garden.

Matthew, red-eyed and periodically tearful, explained why he and his siblings had agreed to speak. They appreciated the intent of the politicians and others around Europe who had denounced their mother's murder and branded it an attack on freedom of expression. But they also found the statements odd. For the brothers, those proclaiming their shock had been far too slow to realise the growing danger in Malta – and elsewhere – to those who challenged powerful vested interests. Matthew returned to the metaphor of conflict.

'It's as if you are in the middle of a war zone, some soldier gets shot dead and you say: "This is an attack on democracy,"' he said. 'The war was already there. It started a long time ago.'

To many outsiders who didn't look too closely, all seemed well on these sun-blessed holiday islands sandwiched between Sicily and the Libyan coast. Malta joined the EU in 2004 as part of the jumbo enlargement that took the bloc from fifteen to twenty-five members. The economy grew fast, albeit partly on the shaky foundations of a property boom, foreign investor tax breaks, flags of convenience for the shipping industry and a 'nationality for sale' scheme. Valletta won plaudits for social liberalisation in areas such as same-sex marriage and gender identity: quite a departure for a nation that didn't even allow divorce until 2011.

'This is where we are,' Matthew Caruana Galizia wrote scathingly in his Facebook post just after the murder. 'A mafia state where you can now change your gender on your ID card – thank God for that! – but where you will be blown to pieces for exercising your basic freedoms.'

As in other societies in miniature, Maltese politics had long featured what is often euphemistically called 'patronage' but is sometimes simply corruption. It underpinned the near-unbroken quarter-century of Nationalist Party rule that ended in 2013. Then the Labour Party came to power and, according to its opponents, began to make up for lost time. Critics said it was a case of – as the title of Michela Wrong's excellent book about Kenya has it – 'it's our turn to eat.'

Daphne Caruana Galizia's Running Commentary blog had drawn a wide audience with postings that ranged from waspish political observations to tales of alleged high-level corruption. Her lawyer said he was defending her in at least forty libel cases, including nineteen filed by a single businessman, when she was killed aged fifty-three.

She stepped up her coverage in 2017, the year of her murder. Building on material from the Panama Papers trove of documents leaked from the Mossack Fonseca law firm, she alleged that officials in Prime Minister Joseph Muscat's office and the premier's wife had received unexplained Azerbaijan-linked money through companies they owned in Panama. All those allegedly involved denied any wrongdoing. An official investigation cleared them in 2018.

Muscat's government held a 'back us or sack us' election in June 2017 in the wake of the original claims – and won handsomely. After the ballot, Caruana Galizia found a fresh target: Adrian Delia, the opposition Nationalists' new leader. At the time of her murder, he had five libel suits outstanding against her. The month before she was killed, she blogged about receiving threats from supporters of Delia, including one urging her to 'take a cyanide pill'. Delia said he had known nothing about the harassment, which he admitted didn't look good.

Daphne Caruana Galizia often found herself playing something of a lone hand. Other journalists on the islands reported honourably and broke stories, but none had the freedom or impact she did. Her work often dismayed her, but she felt she had a duty to raise the alarm. 'She was sick of it but she couldn't stop,' said her son Andrew. 'There was no one else doing it.'

Until the thunderbolt of Brexit, the narrative of the EU had been one of relentless expansion and improvement. The bloc began with six countries in 1958 (as the European Economic Community[4]), grew to nine during the 1970s, and fifteen during the 1990s. Many former Eastern Bloc states came in along with Malta in 2004. Even as Britain negotiated its exit, the European Commission was working closely with six Western Balkan states that wanted to join. Once inside, there are few effective checks on behaviour.

The European Commission had raised concerns about Malta before. A 2014 corruption report highlighted the risk posed by 'executive discretion' to the independence of official investigations on the islands. The commission has since said that no more such reports would be published. The move has drawn criticism. It was a reflection of Brussels' 'unilateral disarmament' of its arsenal to deal with rule of law violations in member states, the

EUobserver, an online newspaper, argued after the Caruana Galizia murder.

The EU's governance problems were in part a hangover from post-Soviet complacency about the triumph of the Western model. For a young European like me entering adulthood in comfortable circumstances in the 1990s, those years were as cosseted as any in human history before or since. But, even in my ignorance and naivety, I always sensed that something was not right. I felt the inequalities of opportunity when I did a student supermarket job. I felt it in the homelessness I saw when I moved to London, and I felt it in the anxiety I saw on reporting trips such as to the Halewood car plant on Merseyside where people's jobs were under threat.

Those sentiments deepened when I began to travel outside Europe and the US for the first time. Three years living in Nigeria during the early 2000s proved a formative experience. Here was a country where the aphorism 'no condition is permanent' had been coined as an emblem of the perpetual promise of improvement. But it had another meaning, too, about the precarity of daily life in a country chafed with conflicts and the fact of mass deprivation amid the riches of oil. When people asked me what the main lessons were of my time in Nigeria, my reply inevitably included some version of the 'fragility of all things'. That sense of living on the edge has spread wider in many European countries as jobs have become more insecure, wages have stagnated and social services have been pared back.

These are among the forces that have allowed chancers to rise to power on the back of their supposed 'populism'. The fight against the false remedies they tout has been hampered by the lofty denunciations levelled against them by some members of shocked elites. This dismissiveness harms progressive causes and alienates further the very people they need to persuade. The pejorative use of the word 'populist' is in itself revealing.

The *Oxford English Dictionary* definition of the word is the quality of 'appealing to or aimed at ordinary people'. That may be deliberately ambivalent, reflecting the many different types of populism of the left and right – but it is not inherently negative.

The damage done by establishment demonisation of populism – as distinct from deserved criticism of the opportunists and racists that harness it – struck me hard when I lived in Thailand. Thaksin Shinawatra, the self-exiled two-time prime minister, had for years been disparaged by his old-money enemies for his 'populist policies'. These included rice subsidies, cheap healthcare and microcredit schemes for small business. Unsurprisingly, these won him millions of votes in vast rural areas long neglected by Bangkok. The frequent attacks on these policies as *morally* bad (as opposed to, for example, poorly managed, badly targeted or prone to corruption) backfired. They revealed more about his enemies' disdain for those they dismissed as ignorant rural voters than it did about Thaksin, for all his serious flaws.

A similar social fracturing can be seen in the post-2008 narrative in the West. The cruelties and hypocrisies exposed in the postwar liberal model have given cover to politicians who appeal brazenly to people's worse instincts. It has also offered a new avenue for manipulation by established interests who realise the populist pose is helpful as a means to discredit opponents – and to distract attention from allegations of venal behaviour.

Laura Codruța Kövesi had enjoyed long international acclaim but now she was under domestic pressure. Romania's chief anti-corruption prosecutor had won plaudits at home and across Western Europe during her almost five years in office, but efforts by her enemies to oust her had swelled alongside the praise. Now, in early 2018, the justice minister was expected within days to announce the results of an investigation into her conduct – and, very possibly, to recommend she be sacked.

Dressed in black blouse and trousers, Kövesi oozed gravitas from her seat in her Bucharest office. The room was brightened by pictures drawn by schoolchildren to show the importance of fighting corruption. The walls were filled with scales of justice and the triumph of figures representing truth.

The idealism contrasted sharply with the real-world problems Kövesi faced, although she tried to make light of them. Long runs helped her keep her equanimity against what she styled a conspiracy against her agency by the politicians and business people it threatened.

'We can face these attacks,' she said. 'We can face these lies and false statements.'

Kövesi had devoted much of her life to combating corruption. Born in Transylvania in the lee of the Carpathian Mountains in 1973, she studied law and joined Romania's prosecuting office in 1995. Since 2000, she had specialised in prosecuting organised crime and financial wrongdoing. In 2013, she became head of the National Anti-Corruption Directorate, known as the DNA. Her tenure had won her awards including France's prestigious *Légion d'honneur*.

Kövesi said the example of her father – a prosecutor for more than forty years – and her teacher mother taught her 'the spirit of fairness and justice'. She decided to focus on corruption because she wanted a 'cleaner country ... a country in which things function as they should, a country in which people don't have to give bribes to get something they're entitled to, and in which nobody can obtain an undeserved status as a result of corruption, regardless of their field of work'.

This was not an outlook universally shared among Romania's political and business elite. In particular, it brought Kövesi into conflict with supporters of Liviu Dragnea, chairman of the ruling

Social Democratic Party and the country's most powerful politician. Dragnea was effectively on a judicial yellow card: he had already been found guilty of electoral fraud and another conviction would see him automatically sent to jail. He had denied wrongdoing in several criminal cases, including a probe into road projects backed by €21 million of EU funding. That investigation was launched after the DNA received information from OLAF, the EU's anti-fraud body.

Kövesi said more than eight hundred people had been convicted and more than €2 billion in proceeds of crime targeted under her stewardship of the DNA. Conviction rates were around ninety percent. Those found guilty included ministers and former ministers, mayors and business people. The results had – she said, with no little understatement – 'led to ample debates within Romanian society'.

Kövesi said the attacks on her agency had three prongs. The first were proposed legal amendments 'meant to diminish the prosecutors' independence and to reduce our investigative tools'. The second were public attacks on the organisation's integrity by people it was targeting and their political allies. The third was paid lobbying by 'companies specialised in denigrating, harassing and intimidating'.

Of these, she saw the legal amendments as by far the most dangerous. They would increase the authority of the justice minister over the corruption prosecutor. They would also oblige the prosecutor to inform anybody against whom a complaint had been made – even if such tipping off might compromise the investigation.

I put it to Kövesi that there were, in fact, aspects of the legal system that ought to be reformed. An unintended consequence of applying EU rules on security of judicial tenure in some former communist countries had been to entrench the positions of justices implicated in corruption or rights abuses during the years of dictatorship. In other cases, old ties allegedly remained between intelligence agencies and prosecuting authorities.

Critics of governments in countries such as Hungary, Poland and Romania said they had cynically used such legitimate points to justify much more extensive – and highly political – overhauls of their legal systems. As one judge campaigning against the Romanian legal amendments put it to me: 'They used the good changes to force through the bad changes.'

Kövesi insisted concerns about the present set-up were over-blown. She said intelligence services were now restricted to providing information to the prosecutor and could not interfere in its investigations. A European court ruling before she took office had stopped the practice of allowing prosecutors to use secret evidence that trial judges would see but defendants could not. Romania's anti-corruption efforts were also subject to a special EU monitoring mechanism imposed when it joined the bloc in 2007.

Kövesi gave a stark warning about the impact of the law changes proposed by the government. What was happening in Romania was a lesson that progress was 'not irreversible', she said. It would send the fight against corruption back to the post-communist years, when only petty matters such as alleged bribe-taking by traffic police and university professors were pursued. All the bigger fish would escape. 'I doubt that there will be any serious investigations involving high officials, people with high positions within the state,' she said.

Proposals to make it harder to prosecute public officials for abuse of office would be especially damaging, she said. More than half the agency's 11,200 cases the previous year had related to some kind of alleged abuse of office. The proposed legal changes would sabotage an expanding effort to stop fraud in public procurement cases. The anti-corruption agency had indicted almost two hundred people in such matters last year, involving official spending of €95 million. 'The conclusion is that we will no longer be able to conduct such investigations,' she said.

Official attempts to set a floor on the amount of money that could be prosecuted would also be harmful, she said. She gave the example of a corrupt hospital manager who could gerrymander drug procurement contracts to avoid breaching the minimum threshold. 'This manager has the possibility of dividing the payment, the total sum, in smaller contracts up to the minimum threshold so that he or she can avoid being investigated,' she said. 'Once they divide these contracts, they can award them, they can grant the contracts to whomever they want without being forced, without being required to explain anything to anybody because it is no longer a crime.'

I countered that there were legitimate questions over the offence of abuse of office. Many countries struggled to define when a bad decision, or serious incompetence, tipped over into criminal negligence. Kövesi retorted that the way the proposals had been floated in Romania showed they were the opposite of a good faith attempt to wrestle with the law's nuances. 'Let's say the content of the law is not very clear,' she said. 'Well, at that point, we need a public, ample, complex debate. We need studies to show us in what cases the law was unclear. We need to identify the points that were unclear. It's not normal practice to issue an ordinance in the middle of the night without having previous consultations, without explaining actually anything to anybody about it.'

Kövesi said the constitutional court had already stymied her agency's work through a ruling the previous year. The judges had decided that violations of secondary legislation, such as government regulations and orders, no longer constituted criminal acts. This meant, for example, that frauds committed during privatisation processes – a rich source of corruption in some former communist countries – could no longer be prosecuted. The court's decision had forced the DNA to close 275 files relating to the alleged misappropriation of €148 million of state funds.

Her detailed account was a sharp reminder of how the rule of law, while much touted by political theorists, is a blunt and inadequate tool without the support of norms and institutions. Legislation can be undone, gerrymandered or worked around: the very act of making it defines what criminals need to do to evade it. What's more, laws alone lack bite unless there is a system of generally agreed customs and ethics around them. It is a lesson the US has had to relearn since the Trump administration took over.

Kövesi said attempts to give the Romanian minister of justice more control over corruption prosecutors were particularly ominous. Independence was not a 'privilege for prosecutors', but a 'fundamental principle for any democratic society', she said. Once independence disappeared, so did the principle of equality of all before the law. She once again referred to the danger that Romania would slip back towards the politicised justice system of communism and its aftermath. 'I am forty-four years old and half of my life I have been a prosecutor,' she said. 'I have known both the times before 2004 and the times after, when Romanian prosecutors became independent and after Romania became a member state of the European Union. When we speak about serious justice, when we speak about the rule of law, and when we speak about the interests of the Romanian citizens, for all these things it is necessary to have an independent justice system.'

I asked Kövesi whether she was worried the attacks on the DNA were hitting home and costing it support, particularly among ruling party voters. Her trenchant reply underscored how – perhaps unwisely – she seemed to have little interest in public relations or emotional appeals.

'It is not my job ... to conduct public surveys to see if Romanian citizens like me or not,' she said. 'It is not my job to be popular. It is my job to conduct high-level corruption investigations.'

I pressed her on the point. While it was true that their work wasn't – and shouldn't be – a popularity contest, surely any institution in any country needed to feel it had public confidence to be credible? She again refused to be drawn. 'I repeat; our job is to conduct investigations,' she said. She added: 'The sociological research, the public pulse over the last years have shown an increase in the trust of Romanian citizens in our activity.'

It was a tough fight, I said. She gave the verbal equivalent of a shrug. 'We chose it.'

Kövesi claimed to be optimistic, but she admitted she was 'very worried' that the proposed law changes would stymie the DNA. Her worry was not for her own position, she said, but for the impact on the country and its citizens.

'We are paid the same if we investigate petty corruption, if we investigate a common theft, or if we investigate and indict important members of society,' she said. 'But corruption will be even more generalised, it will be present in all sectors, they will continue to rob the state budget.'

Less than a week after my meeting with Kövesi, she faced her biggest crisis yet. Justice Minister Tudorel Toader called for her removal, saying that she had gone beyond her authority and hurt Romania's image outside the country. The country's judicial watchdog rejected the application. President Klaus Iohannis, the final arbiter, did too. She had survived – for now.

Few saw that as the end of the matter. They were right. The battle for the soul of Romania was too big and too bitter for that.

Şerban Nicolae was a thickset man who seemed to fill not only his close-fitting dark blue suit but the high-ceilinged room where we met in Romania's gilded parliament building. He had the dominant manner of a power broker who had been in politics pretty much since the fall of the Berlin Wall. A lawyer by profession, he joined the former communists at what he termed the 'beginning of the new democracy', after Nicolae Ceauşescu was ousted and shot in late 1989.

The post-communists had gone through a Pythonesque series of names – the National Salvation Front, Democratic National Salvation Front, Party of Social Democracy – before settling on the Social Democratic Party. Şerban Nicolae had been a presidential adviser, a minister and was now the Senate majority leader: the Mitch McConnell of Romania. He was also a long-time member of the Senate's judicial committee and a main force behind the country's proposed legal system overhaul.

We were meeting late one night in February 2018 in his office. The next room was a red-carpeted chamber where a Social Democrat party caucus now swelled to seventy senators met around a huge rectangle of heavy interlocking wooden tables. The imposing environment was part of a building that was Ceauşescu's most grandiose folly and has been described as 'the world's greatest monument to totalitarian kitsch'.[5] The edifice known in post-communist days as the 'Palace of the Parliament' is a sprawling warren of marbled rooms, carved wood and crystal chandeliers. It occupied the biggest volume of any civilian administrative building in the world and its construction required the removal or destruction of twenty-eight churches, the demolition of 10,000 homes and the eviction of 57,000 families, according to an official website. A project that the former dictator first demanded in the late 1970s was barely half-finished when he was ousted more than a decade later.

Now, it was Şerban Nicolae's base for the modern political power struggle that had pitted his party against Kövesi. He argued some matters pursued as alleged corruption these days were not corruption at all. He cited his party leader Dragnea's legal troubles in connection with a 2012 referendum called by the Social Democrats as part of their long-standing efforts to topple their opponent and *bête noire*, the twice-elected President Traian Băsescu. Dragnea, who was then regional development minister, was accused of leading a campaign of bribery and ballot paper forgery to artificially boost turnout in the vote, so it reached the required threshold of fifty percent of registered voters. The attempt ultimately failed, Băsescu survived – and Dragnea was convicted of electoral fraud.[6] He denied any wrongdoing.

'What was the corruption, what was the personal benefit for Mr Dragnea?' Nicolae asked, adding that in 'other civilised countries' this would not have been a corruption case.

It seemed an odd point. Most people would probably count paying bribes and forging ballot papers as examples of corruption. Further, Nicolae's focus on the lack of immediate personal advantage to Dragnea ignored the political benefits to his party – and the possible indirect benefits to the man himself.

Nicolae pressed on with this line of reasoning. He said Romania had a 'long list of cases where it is inexplicable for people outside Romania' why the crimes were classed as corruption. He cited the affair of Adrian Năstase, a former Social Democrat prime minister, who was convicted in 2012 of using state funds to finance his presidential election campaign and then in 2014 of taking bribes. Nicolae insisted the campaign finance offence was not corruption; it wasn't clear if he felt the same about the bribery case. Năstase also denied any wrongdoing.

Nicolae claimed that the Romanian public was extremely sceptical of Kövesi's anti-corruption agency. He talked about two city mayoral candidates – one from the Social Democrats, one not – who had won resounding victories at the last election despite being under investigation for corruption. 'Two important cases,' he said. 'That was the response from the population from the urban area, educated and informed people – not a rural area, not non-educated people, non-informed people.'

It seemed to me quite a leap to interpret these election votes as a repudiation of the DNA. Even if these electorates didn't trust the agency, it didn't necessarily mean their suspicions were justified. 'The people [are] always right,' he shot back immediately.

In Nicolae's worldview, the people's judgement was not only electorally sacrosanct but axiomatically correct. The people had made a decision to vote for candidates accused of corruption. The people's decision must be honoured. Therefore, the people's decision must also be right – and, by definition, the corruption allegations must be false.

'I will never criticise the people,' Nicolae said. 'I never criticise my people, I never criticise the United States people for electing Mr Donald Trump. I agree with most of his ideas – but that's a different discussion.'

That segue made my ears prick up. I asked which of Trump's views he particularly identified with. 'Political correctness, which is probably the most refined form of hypocrisy ... and the most effective weapon against freedom of opinion,' he said. 'You're not allowed to express your opinion freely because you're affecting certain rules – rules decided by minorities especially – but anyway, any kind of other people's rules. It's punishing a person for expressing their opinion.'

He gave an unexpected example to support his case. 'Let me ask you one thing; the fiancée of Prince Harry; what's her origin?' he said.

He was referring to Meghan Markle, who was due to marry Prince Harry later in 2018. Markle's name had been in the news lately because of racist text messages about her sent by the then girlfriend of Henry Bolton, who was at the time leader of the anti-immigration UK Independence Party.

I replied: 'Well, she's American.'

I asked what he meant by the question. Markle's mother is black and her father white. She has previously described herself as a 'confident mixed-race woman'.

Nicolae launched into a lengthy complaint about what he perceived as the social unacceptability of referring to a person of colour as 'black'. He talked about how 'anywhere in the world you see a black person which is not in Africa ... you have to refer to them as African American or you have to imagine things like African-French, African-British.'

'What is that? What's the meaning of that?' he asked. 'I don't understand why ... I saw a lot of people said, "It does not offend me to say I'm black."'

But nobody is stopping you saying these things, I said: you just said them. 'It leads to sanctions,' he retorted. 'It leads to a punishment if you use that word, if you use that expression, if you express in a certain way [even] if it's non-intentional, if it's not really affecting the person.'

He compared what he saw as the crushing effect of political correctness with the repression of communist-era Romania. He didn't mention that his Social Democrats had grown out of the Communist Party. 'You see, we passed this in Ceaușescu's time; we had a lot of restrictions in terms of expressing our opinion,' he said. 'There were certain terms, certain expressions, certain persons that should not be mentioned in any case; others that should be expressed in a certain way and no other. We passed that period of time and we had that experience and, trust me, it's completely wrong. That's why we had to pass through a revolution.'

I found the analogy bizarre. I did not see how it was reasonable to compare criticism during open public debate with the actions of a dictatorship that arbitrarily arrested people for what they said. In Ceaușescu's Romania, according to the *Encyclopaedia Britannica*, food and other essential items ran short because the regime exported them to pay off debts and raise hard currency, contraception and abortion were outlawed, and doctors monitored women to make sure they remained fertile. The leader installed his wife and other relatives in top government and party jobs as part of his

wider cult of personality.[7] He was also the very definition of a
kleptocrat who had wanted to take valuable portraits from
Romania's central bank but was hoodwinked by officials who told
him the works were painted directly onto the walls. To liken his
tyranny to political correctness in whatever interpretation of that
notoriously slippery phrase seemed cynical, even obscene.

'This is my opinion and you're free to disagree with me,' he said.
'You surely have the right to disagree with me and criticise me
with no repercussions against you.'

That's generous of him, I thought.

Nicolae turned next to a recent US controversy. He said he had
read online that day about how a staging of *The Hunchback of Notre
Dame* 'on Broadway probably' was 'banned' because the part of
Esmeralda – whom Victor Hugo's novel suggests is of Roma
descent – was given to a white actor. 'Some people thought this
was offensive; that role should not be played by a white girl so they
banned the play. It was on the news,' he said.

I said I wasn't aware of the story. When I checked later, he
appeared to be referring to a production of the musical *The
Hunchback of Notre Dame* at a high school in New York, in which
the casting of a white teenager as Esmeralda triggered protests
and prompted the school to pull the show. The decision was
denounced on conservative and far right online media, including
Breitbart News and the neo-Nazi Daily Stormer. Students who
had campaigned against the original casting became the targets of
harassment, including receiving pictures of themselves covered in
swastikas.

The fact that Nicolae seemed to have noticed the fate of the
play was striking (there was no suggestion he had engaged in any
harassment). A cause célèbre seized on by the US alt-right had
been picked up by an Eastern European politician from a nominally left-wing party – a sign that Romania's Social Democrats
were really more like conservative nationalists. The digital age had

linked transatlantic ideological soulmates who might never have come into contact otherwise.

We continued to debate fruitlessly until at some point I said we would have to agree to disagree. 'Sure; a lot of things,' Nicolae replied.

Our back and forth about Romanian politics was one thing. But what struck me most was what I saw as Nicolae's claims of victimhood. Here was one of the most powerful people in the country, complaining that he wasn't allowed to say things he had literally just said. It was like the politicians in Britain who lamented that 'you can't talk about immigration,' even as the national conversation at times seemed to consist of little else.

What people like Nicolae wanted, it seemed to me, was not just freedom of speech: it was freedom from criticism, too. It was the freedom from challenge. They were used to being in charge and to seeing their worldview accepted.

As we left the building, Nicolae's assistant encouraged me to come back for a proper tour of the parliament. It seemed incongruous indeed to have spent an evening in a slain communist dictator's overwrought palace arguing over the supposed new crushing fist of political correctness. But these were topsy-turvy times in Europe – and not just in Bucharest.

It didn't take long to move between worlds in Romania. It was a short ride from central Bucharest to the block upon block of grey suburban Ceauşescu-era dormitories. Communism felt closer here, its architectural starkness unleavened by the capital's ornate monarchist-era curves.

Soon the urban sprawl gave way altogether to wintry fields and sparse settlements where Soviet-era industries once hummed. Signs proclaiming European Union projects appeared frequently, little blue and yellow flashes of colour amid the bleakness.

The journey was a reminder that the so-called miracle of economic convergence within the EU is not all it seems. While countries have moved closer together in income, disparities between regions within countries have in many cases increased, particularly in Central and Eastern Europe. The main reason was straightforward: manual jobs were disappearing, and many of those who once did them were now either out of work or had moved away. While cities such as Sofia and Bucharest fizzed with urban chic, young professionals and tech-based growth industries, some rural areas and old industrial centres were falling further behind.

I was travelling to Cojasca, about fifty kilometres north-west of Bucharest, with Carmen Constantin, a Romanian journalist friend. The community lies on the Ialomiţa River, a tributary of the Danube. Older people and the occasional young mother with children clustered on street corners, plastic chairs and wooden benches, making the most of the afternoon winter sun. Many of the women wore headscarves and the men astrakhan lambskin hats. Piles of horse manure pocked the road to the mayor's yellow-painted office. A handful of young men stood around a kiosk across the street, listening to music and downing Tiger brand energy drinks.

I was received by Victor Gheorghe, the local mayor and also a Roma language teacher. He told me seventy-five percent of the area's population was from the minority ethnic group. He was a paunchy man with a pencil moustache and neatly side-parted jet-black hair. He wore a winning electric-blue shirt and a Seiko watch. A fluorescent green-and-black football perched on a shelf behind him, along with a team photo from his thinner days. One corner of the room was dominated by a tall brown stove; the other by a large EU flag.

Places like Cojasca are part of the rural heartland of Social Democrat support where recent Romanian elections have been won and lost. Gheorghe was now in his fifth four-year term as mayor. He said he normally received about sixty percent of the vote.

He told me many people in the district worked in construction and livestock, although a good number of younger residents had moved to big cities in Romania and elsewhere in Europe in search of work. The town's 8,400 population now included only about 1,400 children under eighteen – a proportion lower even than in some ageing Western European countries such as the UK. The high school was vocationally focused and trained people up for jobs such as seamstresses and agricultural machinery operators and engineers. Older people mostly had meagre pensions, leaving the community heavily dependent on remittances from family members who had jobs elsewhere.

Gheorghe said life had improved in Cojasca in the past few years, partly thanks to EU-funded projects. Almost all its roads were now paved, it had piped water, and it was now on the electrical grid – which was more than could be said for some Romanian villages. It had good communications networks and a hospital. He had plans for an old people's home, waste recycling, LED lighting for streets and an ambulance service.

But he said the area also urgently needed an economic stimulus. He said the local authorities would gladly give land and administrative help to companies that wanted to come. 'My biggest concern for the community is the lack of investors,' he said. 'We really hope we can find an investor to build a factory here so the youngsters can find steady jobs and not leave the village any more.'

He added: 'It's not only my place as a mayor to be concerned about it. The government should also be really concerned about it because it's a national-level phenomenon.'

Gheorghe said his job had become much easier now the Social Democrats he represented were in power nationally. When the opposition was in charge, he'd sometimes found it hard to get money. Since his party had returned to office, it was far simpler for him to access both official cash and technical support. 'I just get the answer a lot quicker and the money a lot easier,' he said.

He said his administration still sometimes struggled to find the necessary matched funding to access EU money. This is a chronic problem for Romania and some other recipients of development money from Brussels. It means they consistently underspend their allocations. 'We had a lot of aid. The problem is we as a country are not able to get what's offered to us,' he said, adding that the process was too bureaucratic. 'And that's not the EU's fault – it's our fault.'

I'd been told that social benefits had become an important tool in Romanian elections. Since they were distributed at a local level, parties could give them out or withhold them in exchange for votes. Gheorghe denied any such conditionality. 'My experience is that people who receive social benefits don't vote for me. I have never asked them and I'm not going to,' he said. 'Eight years ago, I had 550 families that received local benefits. If I could have depended on the votes of these people, I wouldn't have needed to campaign.'

I was interested to see he had an EU flag on display in his office, given the increasing tensions between his party and Brussels. I asked him why. He seemed puzzled by the question. 'I am a European citizen. What should I do – put up the Hungarian flag?' he said. 'I do believe myself to be a European citizen. I do believe I am so and I am proud to show it.'

His logic was the flip side of Brexit. He believed that 'a strong and united Europe is necessary.' 'Maybe there are countries that are in even worse shape than us,' he said. 'Otherwise, I am very content that as a Romanian citizen I can go and work anywhere. I can go to the doctor anywhere if I don't trust the medicine here. And also because the borders are no longer there.'

I asked about the EU's concerns about corruption in Romania. In November 2018, the European Commission would issue a stinging report alleging that Bucharest was backsliding in its anti-corruption efforts. Gheorghe sidestepped my question and added a rider that showed the limits of Brussels' writ. 'It's not my place to say something about it,' he said. 'As a simple citizen, I would say it's not correct on their part to get into our affairs. Because we are a sovereign state.'

Gheorghe had been mayor for eighteen years and a local government administrator for thirty-five. He used to be a tax officer and a cashier. He must have seen corruption, I said. But he was again coy. 'You know what you see on TV, you know what you see in the media,' he said insouciantly. 'I never had any specific situations regarding corruption – only what I saw on the news.'

As I left and we shook hands, he asked if he could ask me a question. Sure, I said. He grinned mischievously. 'Why did Britain vote to leave?' he asked.

Outside the mayor's office, I chatted to some of the young men milling about outside the vendor's kiosk, empty cans littered around them. I asked them about local politics. One man dressed in a black leather jacket told me: 'We have been voting for the Social Democrats in this community for a long time. Because the Social Democrats did more for us than other parties.'

No sooner had he spoken than an old man who had been wheeling his bike away rounded on us with sudden anger. 'They lied more to the people,' he said of the Social Democrats. 'It's like that in all of the country. I am so fed up with this – Iliescu, Dragnea, Ponta,' he continued, reeling off some of the party's leading personalities.

Ion Iliescu, a former communist official who headed Romania's interim government after Ceauşescu fell, was later elected president three times. In 2018, the country's general prosecutor indicted Iliescu for alleged crimes against humanity over the events of the

1989 revolution and its bloody aftermath, during which more than a thousand people died. Iliescu has branded the pursuit of him 'a farce, insulting the sacrifice and memory of those who fought for freedom and democracy'.[8]

Victor Ponta was a former prime minister who was indicted by Kövesi's anti-corruption directorate in September 2015 over allegations including forgery and money laundering. He denied wrongdoing but quit office in November of that year after a fire at a Bucharest nightclub killed sixty people and triggered protests calling for his resignation. Ponta was acquitted of the criminal charges in May 2018 and joined a new political party.

The man on the bike was into his stride now. He gave his name as George and his age as fifty-four – although he looked older. 'What do we have in terms of employers and jobs? The only thing that they are trying to do is get more money for themselves. The only thing they do is make promises without honour.'

George said he was a tractor driver but hadn't worked for five years. It was a reminder that it was not only Western Europe that could be a cruel place for manual workers, especially once they hit middle age: 'Everybody tells me I am too old to get a job! Nobody tried to help me get a job!' George fired as a parting shot, before switching his fury to the task of cycling quickly away.

Cojasca town felt hollowed out: an old person's enclave on an ageing continent. It was the middle of the working day, but the mayor said many of the younger people wouldn't be back later either as they were abroad. Quite a few worked on construction sites in Germany.

I wondered what Cojasca would look like if I returned in ten or twenty years' time. A great deal is said and written about the impact on richer EU states of migration from poorer ones, but much less is heard about the impact on the countries of origin. EU membership has offered opportunities for younger people in Romania and its neighbours to emigrate and send money home, but it has also hollowed out rural communities by tempting away some of their youngest and most energetic members. An old way of life was disappearing and it was not clear what would replace it.

As I was leaving Cojasca, I stopped to talk to a middle-aged woman who was walking slowly down the main road. Maria Constantin wore a dark headscarf, along with a white fleece and a patterned green lower body wrap. I noticed her blue Croc-style shoes had a rather fetching furry lining.

'I am with the three roses,' declared Constantin, referring to the Social Democrats' party symbol, when I asked her about politics. 'I always think the roses are good for this country.'

She praised the party for raising pensions and holding down the cost of living. She and her husband lived on his pension of 700 lei (£130) a month. He'd been a dustman, while she was a housewife. Her two sons were day labourers.

I asked if she was worried about the corruption allegations against some senior Social Democrat figures. 'I saw they are fighting a lot,' she said. 'I am not very attentive to that, I have to say. I am just a simple woman.'

It always dismayed me to hear people doing themselves down, as if their opinion was not cogent or important. Constantin's position was in any case very reasonable. The myriad twists and turns of Romania's corruption cases, and the endless claims of politicisation, did make it hard to work out what was going on. The problem was not too little data but too much – or, perhaps, that no politician or anyone else presented it sufficiently accessibly. As Constantin put it: 'Even if I have information, I don't really understand what they say.'

In June 2018, Liviu Dragnea was convicted of corruption and handed a three-and-a-half-year jail sentence. The backlash did not take long. Within weeks, parliament overhauled abuse of power laws in ways that critics said would hamper efforts to tackle graft.

Days later, Laura Kövesi was toppled. The constitutional court ruled that President Klaus Iohannis did not have the power to oppose the justice minister's demand to oust her, unless the request was illegal. In July, Iohannis fired Kövesi, insisting he had to honour the court ruling. Kövesi said her downfall was the work of politicians trying to escape punishment for 'past, present and future' acts.

The European Commission said it was 'following closely and with growing concern the ongoing developments in Romania', including the changes to the criminal code, the judicial overhaul and the justice minister's putsch against Kövesi. 'We, as well as other international partners and member states, have repeatedly stressed that the fight against corruption and ensuring an independent, professional judiciary is of paramount importance,' it said. 'It is crucial for Romania now to intensify efforts and avoid backtracking on past achievements.'[9]

In February 2019, Romanian authorities set up a new prosecutor's office that critics branded a political creation designed to pursue cases without submitting to the authority of the general prosecutor. Within forty-eight hours, the new body was reviewing a criminal complaint that alleged two European commissioners had made false claims about the decline of the rule of law in the country. Brussels brushed the matter off – but it was another clear warning shot from Bucharest. In May, Liviu Dragnea began a three-and-a-half year prison sentence after the supreme court upheld his corruption conviction.

In Malta, three suspects were arrested in December 2017 and charged with Daphne Caruana Galizia's murder. They pleaded not guilty. Details of the case against them, including their alleged motivations, remained unclear in the months after. Caruana Galizia's sons have called for a public inquiry independent of Malta's police, government and politicians to provide a 'full and complete picture' of their mother's death. They said the probe should examine whether the government breached her right to life under European law.[10] The Maltese authorities said such an inquiry could prejudice the case against the three accused.

The EU's internal divisions over how its members governed themselves were deepening. As states sparred with each other, it appeared that so-called European values were neither universally shared nor, indeed, what people had fantasised they were. After years of reporting from autocratic states of various stripes around the world, I felt many people in Europe still underestimated the danger of the moment – and how far and how fast apparently stable countries could slip.

9

The Post-Napoleonic Wars

The wolf packs of Nazi submarines lay in wait as Joseph Knott prepared to join his first homeward Atlantic convoy. The teenage radio officer was returning to Britain in the late autumn of 1941 after a trip to South America to pick up vital supplies for the embattled homeland. His merchant ship the SS *Sabor* had taken on board wheat, cowhides and Fray Bentos canned meat to feed and clothe a country hemmed in by Hitler's European conquest. The voyage had already been eventful: Knott had celebrated his sixteenth birthday in Rio de Janeiro and later been caught by the tail end of a Caribbean hurricane that had forced the *Sabor* into port for repairs.

The journey home from the rendezvous point in Canada would be even more perilous. A typical British wartime convoy of dozens of vessels would typically spread out over many kilometres of ocean. But it would have only a handful of warships to escort it: the US had not yet joined the conflict, so Britain relied on its own fleet with Canadian support.

The *Sabor* and its fellow ships made their three-week voyage under constant threat of German U-boat attack. Knott was on the bridge one night when one struck. 'There was a tanker went up. She got torpedoed, and she was carrying aviation spirit,' he recalled.

'She just went up like a sheet. There was stuff coming up from her, flying all over.'

The *Sabor* was luckier and made it to port in Britain. Knott, still not old enough to buy a celebratory drink in a pub once ashore, was already on his way to earning his first two wartime medals. He went on to serve throughout the conflict on merchant vessels ferrying troops and goods across a war-racked world. At least two of the ships he served on were later sunk by U-boats. One was the *Sabor*.

Now, at the age of ninety-three, Knott was almost thirty years into retirement from his postwar career as a head teacher. He was also one of the 17.4 million people who in June 2016 had voted for Britain to leave the European Union. The two years that followed the Brexiters' victory by fifty-two percent to forty-eight percent had been turbulent and often bitter ones in the UK. The conditions of the country's planned departure from the bloc were still uncertain – and people were getting jumpy. Some Remainers had intensified their warnings that Brexit would be disastrous for Britain socially, economically and culturally.

Knott deplored what he saw as the pessimism about the country's post-Brexit future. He cited the British defeat of French emperor Napoleon Bonaparte in the early nineteenth century, invoking a narrative of two centuries of island resistance to threats from Europe. 'I suppose I have that feeling, that we can surmount odds,' the former merchant navy man said, as he segued from his wartime experiences to his views on Brexit. 'I think people in those days suffered a lot more than ever they would suffer now.'

Knott exemplified what I felt was a great under-reported story of Brexit. Even as the battle over the terms of Britain's exit from the EU grew in intensity in late 2018 and early 2019, it still felt as if the country had not processed what the vote truly meant. Many commentators – some of them well meaning – were still stuck on the idea that the referendum result was mostly a revolt of people pounded by deindustrialisation and globalisation. Yet Knott and millions of other Leave voters did not fall into this settled narrative. Their motivations were different and needed to be understood for Britain to find a way to reconcile with itself.

The task was becoming increasingly urgent. Almost three years after the MP Jo Cox was murdered by a far right extremist during the referendum campaign, the rhetoric around Brexit was becoming increasingly aggressive. In April 2019, Nigel Farage launched a new Brexit party to fight what he said had become a 'battle between the people and the politicians', after the 'establishment' had betrayed the public by failing to pull Britain out of the EU.[1]

Knott's vote was not a shout of anger from someone 'left behind' economically and in life. That portrayal of Leave had gained force as a useful propaganda tool for politicians of both left and right, allowing them to present the referendum result as a justified repudiation of 'elites'. These partisans differed greatly on what they thought a post-Brexit future should look like, but they shared an interest in making quitting the EU seem a righteous impulse.

It had parallels with the battle over narratives that had erupted stateside after Donald Trump's election victory. Many liberals as well as conservatives had more or less accepted his victory as a great cry of pain from economically devastated former industrial heartlands: what one commentator dubbed the 'Calamity Thesis'.[2] Yet this ignored crucial evidence such as Clinton's lead among voters earning less than $50,000 a year – and the pronounced advantage Trump enjoyed among white voters of all social classes.

Many British pro-Brexit voices had spent two years portraying the vote to leave as the authentic voice of some downtrodden but indomitable Briton. It made an effective counterpoint to a caricature of Remainers as the entitled middle classes who wanted to keep their perceived social inferiors in their place. But neither of those archetypes teased out anything like the whole truth. The deliberate suppression of that complexity hobbled attempts to deal with Brexit. It also made it likely that many people on both sides of the ballot would feel cheated by the process – and become angrier still.

Knott now lived in Torbay on Britain's south-west coast, in a house set back from the cliffs and fronted by a large privet hedge. He appeared at the door with military precision before I'd even rung the bell. He was reassuringly mobile and was wearing a dark blue Six Nations rugby tournament top with the pennants of the competing countries. The sextet – England, France, Ireland, Italy, Scotland and Wales – spanned four EU states.

I went upstairs to use the bathroom, via a stairway covered with the family photos of a lived life. One that caught the eye was of Knott and his wife Joan out on a sunny day in 1960 on their way to France. Joan smiled to the camera from the front seat of their red British Triumph TR3 sports car. Knott stood beside the left rear wheel, his right hand on the furled canvas hood and his left on his waist, with the easy pose of a man for whom things have turned out pretty well.

Downstairs, Knott offered me a cup of tea and we went to the kitchen together to make it. I looked out of the window and complimented him on his attractively spacious back garden. A small St George's flag flew at one end. 'It's secluded,' he said, with a twinkle of the bravado of the young man in the photo. 'You could go naked in the garden – nobody would be offended.'

He took milk from the fridge, where a couple of ragged pieces of coloured paper were coming unstuck from the door. They were old primary school achievement certificates from grandchildren who had now grown up. He considered the documents for a moment, lost in thought. 'It's just a memory, isn't it?' he said.

'Every time I look at them, I think, "They should come down."
But I can't bear to take them off.'

We went to a front room festooned with many more family
photos. One was of his ten-year-old grandson sailing a small boat
on Devon's River Teign. Another was of the graduation of a
granddaughter, a biologist who now worked at Paignton's large
zoo. Knott handed me a photo of him with other veterans at the
local D-Day celebrations a couple of months before, his wartime
medals pinned to his silver-buttoned dark blazer.

He gave me a coaster and gestured to a spot on the end of a sofa
covered with a colourful blanket. 'Take your mother's seat,' he said.
'That's where she always sits when she comes.'

I had first met Knott in very different circumstances almost
thirty-five years previously. He was a stern but distant presence as
head of my primary school in neighbouring Torquay, the biggest
town in the area of Torbay. My mother had also taught at the
school and later became the head when Knott was a school governor. She and Knott – who still called her 'Mrs Peel' – had become
friends and chatted regularly, especially once they had both retired.

My mother had piqued my interest when she told me about a
discussion she and Knott had about why he voted Brexit. He had
described it in stirring terms, citing a Winston Churchill quote: 'If
Britain must choose between Europe and the open sea, she must
always choose the open sea.' It was a quote reportedly shouted
in anger by the British wartime leader to France's General Charles
de Gaulle shortly before the D-Day landings.[3] It had become a
favourite of modern Eurosceptics, some of whom had been
accused of distorting it by taking it out of context and splicing it
with other Churchill sayings.

I lived in Torquay for about seven years, from the late 1970s to the
mid-1980s. I'd been back only rarely for odd days since, when

visiting my parents elsewhere in the county of Devon. I couldn't claim to know Torbay well; on the other hand, the formative years I spent there were part of the bedrock of my memory. I still felt a prickle of recognition at familiar landmarks and a small existential pang over those that had gone.

Torbay's history was notable for its leading role in the first golden age of tourism. The area that styles itself the English Riviera was once a favoured resort for the famous. Nineteenth-century prime ministers William Gladstone and Benjamin Disraeli holidayed there and Disraeli even bought a villa. The Grand Hotel, where the Torquay-born crime writer Agatha Christie honeymooned in 1914, still loomed over the coast road on the way to Knott's house.

Torbay had fallen on harder times in the era of mass-market foreign holidays. The inward migration from the UK was now as likely to be people coming down from points north to look for work in pleasant surroundings and a better climate. By the time I met Knott, around a third of Torbay's residents lived in areas that ranked among the twenty percent most deprived in England; it also had notably affluent enclaves. Torbay was also ageing even more than the country as a whole: it was estimated that by 2030 almost a third of people there would be sixty-five or over.

Knott lived in the town of Paignton, where the centre had a scrappy and dated feel. There was an exotic pets shop and another devoted to beads and knitting. Plans to regenerate the area had been stymied by Torbay Council's funding shortages. The rising hinterland was dotted with retirement communities and neat detached bungalows, many of them owned by older people. According to one council document from 2013, more than a quarter of Paignton's population were either 'affluent greys' or 'prudent pensioners'.[4]

Knott was born in August 1925 in Yorkshire but soon moved to Dover on the south coast. His stepfather served in the army and then the Ministry of Defence. The first of many intertwinements between Knott's life and continental Europe came when the family went to live in France for a while when he was a boy. His father was working on a project linked to the Maginot Line of fortifications and other installations vainly set up to stop a future German invasion.

On his return to England in the 1930s, Knott recalled an atmosphere of social hardship and remembered trauma from the last great conflict. 'I used to know quite a number of people who were the remnants of the '14–'18 war,' he said. 'There were a lot of them there with shell shock.'

Britain declared war on Nazi Germany in September 1939, just a month after Knott's fourteenth birthday. The teenager was 'determined' to get into the battle. 'I wanted to be there. I wanted to be a soldier or sailor, I wanted to be fighting,' he said.

Knott's parents put him down to study navigation at a navy school in Wales but he failed an eye test. He was able to switch to a sister college to study to become a radio officer instead. By May 1941 – still several months short of his sixteenth birthday – he had passed the exam and was ready to go to sea.

After his spell on the *Sabor*, he had a lucky escape. He sailed on the steam merchant ship *Dorington Court* on an unescorted voyage to India. Once he reached Asia he received fresh orders to transfer to a troop carrier. The *Dorington Court* sailed back for Britain without him. It was torpedoed en route, off the coast of Mozambique.

After the war, Knott returned to the UK to train as a teacher. Both study and career advancement were fast-tracked to help fill a postwar shortage in the profession. He went to work in the southern county of Sussex. Before he was thirty, he was the relieving head for schools in the area.

Knott then began his second spell overseas, this time for about twelve years. It would cover what are today three different EU states. It also left an enduring personal mark. Two of his daughters were born in France and one in Belgium. He and Joan gave all three French names: Francine, Martine and Delphine.

Knott worked first of all for a British service school in Cyprus, during the growing crisis between the Mediterranean island's Greek and Turkish communities. He recalled it being an edgy time: he carried a gun belt that he would have to place carefully in the bunker during golf rounds if he had to play a delicate shot. 'They shot people in the back, so even if you had a gun it didn't make any difference,' he remarked mordantly.

In Paris, he worked in an international school before moving to the heart of emergent European cooperation. He helped set up the school at NATO's Supreme Headquarters Allied Powers Europe (SHAPE), in the Belgian city of Mons. During the planning phase, he recalled travelling from Paris to Brussels once a month on a Friday and staying the night at the art nouveau Metropole Hotel, ahead of meetings with Belgian officials the following day. He showed me a picture of him standing in the background at the official signing of the documents to set up the school. He said his French used to be serviceable, if focused on education vocabulary. Now it was rusty from lack of use. '*J'ai oublié beaucoup de mots*,' he said regretfully.

Knott came back to the UK and worked briefly at a school in Romford, north-east of London. That ended in a hurry when he was ordered by education authorities to close the place down because the ceiling in the main hall started crumbling away. He and the family moved to Devon, where Joan had roots. That was where his life first crossed with mine, a schoolboy almost fifty years his junior.

Knott's wartime experiences were understandably hugely formative. They also coloured his view of Brexit now. He was a mild-mannered and agreeable man, not aggressive in his tone. So it was all the more striking when he launched into a trenchant denunciation of those who opposed Britain leaving the EU. Consciously or not, it echoed tropes being pushed by pro-Brexit newspapers about the country's enemy within.

Knott spoke of how he and other children had disparaged people in the late 1930s who had been against Britain going into the war. 'We treated those sort of people as being non-loyal, you know, they weren't part of the flag, they weren't part of the system,' he said. 'And when I come back to this business of Brexit I have some of those same kind of feelings. People like that, the appeasers if you like, you have got that in your mind and you can see these people who are doing the moaning . . . they have the same sort of attitude – or to me they do.'

I asked him to explain in more detail why he voted for Brexit. He said he was 'appalled' at the way EU justice was 'denigrating' the English legal system. 'Most of those people who went down and voted [in the referendum], when they put their cross down they didn't really know what they were voting for,' he said. 'But a lot of them did know that if they voted, that . . . our own country's laws would become superior.'

He mentioned in particular the problems Theresa May had experienced as home secretary in trying to deport Abu Qatada, the militant cleric, to his native country of Jordan. The European Court of Human Rights blocked the repatriation in 2012 on the grounds that Jordanian authorities might try Abu Qatada using evidence obtained under torture. He was eventually deported in 2013 after London made an agreement with Amman that any trial would be fair. A Jordanian court cleared Abu Qatada of terrorism charges the following year.

In a narrow sense, Knott's use of the Qatada case to criticise the EU was founded on a misunderstanding. The Strasbourg-based European Court of Human Rights is not an EU institution. It was set up to deal with alleged violations of the European Convention on Human Rights, which was signed by members of the Council of Europe in 1950 in an effort to safeguard against atrocities like those seen in the Second World War. The Council of Europe now includes all twenty-eight members of the European Union, as well as nineteen other countries, among them Turkey and Russia.

Knott's error was understandable and not something that deserved to be mocked. The alphabet soup of international courts and related treaties is complicated. Even the European Court of Human Rights' own official fact sheet has a dedicated 'not to be confused with' section. It lists the European Court of Justice (EU), the International Court of Justice (UN), the Universal Declaration of Human Rights (UN) and the Charter of Fundamental Rights (EU).

Looking at the point more broadly, I said I thought that cases like Abu Qatada's were not straightforward. The reason why the human rights court ruled against his deportation from Britain was because of the risk of torture in his home country of Jordan. It seemed legitimate that the right of states to deport people should be balanced against the rights of those they were expelling not to be tortured or killed.

Knott said he agreed. 'I would be the last person to say "that person has got to go back to France ... he's going to be guillotined,"' he said. 'I couldn't do that. That would never be for me. But it is a question of: what do you do?'

He added: 'There was a time in this country where they would just be hanged because of what they have done. But now we don't do that sort of thing.'

I was interested to hear him mention the death penalty, which was last carried out in Britain in 1964. Research on the referendum had found that backing for capital punishment was one of the best predictors of Leave support. That goes some way to giving a sense of the breadth of the Brexit vote, since pro-hanging rhetoric cut across differences in class, wealth or geography. It was something you might hear in a hard-hit northern former industrial town, or in a prosperous provincial enclave. Its wellspring was cultural, not economic – an indicator of a view of life that shaded towards the authoritarian.

It was also indicative for Brexit in another way: enthusiasm for capital punishment was principally a phenomenon of the older generation. Support for it had been falling for many years. In 2014, the British Social Attitudes survey found that fewer than half of people supported the death penalty, the first time the number had fallen below fifty percent since the question was first asked in 1986. Again, there was nuance in the generalisation of it as something favoured by the old: forty-three percent of eighteen- to twenty-four-year-olds still backed it. No one could be certain how a referendum on it held now would go.

I asked whether Knott thought the death penalty should be brought back. He paused to think. 'No. I don't agree with it,' he said. 'I don't think any human being has got the right to take the life of anyone else like that.'

He went on to reflect that he would 'willingly have stuck a knife in a German or an Italian during the war'. He used to man the Oerlikon anti-aircraft cannon on the bridge of the ships he sailed on. 'I'd fire it when we were attacked by planes and I'd fire it hoping I'd hit,' he said. 'But in cold blood, no, couldn't do it – and wouldn't want to do it. And I don't think many people would. I think the majority of people, if you said "do you want the death penalty back?", they would say "no".'

He took a similar position on prisons. He spoke with what appeared to be a certain wistfulness of the supposed deterrent effect of convicts doing hard labour 'breaking up stones' at Dartmoor Prison, north-west of Paignton. The forbidding granite-walled jail set in the bleak moorland became an emblem of Victorian penal harshness. Its modern museum displayed manacles, a straitjacket and flogging apparatus used in the old days; it looms to sinister effect as the fictional Princetown prison from which the murderer Selden escapes in the Sherlock Holmes adventure *The Hound of the Baskervilles*. The jail had changed over the years and was now a category C training prison. According to the UK Ministry of Justice website, it had 'done much in recent years to shake off its historically austere image'.[5]

I asked Knott if he thought Dartmoor and other prisons should revert to their former regimes. Again, he demurred. 'It's like living in a place for five years or six years, going away and then going back again. It's never the same place you had when you were there,' he said. 'And I think that is the same thing. If you've moved on from something you didn't want at the time, why would you suddenly want it to come back?'

But he added the rider that he would like to see 'stricter or more direct control over the prisons'. He was also concerned that too many people were being given parole too early.

Knott returned to the idea of the Napoleonic Wars as a forerunner of Brexit. The French commander loomed large in the history of Torbay: it was there that he was held on HMS *Bellerophon* in 1815 while the British authorities decided what to do with him after his defeat at the Battle of Waterloo. Napoleon was supposedly struck by the area's beauty and resemblance to the island of Elba, where he had previously been exiled. He petitioned to be allowed to claim asylum in North America, or if not, to live in Britain. His requests were denied and he was eventually transferred to HMS *Northumberland* to make the long journey into final exile, on the remote South Atlantic island of Saint Helena.

Napoleon had conquered much of Europe but not the British, Knott said. 'That little bit of water in between was enough to save us and that's it,' he said. 'We managed to survive that. And we managed to then knock him off his perch and change the whole system.'

He extended his argument to the Second World War. France 'capitulated, they gave up', he said, harshly. Until the US entered the war after Pearl Harbour in December 1941, Britain 'stood alone against everybody else', he said, reflecting a common myth in the UK. 'There were a lot of people who wanted to jack it in – some very notable people, wealthy people,' he said. 'But the ordinary working-class person didn't want that. People are saying [now], we can't manage on our own. Well, we've managed on our own before.'

I asked whether he thought the EU had any value in keeping the peace in Europe. Some other Second World War veterans had said publicly that they thought so. Franklin Medhurst, a ninety-six-year-old ex-Royal Air Force airman, had written a letter to the *Guardian* just before the referendum urging Britain to stay in a union 'formed from the wreckage of a continent'. 'That victory for the democracies has given Europe 70 years of peace and security in a widely unstable world,' he wrote. 'The "leave" chancers are campaigning to abandon this steady progress, citing values false or irrelevant, while they have no plan of what to do after jumping ship.'[6]

Knott saw the Western military alliance NATO as far more important than the EU as a stabilising force. He also noted that other countries had previously survived rifts with their partners in international organisations. He referred to how France hadn't suffered from President Charles de Gaulle's 1966 decision to pull the country out of NATO's integrated military command structure (though it always retained its political membership). 'I don't see that as being a problem at all,' he said. 'I think we as a nation can stand on our own. And I think we can manage quite well. And if we can't, there's something wrong.'

I agreed with him the country was unlikely to collapse because of Brexit. But I asked whether the historical analogy held up: managing and making sacrifices in wartime when forced to do so was one thing, but leaving the EU was a voluntary peacetime decision. Wasn't the idea of merely coping post-Brexit a rather low ambition and an implication that something was being lost?

Knott didn't see it that way. He said the relationship 'between France and England, Germany and England, Spain and England, that can be what it always was'. It had worked well before Britain joined the EU and would do so again. Britain was better off out of an organisation in which 'like anything else, the best players, the big players, the moneyed players, the top dogs, Germany and France, they are going to monopolise'.

I said that surely Britain had enormous influence on the EU, as – until recently – its second largest economy and a driving force behind big developments such as the single market. Knott insisted it was not so. He cited Prime Minister David Cameron's much-criticised efforts to secure concessions ahead of the Brexit referendum: a sign of how the former premier had erred badly in his approach. Cameron's petition to fellow EU members was meant to show strength but instead suggested weakness, as it reinforced the idea that Britain was being pushed around. As Knott put it: 'We were big – but we don't have any stoppages in any way about some of the stuff they brought in.'

I asked him to what he was referring. 'I don't know,' he said. 'Rules and regulations on what they could do and what they couldn't do.'

Did he have anything in particular in mind, I asked. 'Nothing that affected me,' he replied. 'It's the thought that they can.'

I asked if he was worried that the UK would lose influence in the world if it were outside the EU. 'Nothing really worries me badly. At ninety-three years of age I don't think I should be worried about the future too much,' he said, though he added that of course he was concerned for the futures of his children and grandchildren. I asked what his daughters thought about Brexit. He said he didn't talk politics with them.

Knott did not live extravagantly but he was comfortable in his own house and with his teacher's pension. Joan had died four years previously, but he had plenty of contact with his family. Two of his three daughters still lived in Paignton and the third was only a short drive away in Newton Abbot. Their families would often get together for Sunday lunch at his house, firing up the barbecue in the garden if the weather was good.

'I'm not disgruntled because I've had a wonderful life,' Knott said. 'And I've had a very, very lucky life, in a way. I've lived through some very bad times, wicked times, but at the same time, really, my ninety-three years have been enjoyable. And the more I think about it, the more I appreciate it.'

He viewed Brexit with a similar tranquillity. He said he did talk about it over beer and snooker at the local Conservative club, although he said he was 'not really a good Tory'. His friends there included both 'ardent Leavers' and Remainers who 'think we shouldn't do it'. 'But it doesn't really matter at the end of the day,' he said. 'Whatever happens I am sure will be for the good of mankind. So it will be all right.'

He added: 'The worst of it, Michael, is that now we have got to a stage where people have said so much about it, they are so committed, that they cannot find it in their hearts to change their mind.'

At the same time, he indicated that Brexit was not existential for him. He'd said at the beginning of our conversation simply that he was asked to vote and so he voted.

That attitude was quite common in a country where there was no overwhelming popular call for the referendum to be held. By forcing people into a binary choice that many on both sides didn't feel any overwhelming need to make, the referendum created a false sense of two blocs of monolithic and implacably opposed worldviews. It obliterated the nuance that should have been every-thing in a serious debate: the 'yes, but ...' or 'no, but ...' opinions that would have told us what people really thought. Instead, the crude formulation of the referendum had allowed politicians freedom to project their own fantasies onto the public.

Knott said he wouldn't 'lose any sleep' if there were a second plebiscite and Remain won. 'I will just feel that they have got the wrong decision and that's it,' he said.

I asked Knott whether it gave him any pause that many younger people were against Brexit. One concern was that the referendum could stoke intergenerational tensions, because support for leaving the EU was so heavily skewed towards older people. This senior generation was a stark mix. Some were squeezed by Britain's relatively stingy state retirement benefits. Others, by contrast, made up a uniquely lucky demographic cohort, sitting pretty on property, final salary occupational pensions and other investments part-funded by generous tax breaks.

'Ah ... well, I don't know,' Knott said. 'I don't know what the score is with them because I don't mix with young people. I don't see many people on the younger side. I don't know.'

Knott's was essentially a romantic view of Brexit that tapped into longstanding tropes in popular culture. He had a very particular belief, rooted in his own experiences and a certain era, about Britain's singular character and elevated place in the world. It was a perspective that appeared from opinion polls to be quite widely shared – but was also fiercely contested.

The referendum had triggered a slurry of ugly discourse. Lamentably, there were Remain voters who unleashed their prejudices over this unwanted event they could not control. Their tantrums – amplified by social media – were often the loudest contributions from those who wanted to stay in the EU. They scorned Leave voters as ignorant and racist. These huffy Remainers might have voted the same way as me in the referendum, but their rhetoric disgusted me. It also exposed a deep condescension that thrives among some people – across the political spectrum – who feel their fortune in having had educational opportunities makes them superior.

This pique also played into the hands of prominent commentators who promoted misleading tropes of Remain as the bloc vote of the entitled liberal middle class. Giles Fraser, former canon of St Paul's Cathedral and a vocal Leave supporter, styled Remain as 'all about ever new opportunities for the rich' while Brexit sought a 'reclamation of something we have lost'.[7] In other words, his worldview implied, Brexit was morally virtuous and the ideology of its opponents despicable.

But Fraser and his ilk committed the same sin of unfair generalisation. Just as it would be wrong to characterise the Leave vote only by its darkest underbelly, the same was true of the other side. Both camps were much more heterogeneous than the shrillest commentators would admit. Among other things, that created a fatal problem for the effort to present Brexit as an uprising of the masses against their elite oppressors.

None of this is to argue that the serious social problems in many Brexit-majority areas should be ignored. On the contrary, it is a scandal that they have been disregarded for so long. I would feel reconciled to leaving the EU if I thought that a consequence of it would be to narrow Britain's inequalities and give people the chance to live with greater dignity. My opposition to Brexit is because I fear the opposite will be the case.

A fundamental point often overlooked is that Brexit is predominantly a big-C Conservative phenomenon. The relentless focus – including by liberal media outlets – on Leave voters in traditional Labour strongholds in the post-industrial Midlands and north often masked this basic fact. About sixty-one percent of people who voted Conservative at the 2015 general election backed Leave, according to the pollster YouGov, against just thirty-five percent of Labour voters.[8] (Lord Ashcroft, the ex-Tory deputy chairman turned pollster, put the figures at fifty-eight percent and thirty-seven percent.) At its heart, Brexit was – as the Green MP Caroline Lucas put it – a 'project for the right, by the right'.[9]

This matters because it runs counter to the idea of the Brexit vote as a mass protest against political disenfranchisement. At the time of the referendum, the Conservative Party had already been in government for six years, ruling alone for a year. The Conservatives had a history of governing Britain for most of the twentieth century. Whatever else Conservative-supporting Leave voters were, they were not electorally emasculated: to the contrary, they mostly got their way. Even the Labour Party's own hold on power for thirteen years in the late 1990s and 2000s drew on much of the ideology of the eighteen-year Tory hegemony that preceded it.

Other polling data also torpedoed the idea that Brexit was simply the revenge of the oppressed. Perhaps the single most interesting statistical account of the referendum came from the independent National Centre for Social Research, which brands itself NatCen. It runs the highly regarded annual British Social Attitudes survey and works across fields including health, education and crime. Its analysis of the demography of Brexit is based on two surveys in May/June and September 2016 – before and after the vote. Its conclusions contain their own generalisations, but the underlying data are persuasive and illuminating.[10]

The headline point is that the main foundation of Brexit was not Britain's poorest people, but a group NatCen describes as 'affluent Eurosceptics'. Accounting for twenty-three percent of the country's population, they supported Leave by a margin of three to one. They also turned out in large numbers. They were by far the biggest single source of Leave votes, and eighty-four percent of them have a household income of more than £2,200 a month, roughly the UK average wage. Only thirteen percent of them said they were 'just about getting by or finding it difficult financially'.

The other two main pro-Brexit groups were more familiar from the standard narrative. But they were smaller – and there were interesting nuances here, too. The 'older working classes', accounting for about sixteen percent of the population, went seventy-three percent for Leave. They were retirees on average and far from rich: more than four fifths of them had a household income of less than £2,200 a month. But neither did most of them consider themselves needy, perhaps because some owned their homes and so had no housing costs: fewer than a quarter of them said they were 'just about getting by or finding it difficult financially'. People whom NatCen described as 'economically deprived, anti-immigration' did go overwhelmingly for Leave – but they were barely half as numerous in population terms as their affluent Eurosceptic fellow Brexit supporters.

NatCen's findings also complicated the received wisdom about the Remain vote. Again, the standard analysis is not wholly false: the research did conclude that 'middle-class liberals', accounting for a quarter of the population, made up the core of Remain support. But members of this group gave very similar answers to affluent Leave voters on the researchers' questions about their economic standing. So if you – rightly – consider liberal Remain voters as advantaged financially, then you have to acknowledge the same of their well-off counterparts on the Leave side. In other words, the biggest blocs behind both the Remain and Leave votes were financially reasonably comfortable – as one would expect in a rich country like the UK.

NatCen also found that younger working-class voters, many of them Labour supporters, leaned significantly to Remain. Accounting for another quarter of the population, these people were thirty-seven years old on average and opposed Brexit by sixty-one percent to thirty-nine percent. Two thirds of them had a household income of less than £2,200 a month, while more than half of them said they were struggling financially or just about getting by. The problem from a Remain point of view was that they did not make it to the polling stations: only sixty-seven percent of them voted in the referendum, compared with eighty-nine percent for the older working classes and ninety percent for affluent Eurosceptics. That yawning turnout gap was a big contributor to Remain's defeat, among the many contingencies that could have tipped the result the other way.

The NatCen research concluded, a little glibly, that the referendum was 'less a traditional left–right battle, and more about identity and values (liberalism vs authoritarianism)'. It read the vote as a 'strong sign that the so-called "culture wars" of the US have arrived in Great Britain in earnest'. Its final words seemed almost painfully utopian in the rancorous post-referendum political climate. 'It is important now to have measured debates about the nature of "Brexit", and to find an arrangement that allows as many as possible to feel a stake in the post-EU future,' it said.

Adrian Sanders once had a similar sense of idealism about how Britain might navigate its relationship with the rest of Europe. A Liberal Democrat MP and strong supporter of staying in the EU, he had voted with Eurosceptic Conservatives in 2011 in an earlier failed attempt to trigger a referendum on membership of the bloc. He had written stirringly of his reasons for backing a public vote, citing a former Liberal prime minister. 'It was Gladstone who once said that "liberalism is trust of the people tempered by prudence; conservatism is mistrust of the people tempered by fear,"' he wrote.[11]

Sanders lived in the next street to Knott. It was a small junction between Brexit and Remain, the two roads meeting where

Oaktree Motorbodies garage offered car crash repairs and resprays. The two men didn't know each other, but they occupied the same kind of houses in the same district with the same everyday environment.

The overlap didn't end there. Knott was part of the disparate voting bloc that had elected Sanders as the MP for Torbay for almost two decades, somewhat against the odds in a natural Tory seat. Now Sanders was out of office, swept away by the 2015 tide that punished his party for going into coalition with the Conservatives and, as a by-product, helped entrench the Tories in power. That in turn paved the way for the Brexit referendum, which the Liberals would almost certainly have blocked had they remained in government.

I reminded Sanders of his earlier pro-referendum comments. 'I hadn't foreseen this,' he said with a rueful laugh, contemplating the vote and everything that had followed. 'People did warn me.'

The ex-MP's twelve-year-old golden retriever, Coral, joined us and lay down under the table by my feet during the interview. She was the latest retired guide dog Sanders had taken in. The shelves of his front room were filled with vintage cameras and green bound copies of Hansard, the official parliamentary record.

Sanders was a jovial man who wore a white beard and checked shirt. He now spent much of his time working on an international inter-parliamentary campaign on diabetes. He was a Type 1 sufferer himself. He told me he had just prepared a brief on a sugar tax for a Bermudan MP. He chuckled as he told a story about Mike Huckabee, the right-wing former Republican governor of the US state of Arkansas and the father of former White House spokesperson Sarah Huckabee Sanders. Huckabee had backed various publicly funded diabetes programmes after discovering he had the Type 2 form of the disease. 'The most socialist MP you will ever meet is a conservative with a personal interest,' Adrian Sanders noted wryly.

Sanders was born in Paignton in 1959 and grew up there. He worked in the insurance industry before going into politics. In the early 1990s, he joined the office of then Liberal leader Paddy Ashdown. He reached Parliament at the 1997 election that yielded a landslide for Tony Blair's Labour Party, on a promise of national renewal after an increasingly sclerotic eighteen years of Conservative rule.

Sanders chiselled out an impressive coalition of support in what had been a Conservative seat since the 1920s, as Torbay and its previous incarnation as Torquay. He had squeaked home by just twelve votes in 1997 against Rupert Allason, a spy novelist and noted Eurosceptic. Sanders increased his lead to more than 6,700 in 2001 and held the seat at further polls in 2005 and 2010. He was untarnished by the MPs' expenses scandal of the late 2000s and had a reputation as a good constituency representative. He noted his role in helping secure local projects such as the Newton Abbot bypass and the early roll-out of broadband.

He was also no slavish follower of his party's line in its coalition with the Conservatives. He rebelled against the leadership on contentious subjects such as university tuition fees, although at other times he followed the party whip. He noted drily that his record helped scotch any chance he might have had of advancement to government office.

Sanders dated his own Europhilia to his parents' hosting of foreign language students who thronged Torbay each summer. His family then used the proceeds to go on holidays to the continent. 'We had Norwegians and Dutch and Germans and Italians' as lodgers, he recalled. 'And I love to travel. To me it's an adventure getting on the train at Newton Abbot, even going to Bristol.'

Despite his personal enthusiasm for the EU, Sanders said he wasn't surprised 'one little bit' by the Brexit vote of more than sixty-three percent in Torbay. He pointed to the area's long-standing iconoclasm. 'It's built on hills that are looking out to sea rather than back at the hinterland, so it's never really viewed itself as part of the West Country,' he said. 'It's always had a slight independence of mind about it.'

I said that to my childish eyes the city of Plymouth – about forty-five minutes' drive away – had always seemed like another country. 'It still does!' Sanders shot back.

He said the support for Brexit in Torbay was also unsurprising given that the wider Devon economy was built on tourism, farming, fishing and the military. He recalled opposition to what was then the European Common Market even when he was growing up. Torbay had a long history of right-wing conservatism: for many years the MP was the Tory Sir Frederic Bennett, whose *Guardian* obituary in 2002 described him as 'rich, truculent and litigious'.[12] He was a virulent anti-communist who wrote a pamphlet entitled 'Reds Under the Bed?' and supported avowedly anti-communist dictatorships such as General Zia-ul-Haq's in Pakistan. He also reportedly oversaw an initiative to mint gold medals to honour athletes who joined the American boycott of the 1980 Olympics in Moscow.[13]

Sanders said a vision of the EU as alien and ganging up against Britain had been allowed to take root. He said the bloc received no credit even for initiatives that he felt had helped Torbay, such as the Blue Flag clean beach certification it promoted. 'People used to come to my [MP's] surgery and complain, "why are we still members of this awful institution?"' he said. 'And I always used to pose the question: "Can you name three things that you used to do personally that you cannot do any more?" And they could never come up with one.'

He said the narrative of those angry constituents had never been properly challenged. He felt his own party bore a particular responsibility for this, given its avowedly internationalist and pro-EU positions. He said: 'Part of the problem was that the leadership of the Liberal Party and the Liberal Democrats were so enthusiastic about the [European] political project that they were never interested in selling what the purpose of the political project was.'

Sanders identified the 'forward to a better yesterday again brigade' as one of the main animators of Brexit in Torbay. He spoke of the anti-EU sentiment among retirees in the bungalows scattered among the hills. He said many were 'lower-middle-class retirees who perhaps have a chip on their shoulder that they could have done better but didn't – a sales negotiator at an estate agent, never the owner of it.' Some were former bed-and-breakfast proprietors who had sold out at the right time, just before the industry withered in the face of chain hotels. Many complained about 'political correctness' and censorship that didn't exist.

'They think they can't say something when they can,' Sanders said. 'They think they can't fly the Union Jack when of course they can fly anything they blooming well like on their flagpole. But they feel they can't.'

Voting is always driven by emotion, but what marked Brexit out was the way this impulse had leeched into supposedly empirical policymaking, too. I was reminded of an extraordinary statement in the government's Brexit White Paper. 'Whilst Parliament has remained sovereign throughout our membership of the EU, it has not always felt like that,' it read.[14]

Sanders said many retiree EU critics in Torbay felt frustrated and didn't like what they saw on the news about the way the country was changing. They were 'perhaps the victims of the global media' more than any previous generation, he added. 'They have more time on their hands and there is more news being focused at them than at any other time in their lives,' he said.

It is one of the biggest enduring contradictions in the idea of Brexit as anti-establishment insurgency that the vast majority of the most-read news outlets supported Leave. The *Sun*, the *Daily Mail* and the *Daily Telegraph* – the most popular newspapers appealing to various social classes – all campaigned for Brexit. A Reuters Institute survey of nine national newspapers during the four months of the referendum campaign suggested pro-Leave stories outnumbered anti-Leave stories by about three to two in the run-up to the vote, marking a 'dominant pro Brexit bias'.[15]

Sanders also warned that any kind of overgeneralised pen picture of Leave voters in Torbay was 'going to be wrong'. He mentioned how he'd come across a retired nurse and a coastguard officer who supported the UK Independence Party (UKIP) formerly led by Nigel Farage. 'Maybe their incomes fit that kind of [pro-Brexit] lower middle class – but their life experiences don't necessarily,' he said.

He'd also noticed that certain questionable Eurosceptic tropes had become firmly anchored in people's minds. One example was the repeated references by Leave campaigners to Britain's power as the fifth-largest economy in the world. People took that as meaning Britain was the fifth-richest country in the world in the sense of per capita income, when in fact the UK didn't even make the top twenty by one well-established measure. 'In the eyes of most people, "We are the fifth-richest country – why aren't we doing better?"' Sanders said.

He saw this as part of a damaging wider phenomenon of politicians' refusal to admit to the public the full extent of the UK's declining power in the world. It had struck him very strongly during his time as an MP. 'This is something I've noticed up close and personal: that there is a charade played in Westminster that Westminster is still the centre of the world,' he said. 'It reeks of that, whether you are walking around the House of Commons, or whether you visit the Foreign and Commonwealth Office.'

Sanders recalled the antics in the Commons tea room of a 'particular type of Tory MP who does seem to wish they'd been born in the early 1920s and they could be a Spitfire pilot'. He said it was 'sort of like Biggles' – a fictional British aviator whose adventures spanned both world wars. 'It was, "Oh, Squadron Leader, how you doing?" And they hadn't been in the services! They were play-acting at it.'

The language of conflict cropped up often over Brexit. People from both sides used it, but it was notably strong among Leavers. Some commentators described the dispute over Brexit as a 'civil war', while others urged their compatriots to show a 'Blitz spirit' should there be goods supply shortages or other hardships. It felt to me that only people with no experience of what war was like – and a complacency about what it meant – could speak of it so loosely and casually. The metaphors of bygone conflict also highlighted Britain's strong nostalgist cultural streak: in 2017 alone, cinema releases included two films about Winston Churchill and one about the 1940 Dunkirk evacuation.

The wood-panelled walls and portraits of great historical figures in the Houses of Parliament stoked Britain's delusion that it was still a great power, Sanders said. 'You could be lulled into a feeling that you are so important when all these ushers and security people were doffing their caps to you,' he said. 'I just never bought into that. But that must permeate out. It must find its way down and find its resonance with people.'

Sanders said he did not think in hindsight that he had been naive to call for a referendum on EU membership. He blamed defeat partly on Labour leader Jeremy Corbyn's tepid support for Remain – including his reluctance to appear on a platform with Cameron. Sanders also thought Remain could have won had it run a more passionate campaign, rather than focusing on 'dull and boring' items such as Cameron's EU reform package. 'Whereas the other side, it was all an emotional argument – about "we are being dictated to, let's take back control,"' he said.

He identified a similar sentimentalisation in Leave campaigners' paeans to Britain's creaking democratic infrastructure. He ticked off what he saw as the flaws in the UK system: a hereditary head of state; a second chamber of parliament that was still partly hereditary and stuffed with political appointments (as well as bishops); no written constitution; and an electoral system that grossly under-represented smaller parties like the Liberal Democrats (as well as UKIP and the Greens). Party funding was still open to 'all sorts of scams and unaccountable manoeuvres, which is wrong – and all parties are guilty of that', he added.

'So I worry that our democracy is not in a very healthy state at all,' he said. 'And the last two years sidelined any attention on our own shortcomings.'

His election defeat in 2015 clearly still hurt. He was the victim of a national swing against the Liberal Democrats. The party's decision to govern with the Conservatives drove away many of the anti-government and tactical anti-Tory voters he had relied on to buttress his core natural Liberal supporters. I asked him if the loss felt personal. 'Oh, it does,' he said. 'It shouldn't, but it does. And I think the thing that hurts the most is the people who abandoned me in 2015 who had previously voted for me are the ones who are now most angry about there being a Tory MP.'

Another dimension of his defeat dismayed him. Torbay was one of more than a dozen marginal constituencies investigated by police over possible breaches of electoral funding laws by the Conservatives during the 2015 campaign. In March 2017, the Electoral Commission watchdog fined the Tories £70,000 for failing to declare or misclassifying funding. Two months later, the Crown Prosecution Service announced that no criminal charges would be brought.

Kevin Foster, the Conservative who beat Sanders in Torbay in 2015, welcomed the prosecutor's decision. He said that clarification needed to be provided as to how police probes into campaign finance related to the work of the Electoral Commission. He also took a dig at his beaten Liberal rival, saying that the 'weight ...

given to the statements of defeated general election candidates also needs to be taken into consideration'.[16]

Sanders – along with some other observers – had said the investigation highlighted the need for tougher rules on election funding. At the heart of the affair was the question of whether the Conservatives were avoiding strict limits on local campaign spending by attributing costs under the far more generous national financing rules. Police examined spending ranging from hotel rooms for activists to visits by the Tory 'Battle Bus' that toured marginal constituencies. Sanders also said there should be tighter rules to stop political parties classing targeted mailshots tailored to local constituencies as national spending. 'The law needs changing,' Sanders said. 'I was somewhat disillusioned by everything as a result of that experience.'

Sanders had wider fears for Britain in the aftermath of Brexit. He pointed to the influence of Conservative hard-liners who appeared to want the rupture to be as big as possible. He compared them to drivers of a car barrelling towards a famous Torbay promontory near where Napoleon was once held at bay.

'They are on a vehicle that's going hell-bent towards Berry Head – and no one is willing to change gear, never mind apply the brake,' he said.

I wasn't surprised by the victory for Brexit as I watched it from ten thousand kilometres away in Bangkok. Perhaps it was easier to see from a distance. I'd always thought a Leave vote quite likely, both because of the nature of Britain and because of the way anti-EU coverage had dominated in the media for the thirty years I had been following politics. I did not see how three decades of negativity could be reversed in a three-month referendum campaign, especially one as lacklustre as Remain had run.

European expatriates I spoke to in South-East Asia in the weeks before the referendum were stunned when I told them I thought there was a ninety percent chance of a Leave vote. On polling day, sterling surged to its highest level for months against the Thai baht. It seemed to me that the markets hadn't priced in the chances of Brexit. At the time, I was paid in sterling and transferred money to Thailand when the exchange rate was favourable. I wired the latest tranche to Thailand on referendum day. Sure enough, less than twenty-four hours later, the pound had plunged about fifteen percent against the baht. The effectiveness of my small personal financial protective measure made me think how much those with serious money to invest in Brexit chaos would be making.[17] Some hedge funds reaped big windfalls after betting on a Leave vote.[18]

My first appointment the morning after the referendum, just an hour or two after the result had been confirmed in the UK, was with a Singapore property developer in Bangkok. He asked how I felt about the result. I told him I saw it as a big mistake. I asked what he thought. 'This may surprise you to hear, but I'm for it,' he said.

He explained that sterling's plunge would make his Singapore dollars go further towards school and university fees for his three children studying in the UK. It would also make it cheaper for him and his wife to buy a property they wanted in London's West End. It seemed a telling early sign that the biggest winners of Brexit might not be those whom its promoters had promised would benefit.

The referendum result also seemed entirely consistent with what surveys showed about people's perceptions and misperceptions about the EU, British society and the UK's place in the world. In a poll ahead of the referendum, Ipsos MORI found that Britons – and especially Leave voters – greatly overestimated how many people born elsewhere in the EU were in Britain. Brexit supporters put the figure at twenty percent of the population, instead of the official number of five percent. Almost four in ten people thought the number of children in EU countries receiving child benefit from the UK was at least forty times the actual level. Most people also called the referendum result wrong: only twenty-three percent predicted Brexit.[19]

Other Ipsos MORI polls in its 'Perils of Perception' series suggested people's impressions about the make-up of the society they lived in were often wildly wrong. They were almost always in line with moral panics stoked by conservative media – and they played into the mantra of a country out of control. In 2013, the pollster found that people estimated that £24 of every £100 of benefit money was claimed fraudulently – more than thirty times more than the official estimate of 70 pence. Almost a third of people thought the government spent more on the Jobseeker's Allowance than pensions, when in fact the spending on pensions is fifteen times greater. People also estimated that the UK population was twenty-four percent Muslim and thirty-four percent Christian, when in fact the figures were five percent and fifty-nine percent, respectively, in England and Wales.[20]

On an even more visceral level, the Leave campaign tapped effectively into entrenched beliefs and unacknowledged anxieties about Britain's international standing. Most countries struggle to deal with decline and shameful aspects of their past and Britain has much more to reckon with than most. Like many UK schoolchildren, I never studied the British Empire and its legacy in any detail. This attitude of organised forgetting was summed up by the Labour Chancellor and future prime minister Gordon Brown in 2005. He declared on a visit to four African countries that the 'days of Britain having to apologise for its colonial history are over'.[21]

His view seemed to echo that of a majority of the public. A 2014 YouGov poll found that fifty-nine percent of people said the British Empire was more something to be proud of than ashamed of, against just nineteen percent who took the opposite view. Almost half of respondents thought ex-British colonies were better off for having been part of the empire, against just fifteen percent who disagreed. A third of people said they would like it if Britain still had an empire.[22]

It was a view of history that surfaced in rhetoric about the UK 'liberating itself' or 'throwing off the yoke of Brussels'. It was part of a linguistic style that cast the UK in a strange and contradictory position, at once a dominant world power yet also dominated by its neighbours. It seemed to me offensive for a former imperial oppressor such as Britain to apply the language of freedom struggle to the process of leaving an international organisation that it had joined voluntarily – and in which it had wielded great influence as one of the largest member states. It also played to the curious sense of victimhood that some leading Brexit campaigners seemed to nurse and cultivate even as they crowed about their win.

Brexit and its aftermath appeared to me at times to have a poetic quality. The process was exposing self-delusions to which Britain had obdurately clung. As Laurie Penny wrote in the *New Statesman*: 'Britain has no idea what it is because it hasn't a clue what it was, because it chooses not to remember.'[23]

I hope I was never starry-eyed about the EU and its failings. Once I arrived in Brussels in 2017, I found not only many perceptive and diligent officials, but also vested interests, indulgence and waste, and a streak of self-righteousness. It was also, at the levels of both the institutions and the press corps, startlingly white (myself included). The EU was racked by existential disputes over questions ranging from the fate of the euro to the management of migration – as well as tensions over the dominance of influential western European country agendas, amid the bitter fallout from Greece's financial crisis. The almost cultish early enthusiasm for France's President Emmanuel Macron as a saviour of centrist Europhile politics always struck me as a keen mark of desperation.

There were mixed emotions about Brexit in Brussels. These included genuine regret from countries that had made common cause with Britain over the years. Late in 2017, I chatted about Brexit with an EU official from an Eastern European state with generally good relations with London. I spoke of the possibility that the obstinate British approach to the exit negotiations would lead the country into deeper trouble. 'Maybe you need to go off the cliff edge,' he shot back. 'That's the only way to get change. It might take five, ten years, and need two or three governments. Then you can decide on what kind of country you want to be.'

My mum drove me from Joseph Knott's house, along the coast road arc of Torbay, whose slipways had once despatched boats to Utah beach in Normandy on D-Day. We passed Torre Abbey Sands, where I had as a boy foolishly buried my favourite Matchbox toy cars and lost them to the advancing tide. On the other side of the road, the August bank holiday fairground obscured the Abbey ruins and the meadows where we used to play French cricket and crazy golf. It always seemed to be summer in my Torquay memories.

I passed the library, a formative place where I went to choose my four books each Saturday. I remembered an epic library reading scheme on which you had to amass a thousand points from works of fiction colour-coded according to their difficulty. It was a task of many months, a veritable football season of reading.

I walked down to Union Street, gateway to the harbour and seafront. It seemed much shorter to my adult eyes. It also felt less thriving: Torquay's town centre, like so many others, has been gradually hollowed out by chains and out-of-town retail. This had been a place of childish excitement, where on special days you would turn right and climb the steps to the Odeon cinema – with maybe a takeaway afterwards from Piggy's burger bar on the

harbour if you were lucky. Now I saw a Cash Generator second-
hand shop, a British Heart Foundation outlet and an American
Delights candy store.

I had tried to find a good independent tearoom or coffee shop
online but there were none that seemed to be open so late in the
afternoon. So, with a slight feeling of regret, I chose a branch of
Costa Coffee as the rendezvous point with my next three
Brexiteers.

I had contacted the trio via a request I made through a local
charity for older people. The most senior of the three was Joyce
Mitchell, a white-haired and warm eighty-four-year-old –
or 'twenty-one for the fourth time', as she put it. Mitchell had
lived in Australia for many years, where she'd worked as a dress-
maker. Her husband was a builder. She had known personal tragedy and she had also been caught in the vagaries of the welfare
state. She produced documents to show me how she had struggled
to establish her pension rights in Australia despite her long
residence there.

Opposite Mitchell was Carol Kendall, a youthful sixty-three-
year-old who was Devon born and bred. Kendall, a colourful presence in her flowing skirt and long loose orange cardigan, had
married and divorced young. She'd had health problems since,
restricting her ability to work. She now devoted much of her time
to work for voluntary organisations.

They were joined by Frank Wye, seventy-seven and weathered,
though still looking fit. He was born in Ireland and had lived for a
long time in the English Midlands. He was a retired telecommu-
nications engineer whose no-nonsense manner was leavened by a
hint of mischief.

Wye had travelled widely for his work, including to China, and
had lived for several years in Moscow. He claimed the EU was
'more bureaucratic than any communist state you'll ever come
across'.

He further accused the EU of throwing around money 'like it goes out of fashion'. He cited as particularly wasteful the practice of holding some sessions of the European Parliament in Strasbourg (he might also have mentioned the ministerial meetings in Luxembourg three times a year). He highlighted that the bloc 'spent £40 million on translators last year' – an apparent reference to the revenues reported by the EU's shared translation centre, which were forecast to be €48.5 million in 2018. He quoted Churchill's dictum – 'I like Churchill quotes, I have to say' – that governments 'have nothing to give but what they have first taken away'.[24]

Kendall said she voted Brexit 'along the same lines'. She mentioned her worries about the (distant) prospect of a European army, the spread of the euro, and 'the bureaucracy, all the rules and regulations'. Britain was more naturally independent, an island that had 'done a great deal in the past, good and bad'.

'How can we be ruled from Brussels?' she asked. 'How can one rule fit all European countries and make sense?'

Mitchell was worried the UK was short of money to fund services such as healthcare and social welfare. She referred disparagingly to the – much misrepresented – EU regulations on banana quality and shape, a favoured target of Brexit campaigners such as Boris Johnson. She said the UK had thought it was joining a trade organisation, not a political project.

'So we were coerced into joining under false pretences in the first place,' she said. 'So having said that, I can't see that we can undo what's been done – except by saying we won't belong any more so we have to come out.'

I said that public spending was surely mostly to do with national government policies, not the EU. Wye agreed but argued that a UK administration could be voted out if they were 'not spending it on the things that you and I want'. He added that he had started watching RT, the Russian government-funded channel, for an alternative political view, even though he regarded it as 'complete rubbish'. He had voted UKIP in the past to 'frighten the life' out of Britain's two main parties. Kendall chipped in that she had also voted UKIP to 'kick arse'.

'Our system isn't the best system in the world but it's still better than the EU,' Wye said. 'Maybe proportional representation is the answer.'

For all the trio's shared support for Brexit, the differences between them were as noticeable as the common ground. Mitchell launched into a ringing liberal defence of immigration. She described it as the 'primary instinct of self-preservation'. Wye – who had, like her, once lived outside the UK – objected. 'Yes, but you can't have the whole of Africa coming to Europe,' he said. 'There have to be limits. Yes, of course you have to help people. But you can't allow everybody to come in.'

Mitchell said there shouldn't be any laws on immigration. 'We should be free to come and go as we want. It's freedom of movement. It's a human right,' she said.

I said that I thought all of us sat at the table and many other people, Leave or Remain, wanted similar things for our country: decent healthcare, pensions, housing, rights for workers and so on. I asked my coffee companions if they thought there was a danger that the Leave vote had empowered people who had the opposite aim – to slash public spending and regulations that protected citizens. The EU had its own vices, but I was worried about the consequences of leaving, especially in the chaotic manner Britain was doing. In particular I feared it would be a Trojan Horse for the kind of anti-statists who wanted to destroy aspects of public life valued by many Leave and Remain voters.

'Possibly. Possibly, yeah yeah,' Wye said. 'There is a risk, but then life is about having risks,' he said. 'All my life I've volunteered to do things that people have told me are crazy. You have got to take a risk to try to resolve something.'

Kendall said she hoped that in fifty years all the arguments over Brexit would be viewed as a 'hiccup' or a 'ripple in time'. She said she was not naive: she had not believed the notorious suggestion on the side of the Leave campaign bus that Britain paid £350 million a week into the EU and could spend the money on the National Health Service instead. The claim had still resonated with her, though. 'It was the amount of money we were putting in [the EU] that was the shocker for me,' she said, 'whether it was that amount of money or not.'

I asked whether they thought society had changed for the better or worse since they were younger. Their assessment was overwhelmingly negative. The only positive point they mentioned was that Kendall thought housing quality had generally improved, though even here she added the caveat of the problems faced by many private renters.

Mitchell said there were 'more cases of poverty, homelessness, sickness, illness', while social services were 'just disappearing'. Kendall spoke of a loss of community in the much expanded village where she had grown up, adding that her son – an online journalist – had to move away because he 'couldn't get a job down here'. Wye said he would 'hate to be a young boy these days', with the pressures created by social media. He lamented the number of children on antidepressants now, saying that nobody he knew when he was growing up was depressed. 'So I think for youngsters the world is a bloody sight worse than it ever was,' he said.

I listened to what they said with mixed feelings. Everything they mentioned was valid to some degree, showed a social concern – and, often, a regard for the younger generation. But it also seemed to discount ways in which the world had got better, particularly in areas such as public health, opportunities for women and racial discrimination. It surely also underplayed the scale of social problems, many of them hidden or ignored, when they were growing up. We saw our troubles more clearly now in part because we understood, investigated and publicised them more.

Mitchell did note that poverty had curtailed her education. She won a scholarship to a local grammar school but left at fourteen because her parents were poor and couldn't afford uniforms 'to allow me to fit into that level of society'.

'I always say that they taught me how to think but they didn't teach me what to think because I wasn't there long enough,' she said of her schooldays. 'So since then I have been self-educated in the University of Life.'

It was coming up to closing time at Costa and we were the only customers left. Holidaymakers were drifting up from the harbour area past the shopfront. I asked Kendall, Mitchell and Wye to tell me in one sentence what they thought the meaning of Brexit was.

'Independence, self-determination', said Wye.

'Right now, confusion', said Kendall. 'Right now, total confusion – lack of direction and just mess.'

Mitchell said: 'I think it promised democracy but it didn't deliver.'

Wye had the last word. 'Can I give you a quote from Churchill on democracy?' he asked. 'If you want to know what's wrong with democracy, talk to the average voter for five minutes.'

It is an oft-cited line. But winstonchurchill.org, a website overseen by the International Churchill Society, listed it among 'Red Herrings: Famous Words Churchill Never Said'. The site noted: 'Though he sometimes despaired of democracy's slowness to act for its preservation, Churchill had a more positive attitude towards the average voter.'[25]

Brexit had many fathers and mothers. The idea that it could be presented as a coherent statement, or that its supporters formed a well-defined group, flew in the face of all the evidence. It was a switch people pressed, for widely differing reasons. It was a moment of entropy, not order.

All this nuance had been crushed by a binary narrative that set against each other people who in other respects had much in common. I believe most voters on both sides valued many of the things that make life in Britain decent, including a social solidarity expressed through enterprises such as universal healthcare, good education and attractive shared public spaces. The hard-right state destroyers – and their leftist mirror images preaching revolution from positions of personal comfort – had always been minorities. Jacob Rees-Mogg had long cut a self-consciously idiosyncratic figure, his socially illiberal views at odds with much of modern Britain. Yet the referendum catapulted him to the status of power broker. The rule of the plebiscite had the paradoxical – though predictable – effect of empowering the marginal and the extreme.

Another contradiction was in my view even more destructive for British society. Delivering the referendum mandate required British politicians to routinely dissemble and go against what they believed. MPs voted by a large majority to trigger the Article 50 EU withdrawal process without a plan, even though a large majority of them thought Brexit a bad idea in the first place. Both Theresa May's Conservative government and Jeremy Corbyn's Labour opposition consistently played down the negative effects of Brexit and the choices to be made. The free movement of people was portrayed as a one-way street into Britain, rather than a reciprocal right whose conditions London could have made tougher – but chose not to.

Ignoring the referendum result would clearly have been wrong and damaging to the credibility of the political system. But so was the failure to be honest with people about the consequences of Brexit. The official suppression of problems inherent in leaving the EU became its own type of condescension. It cast the British people as infantile, to be protected from reality's full glare. Worst of all, it risked destroying the integrity of the political system.

Before I left Torquay, I took a short drive around the town, a little nostalgia tour of my childhood self. I saw my old school – once Joseph Knott's, and my mother's – still perched with crab-like compactness on a raised corner of two streets. I was pleased to see the shop across the road, where I used to buy distinctly un-nutritious Wham Bar sweets with my pocket money, was still a newsagent.

The house where I had lived seemed to be under renovation, its side covered in scaffolding. A gravel track nearby, where years ago I learned to ride a bike, was overgrown with weeds. The lime trees that had always loomed large seemed even thicker than I remembered, dominating the pavement as vegetation did in Bangkok. Down the road, where my school friend Jason had lived, a large seagull took flight over a garden where we had once battled with sticks in homage to *Star Wars* and the cult TV series *Monkey*.

I resented the way some Leave advocates portrayed those who wanted to stay in the EU as somehow less rooted, less British or less interested in making its society fairer. It was precisely because I cared about the country and its people – my country and my people – that I saw Brexit as so dangerous. My greatest fear was that ultimately the only ones who would be happy with and served by Brexit would be the worst of us. These were the true bigots, the disaster capitalists and the politicians who saw the referendum as their chance to gamble the nation's future in the service of ideology and ambition. I felt anger and a sense of growing foreboding.

I could see how being in or out of the EU might seem a small thing to someone like Joseph Knott, who had once faced the prospect of imminent death in the Atlantic's freezing waters. I envied him the equanimity with which he seemed able to view Brexit and its potential impact from the twilight of his life. I wished I shared his confidence in the direction of a country that, to me, seemed increasingly lost and under the control of people who were not serving its interests well.

'When they say there will be those terrible disasters, I don't believe they will occur,' Knott tried to reassure me. 'There will be bumps, there will be troubles but we will find a way over the top of them. Because that is the natural way of us.'

Epilogue: Banish the Chill

The events I have witnessed on several continents over the past ten years have often been unexpected, sometimes wild and occasionally historic. It has all added up to a crash course in the world of tall tales.

Some of what I saw exposed received wisdom as highly misleading, or simply false. When people spoke of an 'Arab world exceptionalism' that meant people in the region tolerated or even welcomed dictatorship, I found it strange even without having lived in the Middle East. After all, people of other regions, from Latin America to Africa to Europe, had rebelled against tyranny. It turned out Arab states were not such outliers after all.

When I moved to Thailand, I read and heard about how the monarchy was universally loved. Again, it sounded odd: I thought there must be something coercive going on beneath any supposedly unanimous belief. I had the same natural scepticism when it came to the acclaim for Aung San Suu Kyi in Myanmar: surely this person, whatever her qualities, could not be as saintly as she was perceived to be.

Back in Europe, I wondered why there was such surprise at the rise of demagogues who stoked hostility to the other. Their rhetoric seemed continuous with the violent skein that runs through the modern history of the continent, particularly when economic hardships increased people's susceptibility to such messages. Europe was, in one sense, just reverting to type.

These observations were hardly profound in themselves. Each individually would seem commonplace to the many people who knew the particular terrains better than I did. What I had was the opportunity to compare between countries and join various dots of deception. I'd had the chance to take a global view of the exploitation, authoritarianism and social control that keep people in check. I also saw how those who fought these pressures daily and placed themselves in harm's way deserved maximum gratitude and respect.

So much of our understanding of life depends on an awareness of the forces at work on ourselves, our countries and our planet. This is a personal account of what I see as some of the many myths that govern us. We have to keep talking to each other and inter-rogating what we are told. If we don't, one day the fabulists will rule us all.

On All Saints' Day 2018, I went to visit the Belgian church where the seven Congolese people who died in King Leopold's human zoo are buried. It is in the village of Tervuren, not far from the Africa museum's grounds. The remains were moved there from the countryside after the Second World War, Guido Gryseels, the museum's director, told me, after complaints that they deserved a more prominent and respectful resting place. Contemporary activists have campaigned for a memorial to the deceased acknowl-edging them as 'victims of a colonialist crime'.[1]

The graves lay by themselves in the lee of the church's exterior wall, underneath a stained-glass window and next to a paved driveway where a couple of cars were parked. A service had just finished and people were leaving the building. In the village square just beyond, a holiday fairground blared out the cancan and the *Star Wars* theme music.

The graves themselves were simple, fashioned from abutting pieces of grey stone. The faded inscriptions showed a single star – which features on both the colonial and modern Congolese flags – and a sheaf of long leaves like those from a banana plant. They also gave the names of those buried along with minimal details, such as their places of origin or the fact that they had been soldiers.

A small plaque fixed to the church wall behind the graves described how hundreds of Congolese people had been put on display for Leopold's 1897 exhibition nearby. It explained how seven – named as Ekia, Gemba, Kitukwa, Mpeia, Zao, Samba and Mibange – 'didn't survive the chilly summer' and were now buried here. Not all the spellings tallied with those on the graves.

The use of the word 'chilly' – *kille* in Flemish – also jarred with me. It felt to me as if it struck a self-exculpatory note. If only it had been warmer, the sign appeared to be saying, perhaps these people would have lived. On some level, it seemed to be suggesting, their deaths were more the result of bad luck than bad faith.

The inscription writers were not the only people struggling to tell the full brutal truth. A few weeks later, the Africa museum finally reopened, five years after shutting its doors. Not everyone was impressed, with some visitors finding that the style and language of the presentation still glossed over the magnitude of the Congo murder and looting. Some exhibits that cast a positive light on the actions of King Leopold II and Belgium survived.

Gryseels told me before the opening that the museum had been unable to move some artefacts because they were covered by the building's protected status. His answer was to commission works from African artists to respond to the claims of imperial benefi-cence. Two versions of reality would be displayed side by side. It would be left to viewers to make the final judgement.

It was a messy and incomplete reckoning. The rejection of long- and deeply held illusions usually is.

Gryseels acknowledged that the Africa museum had for much of its history been there 'to service colonial activities; we were there for propaganda activities'. Reconciling with that had been the most 'difficult part' of the long renovation, he said. 'The debate about the colonial past has been in full swing in many European countries,' he noted, pointing to moves by French president Emmanuel Macron to return thrones and statues plundered from Benin in West Africa.[2]

When I asked about the graves at the Tervuren church, Gryseels was keen to show he was thinking about them, too. He said he had requested that they be better maintained. He had also enquired as to whether the inscriptions could be made clearer, but had been told this was difficult. The names were sculpted into the stone itself, so alterations were forbidden by law.

I asked whether his museum had any plans to commemorate the sites of the human zoo itself. I pointed out that there was nothing at all to hint at the dark history of this well-tended and much-visited spot. He paused for a moment, the brief silence another small gap between the world as we see it and the world as it is.[3]

'Yeah, absolutely,' he replied. 'We ought to do more about it.'

Notes

Introduction: Civilisation Story

1 'Leopold II' by Adam Hochschild, *Encyclopaedia Britannica*, https://www.britannica.com/biography/Leopold-II-king-of-Belgium (Accessed 6 March 2019)

2 'King Leopold's ghost: Belgium's Africa museum to reopen', Reuters, 1 June 2018, https://www.reuters.com/article/us-belgium-museum-africa/king-leopolds-ghost-belgiums-africa-museum-to-reopen-idUSKCN1IX53V (Accessed 6 March 2019)

3 'Hidden Tribes: A Study of America's Polarized Landscape' by Stephen Hawkins et al., More in Common, https://static1.squarespace.com/static/5a70a7c3010027736a22740f/t/5bbcea6b7817f7bf7342b718/1539107467397/hidden_tribes_report-2.pdf (Accessed 15 April 2019)

4 'Yuval Noah Harari extract: "Humans are a post-truth species"', *Guardian*, 5 August 2018, https://www.theguardian.com/culture/2018/aug/05/yuval-noah-harari-extract-fake-news-sapiens-homo-deus (Accessed 1 May 2019)

1 All Brave Men – And Women

1 'Khashoggi fiancée hits at Trump response, warns of "money" influence' by Guy Faulconbridge, Reuters, 29 October 2018, https://www.reuters.com/article/us-saudi-khashoggi-fiancee/khashoggi-fiancee-hits-at-trump-response-warns-of-money-influence-idUSKCN1N32I2 (Accessed 6 March 2019)

2 'In Extraordinary Statement, Trump Stands With Saudis Despite Khashoggi Killing' by Mark Landler, *New York Times*, 20 November 2018, https://

www.nytimes.com/2018/11/20/world/middleeast/trump-saudi-khashoggi.html (Accessed 15 April 2019)

3 'Saudi Arabia's Arab Spring, at Last' by Thomas L. Friedman, *New York Times*, 23 November 2017, https://www.nytimes.com/2017/11/23/opinion/saudi-prince-mbs-arab-spring.html (Accessed 15 April 2019)

4 'The Obama Doctrine' by Jeffrey Goldberg, *The Atlantic*, April 2016, https://www.theatlantic.com/magazine/archive/2016/04/the-obama-doctrine/471525/ (Accessed 15 April 2019)

5 'Freedom in the World 2018: Table of Country Scores', Freedom House, https://freedomhouse.org/report/freedom-world-2018-table-country-scores (Accessed 6 March 2019)

6 'Saudi blogger Raif Badawi sentence "a slow death", says wife', BBC News, 12 June 2015, https://www.bbc.com/news/av/world-middle-east-33105945/saudi-blogger-raif-badawi-sentence-a-slow-death-says-wife (Accessed 6 March 2019)

7 'Saudi Arabia: 5 Years On, Activist Still Behind Bars', Human Rights Watch, 15 April 2019, https://www.hrw.org/news/2019/04/15/saudi-arabia-5-years-activist-still-behind-bars (Accessed 1 May 2019)

8 'My Sister Is in a Saudi Prison. Will Mike Pompeo Stay Silent?' by Alia al-Hathloul, *New York Times*, 13 January 2019, https://www.nytimes.com/2019/01/13/opinion/saudi-women-rights-activist-prison-pompeo.html (Accessed 6 March 2019)

9 'Saudi Arabia: Reports of torture and sexual harassment of detained activists', Amnesty International, 20 November 2018, https://www.amnesty.org/en/latest/news/2018/11/saudi-arabia-reports-of-torture-and-sexual-harassment-of-detained-activists/ (Accessed 6 March 2019)

10 'Saudis prepare trials of detainees identified as women's rights activists', Reuters, 1 March 2019, https://www.reuters.com/article/us-saudi-women-court/saudi-arabia-prepares-trials-of-detainees-identified-as-women-activists-idUSKCN1QI5E5 (Accessed 6 March 2019)

11 'Emirati convicted for second time of insulting country and leaders' by Haneen Dajani, *The National*, 30 May 2018, https://www.thenational.ae/uae/courts/emirati-convicted-for-second-time-of-insulting-country-and-leaders-1.735523 (Accessed 15 April 2019)

12 'Half the population of Yemen at risk of famine: UN emergency relief chief', UN News, October 2018, https://news.un.org/en/story/2018/10/1023962 (Accessed 1 May 2019)

13 'Saudis Said to Use Coercion and Abuse to Seize Billions' by Ben Hubbard, David D. Kirkpatrick, Kate Kelly and Mark Mazzetti, *New York Times*, 11 March 2018, https://www.nytimes.com/2018/03/11/world/middleeast/

saudi-arabia-corruption-mohammed-bin-salman.html (Accessed 6 March 2019)

14 'Prince Alwaleed "likely to split" $13bn Kingdom Holding Company' by Simeon Kerr, *Financial Times*, 20 March 2018, https://www.ft.com/content/74320eb6-2c01-11e8-9b4b-bc4b9f08f381 (Accessed 23 April 2019)

15 'U.S. Ambassador Hosts Reception at Khalifa Port Onboard USS Rushmore', US Navy, 2 February 2013, https://www.navy.mil/submit/display.asp?story_id=71825 (Accessed 1 May 2019)

16 'In conversation... US top priority is business' by Allan Jacob and Amanda Fisher, *Khaleej Times*, 31 January 2013, https://www.khaleejtimes.com/article/20130131/ARTICLE/301319876/1036 (Accessed 15 April 2019)

17 'What price football and books when an innocent man is jailed in the UAE?' by David Olusoga, *Guardian*, 25 November 2018, https://www.theguardian.com/commentisfree/2018/nov/25/what-price-football-and-books-when-an-innocent-man-is-jailed-in-uae (Accessed 6 March 2019)

18 'Ali on target as Qatar stun Japan to win first Asian Cup' by Nick Mulvenney, Reuters, 1 February 2019, https://uk.reuters.com/article/uk-soccer-asiancup-final/ali-on-target-as-qatar-stun-japan-to-win-first-asian-cup-idUKKCN1PQ582 (Accessed 6 March 2019)

19 'On Relations between Rulers and Citizens: The Need for a New Social/Political Contract in the GCC States', by Dr Abdulaziz Sager, Gulf Research Centre, February 2013, http://newsletter.greengulf.net/mwsubscribe/index.php?what=showarchive&nId=5858 (Accessed 10 June 2019)

20 'Haji Hassanal Bolkiah Mu'izzaddin Waddaulah', *Encyclopaedia Britannica*, https://www.britannica.com/biography/Haji-Hassanal-Bolkiah-Muizzaddin-Waddaulah (Accessed 6 March 2019)

21 'Brunei GDP per capita, PPP, 1990-2017', World Bank, https://data.worldbank.org/indicator/NY.GDP.PCAP.PP.CD?locations=BN&most_recent_value_desc=true (Accessed 10 June 2019)

22 'Human Development Reports', United Nations Development Programme, http://hdr.undp.org/en/2018-update (Accessed 1 May 2019)

23 Judgment of the Lords of the Judicial Committee of the Privy Council, 8 November 2007, https://www.privy-council.org.uk/files/other/Bolkiah.Scott.rtf (Accessed 11 March 2019)

24 'Profligate prince's property expected to fetch £30m' by Alex Spillius, *Telegraph*, 11 August 2001, https://www.telegraph.co.uk/news/worldnews/1337090/Profligate-princes-property-expected-to-fetch-30m.html (Accessed 11 March 2019); 'Prince Jefri's shame goes under the hammer' by Ignatius Stephen and Alex Spillius, *Telegraph*, 12 August 2001, https://www.

telegraph.co.uk/news/worldnews/1337212/Prince-Jefris-shame-goes-under-the-hammer.html (Accessed 11 March 2019)

25 Zaman v. Amedeo Holdings, Court of Chancery of Delaware, 23 May 2008, https://casetext.com/case/zaman-v-amedeo-holdings#c05fea00-64c4-462a-93ec-566de1eeeaf1-fn4 (Accessed 11 March 2019)

26 'The Empire Country Club', Nicklaus Design, http://www.nicklaus.com/design/empire/ (Accessed 11 March 2019)

27 'About Us', The Empire Hotel & Country Club, Brunei, http://www.theempirehotel.com/aboutus (Accessed 11 March 2019)

28 r/Brunei, Reddit, https://www.reddit.com/r/Brunei/comments/bertjb/legco/ (Accessed 1 May 2019)

29 'Brunei imposes sharia-based penal code' by Jeremy Grant, *Financial Times*, 30 April 2014, https://www.ft.com/content/b12f97d4-d043-11e3-af2b-00144feabdc0 (Accessed 23 April 2019)

30 Letter from the Mission of Brunei Darussalam to the European Union, 15 April 2019, https://www.documentcloud.org/documents/5974911-Mission-of-Brunei-letter-to-the-European-Union.html (Accessed 10 June 2019)

2 Don't Insult the Dog

1 'Thai scholar faces royal insult charge over medieval king', Reuters, 20 October 2014, https://www.reuters.com/article/us-thailand-lesemajeste/thai-scholar-faces-royal-insult-charge-over-medieval-king-idUSKCN0I90OS20141020 (Accessed 6 March 2019)

2 'King of Literature', *Bangkok Post*, 22 October 2016, https://www.bangkokpost.com/learning/learning-entertainment/1115041/king-of-literature (Accessed 6 March 2019)

3 'First Reigning King of Thailand Visits America', Great and Good Friends, https://www.greatandgoodfriends.com/our-story (Accessed 12 March 2019)

4 'Thai court jails Thaksin supporter for royal insult' by Kittipong Soonprasert, Reuters, 28 August 2009, https://www.reuters.com/article/us-thailand-lesemajeste-idUSTRE57R0M820090828 (Accessed 6 March 2019)

5 'Dutch Parliament reduces penalties for insulting king' by Christopher Schuetze, *Sydney Morning Herald*, 11 April 2018, https://www.smh.com.au/world/europe/dutch-parliament-reduces-penalties-for-insulting-king-20180411-p4z8yx.html (Accessed 6 March 2019)

6 'When LIFE Photographed Thai King Bhumibol Adulyadej in 1960' by Lily Rothman and Liz Ronk, *Time*, 13 October 2016, http://time.com/4526648/thailand-king-bhumibol-1960/ (Accessed 13 March 2019)

7 'Department of Royal Rainmaking and Agricultural Aviation', Government of Thailand, http://www.royalrain.go.th/royalrain/en/m/royal-rainmaking -technology-15 (Accessed 1 May 2019)

8 'Thailand's Hyper-Royalism: Its Past Success and Present Predicament' by Thongchai Winichakul, *Trends in Southeast Asia*, ISEAS – Yusof Ishak Institute, 2016, https://www.iseas.edu.sg/images/pdf/TRS7_16%20(002). pdf (Accessed 13 March 2019)

9 'Miracles Can Happen: Meeting His Majesty King Bhumibhol Adulyadej and Her Majesty Queen Sirikit of Thailand' by Bridget Winter, A Course in Miracles Archives, http://acim-archives.org/Media/articles/Bridget_ Winter-film_commentary.html (Accessed 13 March 2019)

10 Leaked US diplomatic cable, WikiLeaks, 25 January 2015, https://wikileaks. org/plusd/cables/10BANGKOK192_a.html (Accessed 10 June 2019)

11 'H.M. King Bhumibol Adulyadej', web page, Royal Thai Embassy, Washington, D.C., http://thaiembdc.org/h-m-king-bhumibol-adulyadej1/ (Accessed 13 March 2019)

12 'Former Thai PM Thaksin found guilty of corruption' by Ian MacKinnon, *Guardian*, 21 October 2008, https://www.theguardian.com/world/2008/ oct/21/thaksin-thailand-corruption (Accessed 6 March 2019)

13 'Content Restrictions Based on Local Law', Facebook, 2018, https:// transparency.facebook.com/content-restrictions (Accessed 6 March 2019)

14 'Thailand jails two on royal insult charge over play' by Aukkarapon Niyomyat, Reuters, 23 February 2015, https://www.reuters.com/article/us-thailand-lesemajeste-idUSKBN0LR0CN20150223 (Accessed 14 March 2019)

15 'Historian Summoned Over "Elephant Battle" Lese Majeste Charge', *Khao Sod*, 24 December 2014, http://www.khaosodenglish.com/politics/2014/ 12/24/1419424792/ (Accessed 14 March 2019)

16 'King's Death Left "Hole in Heart" of Loyalist Critic Sulak' by Pravit Rojanaphruk, *Khao Sod*, 27 October 2016, http://www.khaosodenglish. com/news/2016/10/27/kings-death-left-hole-heart-loyalist-critic-sulak/ (Accessed 14 March 2019)

17 'Enticing Patriotism: Thai National Anthems and Elites' Political Interests in the 1930s' by Chanon Adsanatham, *Kyoto Review of Southeast Asia*, 17, August 2015, https://kyotoreview.org/yav/enticing-patriotism-thai-national-anthems-and-elites-political-interests-in-the-1930s/ (Accessed 6 March 2019)

18 'Jacques de Coutre on Southeast Asia: Insights from the 16th and 17th Century' by Peter Borschberg, Academia.edu, 19 November 2013, https:// www.academia.edu/4324418/Jacques_de_Coutre_on_Southeast_Asia_ Insights_from_the_16th_and_17th_Century (Accessed 6 March 2019)

19 'Assets registered to Thai Crown Property Bureau to be held under king's name', Reuters, 16 June 2018, https://www.reuters.com/article/us-thailand -king-property/assets-registered-to-thai-crown-property-bureau-to-be-held-under-kings-name-idUSKBN1JC0EK (Accessed 14 March 2019)

20 'Thai King Now Owns Monarchy Assets. He'll Have to Pay Taxes on Them.' by Richard C. Paddock, *New York Times*, 17 June 2018, https://www.nytimes.com/2018/06/17/world/asia/thailand-king-assets.html (Accessed 14 March 2019)

21 'EU to resume political contact "at all levels" with Thailand – statement', Reuters, 11 December 2017, https://www.reuters.com/article/us-thailand -eu/eu-to-resume-political-contact-at-all-levels-with-thailand-statement-idUSKBN1E51TH (Accessed 14 March 2019)

22 'Politics of Thai zoology' by Duncan McCargo, *Nikkei Asian Review*, 29 August 2018, https://asia.nikkei.com/Editor-s-Picks/Tea-Leaves/Politics-of-Thai-zoology (Accessed 14 March 2019)

23 'Bodies of exiled Thai activists "stuffed with concrete"', Reuters, 23 January 2019, https://www.reuters.com/article/us-thailand-activists/bodies-of-exiled -thai-activists-stuffed-with-concrete-idUSKCN1PH134 (Accessed 6 March 2019)

24 'Thailand's king criticises bid by sister to run for political office' by John Reed, *Financial Times*, 8 February 2019, https://www.ft.com/content/ b7219798-2b4a-11e9-a5ab-ff8ef2b976c7 (Accessed 23 April 2019)

3 Enter the Punisher

1 'Rodrigo Duterte vows to kill 3 million drug addicts and likens himself to Hitler' by Oliver Holmes, *Guardian*, 1 October 2016, https://www.theguardian.com/world/2016/sep/30/rodrigo-duterte-vows-to-kill-3-million-drug-addicts-and-likens-himself-to-hitler (Accessed 14 March 2019)

2 'Philippine president Duterte was "involved in death squad"' by Bryan Harris, *Financial Times*, 15 September 2016, https://www.ft.com/content/ e4951e88-7b26-11e6-ae24-f193b105145e (Accessed 23 April 2019)

3 'Duterte explains rape cases in Davao: "Many beautiful women"', Rappler, August 2018, https://www.rappler.com/nation/210792-duterte-many-rape -cases-davao-beautiful-women (Accessed 1 May 2019)

4 'Philippines president says he once stabbed someone to death', *Guardian*, 10 November 2017, https://www.theguardian.com/world/2017/nov/10/ philippines-president-rodrigo-duterte-says-he-once-stabbed-someone-to-death (Accessed 19 March 2019)

5 'Philippine leader says once threw man from helicopter, would do it again',

Reuters, 29 December 2016, https://www.reuters.com/article/us-philippines
-duterte-helicopter/philippine-leader-says-once-threw-man-from-
helicopter-would-do-it-again-idUSKBN14I0DH (Accessed 1 May 2019)

6 'Duterte gov't allows "drug war" deaths to go unsolved' by Lian Buan,
   Rambo Talabong and Jodesz Gavilan, Rappler, 14 January 2019, https://
   www.rappler.com/newsbreak/in-depth/220595-duterte-government-drug
   -war-deaths-unsolved (Accessed 6 March 2019)

7 'Philippines:The police's murderous war on the poor',Amnesty International,
   31 January 2017, https://www.amnesty.org/en/latest/news/2017/01/
   philippines-the-police-murderous-war-on-the-poor/ (Accessed 10 June
   2019)

8 'Philippine anti-graft official sacked for revealing Duterte probe details',
   Reuters, 1 August 2018, https://www.reuters.com/article/us-philippines-
   corruption/philippine-anti-graft-official-sacked-for-revealing-duterte-
   probe-details-idUSKBN1KM4D2 (Accessed 6 March 2019)

9 'De Lima urges Senate action on human rights measures', Senate of the
   Philippines press release, 11 October 2018, http://www.senate.gov.ph/
   press_release/2018/1011_delima2.asp (Accessed 6 March 2019)

10 'Duterte jokes he'll show De Lima "sex video" to Pope Francis' by Pia Ranada,
   Rappler, 28 November 2017, https://www.rappler.com/nation/189799-
   duterte-jokes-pope-francis-leila-de-lima-rosary (Accessed 2 May 2019)

11 'De Lima-Duterte feud evolves into sex talk' by Christine O. Avendaño,
   Inquirer.net, 27 September 2016, https://newsinfo.inquirer.net/819279/de-
   lima-duterte-feud-evolves-into-sex-talk (Accessed 1 May 2019)

12 'Duterte's Popularity Hits Highest Ahead of Midterm Elections' by Andreo
   Calonzo, Bloomberg, 11 April 2019, https://www.bloomberg.com/news/
   articles/2019-04-11/duterte-s-popularity-back-to-highest-ahead-of-
   midterm-elections (Accessed 1 May 2019)

13 'A Message From Philippine Sen. Leila de Lima', Foreign Policy, 5 December
   2017, https://foreignpolicy.com/2017/12/05/a-message-from-philippine-
   senator-leila-de-lima/ (Accessed 20 March 2019)

14 'Philippines: Outspoken senator marks two years in arbitrary detention',
   Amnesty International, 22 February 2019, https://www.amnesty.org/en/
   latest/news/2019/02/philippines-outspoken-senator-marks-two-years-
   arbitrary-detention/ (Accessed 6 March 2019)

15 'Arrest warrant against Rappler's Maria Ressa shows authorities "railroading"
   case in the Philippines',Amnesty International, 13 February 2019, https://
   www.amnestyusa.org/press-releases/arrest-warrant-against-rapplers-maria-
   ressa-shows-authorities-railroading-case-in-the-philippines/ (Accessed 21
   March 2019)

4 We Are Not a Lie

1 'Patterns of civilian and child deaths due to war-related violence in Syria: a comparative analysis from the Violation Documentation Center dataset, 2011–16' by Debarati Guha-Sapir, Benjamin Schlüter, Jose Manuel Rodriguez-Llanes, Louis Lillywhite and Madelyn Hsiao-Rei Hicks, *The Lancet Global Health*, Vol. 6, Issue 1, 1 January 2018, https://www.thelancet.com/journals/langlo/article/PIIS2214-109X(17)30469-2/fulltext?elsca1= tlpr (Accessed 21 March 2019)

2 'Counting Hell' by Bruce Sharp, Mekong.net, http://www.mekong.net/cambodia/deaths.htm (Accessed 22 March 2019)

3 'Darfur: Counting the deaths: Mortality estimates from multiple survey data' by Debarati Guha-Sapir, Olivier Degomme and Mark Phelan, Centre for Research on the Epidemiology of Disasters, available at https://dial.uclouvain.be/pr/boreal/object/boreal:179719 (Accessed 22 March 2019)

4 'Patterns of mortality rates in Darfur conflict', by Debarati Guha-Sapir, Olivie Degomme, *The Lancet*, Vol. 375, Issue 9711, 23 January 2010, https://www.thelancet.com/journals/lancet/article/PIIS0140-6736(09)61967-X/fulltext (Accessed 10 June 2019)

5 'Now ten years since the UN offered a mortality estimate for the Dafur genocide', by Eric Reeves, Sudan: Research, Analysis, and Advocacy, 22 April 2018, http://sudanreeves.org/2018/04/22/now-ten-years-since-the-un-offered-a-morality-estimate-for-the-darfur-genocide/ (Accessed 10 June)

6 'Darfur Crisis: Death Estimates Demonstrate Severity of Crisis, but Their Accuracy and Credibility Could Be Enhanced', United States Government Accountability Office Report to Congressional Requesters, November 2006, https://www.gao.gov/new.items/d0724.pdf (Accessed 6 March 2019)

7 'Mortality after the 2003 invasion of Iraq: a cross-sectional cluster sample survey' by Gilbert Burnham, Riyadh Lafta, Shannon Doocy, Les Roberts, *The Lancet*, Vol. 368, Issue 9545, 21 October 2006, https://www.thelancet.com/journals/lancet/article/PIIS0140673606694919/fulltext (Accessed 10 June)

8 'Mortality in Iraq – Authors' reply', *The Lancet*, 13 January 2007, https://www.thelancet.com/journals/lancet/article/PIIS0140-6736(07)60063-4/fulltext (Accessed 1 May 2019)

9 Monthly Statistical Report on Casualties in Syria – December 2018, Violations Documentation Center in Syria, http://vdc-sy.net/monthly-statistical-report-casualties-syria-december-2018/ (Accessed 6 March 2019)

10 'Syria emergency', UNHCR, https://www.unhcr.org/syria-emergency.
html (Accessed 10 June)

11 'Tea time at the front: Gains give Syria's regime a new swagger' by Michael
Peel, *Financial Times*, 27 June 2013, https://www.ft.com/content/85886830
-df09-11e2-a9f4-00144feab7de (Accessed 16 April 2019)

12 'Syria's Assads Turned to West for Glossy P.R.' by Bill Carter and Amy
Chozick, *New York Times*, 10 June 2012, https://www.nytimes.com/2012/
06/11/world/middleeast/syrian-conflict-cracks-carefully-polished-image-
of-assad.html (Accessed 16 April 2019)

13 'Asma al-Assad:A Rose in the Desert' by Joan Juliet Buck, *Vogue*, 25 February
2011, archived at https://archive.is/20110225222156/http://www.vogue.
com/vogue-daily/article/asma-al-assad-a-rose-in-the-desert/ (Accessed 16
April 2019)

14 'Beheaded Syrian scholar refused to lead Isis to hidden Palmyra antiquities'
by Kareem Shaheen and Ian Black, *Guardian*, 19 August 2015, https://www.
theguardian.com/world/2015/aug/18/isis-beheads-archaeologist-syria
(Accessed 6 March 2019)

15 'Let's deal with the Devil: we should work with Vladimir Putin and Bashar
al-Assad in Syria' by Boris Johnson, *Telegraph*, 6 December 2015, https://
www.telegraph.co.uk/news/worldnews/middleeast/syria/12036184/Lets-
deal-with-the-Devil-we-should-work-with-Vladimir-Putin-and-Bashar-al
-Assad-in-Syria.html (Accessed 16 April 2019)

16 Labour Party Press Team, @labourpress, Twitter, 8 April 2018, https://
twitter.com/labourpress/status/983053337896595456 (Accessed 16 April
2019)

17 Report of the fact-finding mission regarding the incident of alleged use of
toxic chemicals as a weapon in Douma, Syrian Arab Republic, on 7 April
2018, Organisation for the Prohibition of Chemical Weapons, 1 March 2019,
https://www.opcw.org/sites/default/files/documents/2019/03/s-1731-
2019%28e%29.pdf (Accessed 6 March 2019)

18 'OPCW Issues Fact-Finding Mission Report on Chemical Weapons Use
Allegation in Douma, Syria, in 2018', Organisation for the Prohibition of
Chemical Weapons, 1 March 2019, https://www.opcw.org/media-centre/
news/2019/03/opcw-issues-fact-finding-mission-report-chemical-
weapons-use-allegation (Accessed 6 March 2019)

19 Russian Embassy in the Netherlands, @rusembassynl, Twitter, 1 March 2019,
https://twitter.com/rusembassynl/status/1101536111795552257 (Accessed
6 March 2019)

20 'West hits back at Russian spying activities' by David Bond, Mehreen Khan
and Kadhim Shubber, *Financial Times*, 4 October 2018, https://www.ft.

com/content/b87834d2-c7c0-11e8-ba8f-ee390057b8c9 (Accessed 23 April 2019)

21 'Epidemiological findings of major chemical attacks in the Syrian war are consistent with civilian targeting: a short report' by Jose M. Rodriguez-Llanes, Debarati Guha-Sapir, Benjamin-Samuel Schlüter and Madelyn Hsiao-Rei Hicks, 16 April 2018, https://www.ncbi.nlm.nih.gov/pmc/articles/PMC5901879/ (Accessed 16 April 2019)

22 'Europe sees sharp rise in measles: 41,000 cases, 37 deaths', Associated Press, 20 August 2018, https://apnews.com/baf52965cd5746ffa55f5666d5f003c8 (Accessed 16 April 2019)

5 From Criminal to VIP

1 'The Real Wolves of Wall Street', Global Witness, https://www.globalwitness.org/en/campaigns/corruption-and-money-laundering/real-wolves-of-wall-street/ (Accessed 17 April 2019)

2 'The Edge chairman gifts 1MDB whistle-blower Justo US$2 million', *The Edge Markets*, 31 January 2019, https://www.theedgemarkets.com/article/edge-chairman-gifts-1mdb-whistle-blower-justo-us2-million (Accessed 10 June)

3 'Saudi minister says donation to Malaysia's Najib was genuine: state media', Reuters, 15 April 2016, https://www.reuters.com/article/us-malaysia-scandal-saudi/saudi-minister-says-donation-to-malaysias-najib-was-genuine-state-media-idUSKCN0XC06D (Accessed 17 April 2019)

4 'Malaysia's top lawyer rejected advice to charge PM – source' by Rozanna Latiff and Praveen Menon, Reuters, 27 January 2016, https://www.reuters.com/article/us-malaysia-politics-commission-idUSKCN0V51G0 (Accessed 17 April 2019)

5 'Office of the Attorney General of Switzerland requests Malaysia for mutual assistance', Office of the Attorney General of Switzerland, 29 January 2016, https://www.bundesanwaltschaft.ch/mpc/en/home/medien/archiv-medienmitteilungen/news-seite.msg-id-60510.html (Accessed 10 June 2019)

6 United States of America v "The Wolf of Wall Street", US Department of Justice, July 2016, https://www.justice.gov/archives/opa/page/file/877166/download (Accessed 1 May 2019)

7 United States of America v Certain rights to and interests in the Viceroy Hotel Group, US Department of Justice, June 2017, https://www.justice.gov/opa/press-release/file/973671/download (Accessed 1 May 2019)

8 'Jho Low says it ain't so: Malaysian tycoon denies role in 1MDB "heist of the century"' by Eric Ellis, *Euromoney*, 1 April 2015, https://www.euromoney.

com/article/b12kmz59m12yj8/jho-says-it-aint-so-malaysian-tycoon-denies-role-in-1mdb-heist-of-the-century (Accessed 17 April 2019)

9 '"The Wolf of Wall Street" producers to pay $60 million to U.S. in lawsuit settlement', Reuters, 7 March 2018, https://www.reuters.com/article/us-malaysia-scandal-redgranite/the-wolf-of-wall-street-producers-to-pay-60-million-to-u-s-in-lawsuit-settlement-idUSKCN1GJ0FH (Accessed 17 April 2019)

10 'Singapore shuts second Swiss bank over 1MDB corruption scandal' by Michael Peel, Don Weinland and Ralph Atkins, *Financial Times*, 11 October 2016, https://www.ft.com/content/ec182626-8f64-11e6-a72e-b428cb934b78 (Accessed 17 April 2019)

11 'Jeff Sessions calls Malaysia's 1MDB scandal "kleptocracy at its worst"', Reuters, 5 December 2017, https://www.reuters.com/article/us-malaysia-scandal-doj/jeff-sessions-calls-malaysias-1mdb-scandal-kleptocracy-at-its-worst-idUSKBN1DZ0MX (Accessed 17 April 2019)

12 'Regulators accuse Swiss bank BSI over 1MDB scandal' by Michael Peel, *Financial Times*, 24 May 2016, https://www.ft.com/content/be8247ec-2177-11e6-9d4d-c11776a5124d (Accessed 17 April 2019)

13 'Thailand rejects Swiss request to hand over jailed 1MDB witness' by Michael Peel, Ralph Atkins and Jeevan Vasagar, *Financial Times*, 20 September 2016, https://www.ft.com/content/7d407e22-7f3a-11e6-8e50-8ec15fb462f4 (Accessed 17 April 2019)

14 Transcript of speech by David Cameron at Anti-Corruption Summit, 12 May 2016, https://www.gov.uk/government/speeches/anti-corruption-summit-2016-pms-closing-remarks (Accessed 17 April 2019)

15 'Mahathir Suspects Link to Ringgit's Fall: Malaysian Leader Sees Hidden Jewish "Agenda"', *New York Times*, 11 October 1997, https://www.nytimes.com/1997/10/11/news/mahathir-suspects-link-to-ringgits-fall-malaysian-leader-sees-hidden.html (Accessed 17 April 2019)

16 'Former Malaysian PM Mahathir Mohamad on the rise of China' by Jamil Anderlini, *Financial Times*, 25 May 2017, https://www.ft.com/content/b4affab0-4076-11e7-82b6-896b95f30f58 (Accessed 17 April 2019)

17 'The cover-up: Malaysian officials reveal just how much 1MDB probe was obstructed', *Reuters*, 4 July 2019, https://www.reuters.com/article/us-malaysia-politics-najib-coverup-analy/the-cover-up-malaysian-officials-reveal-just-how-much-1mdb-probe-was-obstructed-idUSKBN1JT2Z9 (Accessed 10 June 2019)

18 Indictment: United States of America against Low Taek Jho and Ng Chong Hwa, 3 October 2018, https://www.justice.gov/opa/press-release/file/1106931/download (Accessed 17 April 2019)

19 'Malaysian fugitive Jho Low, four others hit with fresh 1MDB charges', Reuters, 5 December 2018, https://www.reuters.com/article/us-malaysia-politics-1mdb-financier/malaysian-fugitive-jho-low-four-others-hit-with-fresh-1mdb-charges-idUSKBN1O40AW (Accessed 17 April 2019)

20 Letter from Jho-Low.com, https://static1.squarespace.com/static/53d14d5ce4b0d5933c1dffa3/t/5b9a41a640ec9a28d6519e5b/1536836007338/Letter+English.pdf (Accessed 10 June 2019)

6 Small Americas

1 Press Conference of President Obama after ASEAN Summit, 8 September 2016, https://obamawhitehouse.archives.gov/the-press-office/2016/09/08/press-conference-president-obama-after-asean-summit (Accessed 20 April 2019)

2 'A Journalist Abroad Grapples With American Power' by Hisham Matar, *New York Times*, 28 August 2017, https://www.nytimes.com/2017/08/28/books/review/notes-on-a-foreign-country-suzy-hansen.html (Accessed 20 April 2019)

3 'Trump defends Putin: "You think our country's so innocent?"' by Sophie Tatum, CNN, 6 February 2017, https://edition.cnn.com/2017/02/04/politics/donald-trump-vladimir-putin/index.html (Accessed 20 April 2019)

4 Michael McFaul, @McFaul, Twitter, 5 February 2017, https://twitter.com/McFaul/status/828034509190754308 (Accessed 10 June 2019)

5 'When America No Longer Is a Global Force for Good' by Susan E. Rice, *New York Times*, 20 December 2017, https://www.nytimes.com/2017/12/20/opinion/susan-rice-america-global-strategy.html (Accessed 20 April 2019)

6 'Defending Liberty in a Global Economy' by Richard B. Cheney, Cato Institute, 23 June 1998, https://www.cato.org/publications/speeches/defending-liberty-global-economy (Accessed 20 April 2019)

7 'Trump's Foreign Policy Isn't the Problem' by Jeanne Morefield, *Boston Review*, 8 January 2019, http://bostonreview.net/politics/jeanne-morefield-trump%E2%80%99s-foreign-policy-isn%E2%80%99t-problem (Accessed 6 March 2019)

8 'Communication by the Government of Liberia', International Commission of Enquiry in Liberia, League of Nations, 15 December 1930, https://biblio-archive.unog.ch/Dateien/CouncilMSD/C-658-M-272-1930-VI_EN.pdf (Accessed June 2019)

9 Quoted in 'Nina Simone in Liberia' by Katherina Grace Thomas, Guernica, 19 June 2017, https://www.guernicamag.com/nina-simone-in-liberia/ (Accessed 20 April 2019)

10 'While at NATO, Trump falsely claims for a third time that Reagan lost Wisconsin' by John Wagner, *Washington Post*, 12 July 2018, https://www.washingtonpost.com/politics/while-at-nato-trump-falsely-claims-for-a-third-time-that-reagan-lost-wisconsin/2018/07/12 (Accessed 20 April 2019)

11 'Faith, Certainty and the Presidency of George W. Bush' by Ron Suskind, *New York Times*, 17 October 2004, https://www.nytimes.com/2004/10/17/magazine/faith-certainty-and-the-presidency-of-george-w-bush.html (Accessed 20 April 2019)

12 'Address by Dr. Henry A. Kissinger, September 29 2010', Office of the Historian, US Department of State, https://history.state.gov/conferences/2010-southeast-asia/secretary-kissinger (Accessed 1 May 2019)

7 The Lady Vanishes

1 'Nobel lecture', Aung San Suu Kyi, 16 June 2012, https://www.nobelprize.org/prizes/peace/1991/kyi/26193-aung-san-suu-kyi-nobel-lecture-1991/ (Accessed 10 June 2019)

2 'How Aung San Suu Kyi sees the Rohingya crisis', BBC News, 25 January 2018, https://www.bbc.co.uk/news/world-asia-42824778 (Accessed 21 April 2019)

3 Transcript of speech at http://chnm.gmu.edu/wwh/p/119.html (Accessed 20 April 2019)

4 'Aung San Suu Kyi awarded US congressional medal', *Guardian*, 20 September 2012, https://www.theguardian.com/world/2012/sep/20/aung-san-suu-kyi-medal (Accessed 20 April 2019)

5 'Interviews with Rohingyas fleeing from Myanmar since 9 October 2016', OHCHR Mission to Bangladesh, 3 February 2017, https://www.ohchr.org/Documents/Countries/MM/FlashReport3Feb2017.pdf (Accessed 10 June 2019)

6 Muhammad Yunus, @Professor.Muhammad.Yunus, Facebook, 29 December 2016, https://www.facebook.com/Professor.Muhammad.Yunus/posts/996372943802283:0 (Accessed 10 June 2019)

7 'UN calls Myanmar violence "textbook" ethnic cleansing' by Michael Peel and John Reed, *Financial Times*, 11 September 2017, https://www.ft.com/content/c867eff4-96e3-11e7-a652-cde3f882dd7b (Accessed 21 April 2019)

8 '"Acts of genocide" suspected against Rohingya in Myanmar: U.N.' by

Stephanie Nebehay and Simon Lewis, Reuters, 7 March 2018, https://www.reuters.com/article/us-myanmar-rohingya-rights/acts-of-genocide-suspected-against-rohingya-in-myanmar-u-n-idUSKCN1GJ163 (Accessed 21 April 2019)

9 'Suu Kyi defense of jailing of Reuters journalists "unbelievable" – Haley', Reuters, 13 September 2018, https://www.reuters.com/article/us-myanmar-journalists-suukyi/suu-kyi-defense-of-jailing-of-reuters-journalists-unbelievable-haley-idUSKCN1LT08A (Accessed 6 March 2019)

10 'Amnesty International withdraws human rights award from Aung San Suu Kyi', Amnesty International, 12 November 2018, https://www.amnesty.org/en/latest/news/2018/11/amnesty-withdraws-award-from-aung-san-suu-kyi/ (Accessed 6 March 2019)

11 'South Africa's Tutu asks Myanmar's Suu Kyi to help Rohingya', Reuters, 7 September 2017, https://www.reuters.com/article/us-myanmar-rohingya-tutu/south-africas-tutu-asks-myanmars-suu-kyi-to-help-rohingya-idUSKCN1BI2I0 (Accessed 21 April 2019)

12 'Cate Blanchett Slams Aung San Suu Kyi Over Rohingya Crisis' by Phil Mercer, Voice of America, 24 March 2018, https://www.voanews.com/a/cate-blanchett-aung-san-suu-kyi/4314385.html (Accessed 21 April 2019)

13 Statement from Hillary Clinton on the Burmese Election, American Presidency Project, 11 November 2015, https://www.presidency.ucsb.edu/documents/statement-from-hillary-clinton-the-burmese-election (Accessed 21 April 2019)

14 Tweet by Thant Myint-U, @thantmyintu, Twitter, 4 August 2018, https://twitter.com/thantmyintu/status/1025782319158779904 (Accessed 21 April 2019)

15 'The Burmese Fairy Tale' by Ma Thanegi, *Far Eastern Economic Review*, 19 February 1998, available at http://www.burmalibrary.org/reg.burma/archives/199802/msg00314.html (Accessed 21 April 2019)

16 Transcript of speech by Aung San Suu Kyi, Oxford University, 20 June 2012, http://www.ox.ac.uk/news/2012-06-20-transcript-aung-san-suu-kyi-speech (Accessed 22 April 2019)

17 'Suu Kyi draws rare rancor over Myanmar mine report' by Soe Zeya Tun, Reuters, 14 March 2013, https://www.reuters.com/article/us-myanmar-suukyi-protest/suu-kyi-draws-rare-rancor-over-myanmar-mine-report-idUSBRE92D0OT20130314 (Accessed 22 April 2019)

18 Transcript of Aung San Suu Kyi's Nobel Prize acceptance speech, June 2012, http://speakingfrog.com/?p=1168 (Accessed 20 April 2019)

19 'Aung San Suu Kyi's speech at Nehru', Burma Library, http://www.

burmalibrary.org/reg.burma/archives/199511/msg00096.html (Accessed 1 May 2019)

20 'Myanmar leader says no ethnic cleansing of Rohingya Muslims – BBC' by Guy Faulconbridge, Reuters, 7 April 2017, https://www.reuters.com/article/myanmar-rohingya-suukyi-int/myanmar-leader-says-no-ethnic-cleansing-of-rohingya-muslims-bbc-idUSKBN1772XN (Accessed 22 April 2019)

21 'Rakhine State affair and cooperation', *Global New Light of Myanmar*, 2 November 2017, http://www.globalnewlightofmyanmar.com/rakhine-state-affair-cooperation/

22 Tweet by Zaw Htay, @ZawHtayMyanmar, Twitter, 27 December 2016, https://twitter.com/zawhtaymyanmar/status/813698482498256897 (Accessed 22 April 2019)

23 Press release from Ministry of the Office of the State Counsellor, Government of the Republic of the Union of Myanmar, 9 August 2018, https://reliefweb.int/report/myanmar/government-republic-union-myanmar-ministry-office-state-counsellor-press-release (Accessed 10 June 2019)

24 'Myanmar's need for a shared long-term vision' by U Thant Myint-U, Mizzima, 14 July 2018, http://mizzima.com/news-opinion/myanmar%25E2%2580%2599s-need-shared-long-term-vision (Accessed 22 April 2019)

8 A Question of Values

1 'Viktoria Marinova murder: Bulgarian man says he did not mean to kill journalist' by Toyin Owoseje, *Independent*, 19 October 2018, https://www.independent.co.uk/news/world/europe/viktoria-marinova-murder-rape-bulgaria-man-kill-journalist-stade-severin-krassimirov-a8592051.html (Accessed 6 March 2019)

2 'Jan Kuciak: Slovak man charged over double murder', BBC News, 14 March 2019, https://www.bbc.com/news/world-europe-47568521 (Accessed 1 May 2019)

3 Blog post by Daphne Caruana Galizia, 16 October 2017, https://daphnecaruanagalizia.com/2017/10/crook-schembri-court-today-pleading-not-crook/ (Accessed 22 April 2019)

4 'The history of the European Union – 1958', European Union, https://europa.eu/european-union/about-eu/history/1946-1959/1958_en (Accessed 6 March 2019)

5 Obituary: Anca Petrescu, *Telegraph*, 1 November 2013, https://www.telegraph.co.uk/news/obituaries/10421302/Anca-Petrescu.html (Accessed 22 April 2019)

6 'Romanian minister found guilty of vote-rigging in referendum' by Luiza

Ilie, Reuters, 15 May 2015, https://www.reuters.com/article/us-romania-corruption/romanian-minister-found-guilty-of-vote-rigging-in-referendum-idUSKBN0O00J820150515 (Accessed 6 March 2019)

7 'Nicolae Ceauşescu', *Encyclopaedia Britannica*, https://www.britannica.com/biography/Nicolae-Ceausescu (Accessed 6 March 2019)

8 'Romanian prosecutors indict ex-leader for revolution deaths', Associated Press, 17 April 2018, https://www.apnews.com/de0bd5169f70451698aa69f0b3c9572f (Accessed 24 April 2019)

9 'Romania's chief anti-corruption prosecutor removed from office' by Valerie Hopkins and Michael Peel, *Financial Times*, 9 July 2018, https://www.ft.com/content/03cb2876-838e-11e8-a29d-73e3d454535d (Accessed 24 April 2019)

10 'Caruana Galizia murder: Enemies killed Malta journalist's dogs', BBC News, 9 August 2018, https://www.bbc.co.uk/news/world-europe-45129142 (Accessed 24 April 2019)

9 The Post-Napoleonic Wars

1 'Farage launches the Brexit Party and unveils his secret weapon ... Rees-Mogg's little SISTER: Ex-"Cameron cutie" Annunziata, 40, stuns the Tories by defecting just HOURS before vowing to take on "far-right" UKIP in EU elections' by Martin Robinson, David Wilcock and Tim Sculthorpe, *Mail Online*, 12 April 2019, https://www.dailymail.co.uk/news/article-6914049/Farage-vows-fightback-against-establishment-betrayal-Brexit.html (Accessed 3 May 2019)

2 'The Nationalist's Delusion' by Adam Serwer, *Atlantic*, 20 November 2017, https://www.theatlantic.com/politics/archive/2017/11/the-nationalists-delusion/546356/ (Accessed 24 April 2019)

3 'A revealing deception about Winston Churchill?' by Jon Danzig, New Europeans, 25 January 2015, https://neweuropeans.net/article/604/revealing-deception-about-winston-churchill (Accessed 24 April 2019)

4 'Economic Regeneration', Torbay Council, n.d., http://www.torbay.gov.uk/DemocraticServices/documents/s12713/Appendix%201%20-%20Economic%20Regeneration.pdf (Accessed 24 April 2019)

5 http://www.justice.gov.uk/contacts/prison-finder/dartmoor (Accessed 10 June)

6 'Don't abandon the Europe that I fought for – and my comrades died for', letter to the *Guardian* by Franklin Medhurst, 15 June 2016, https://www.theguardian.com/politics/2016/jun/15/dont-abandon-the-europe-that-i-fought-for-and-my-comrades-died-for (Accessed 2 May 2019)

7 'Why won't Remainers talk about family?' by Giles Fraser, *UnHerd*, 22

February 2019, https://unherd.com/2019/02/why-wont-remainers-talk-about-family/ (Accessed 10 June 2019)

8 'How Britain voted',YouGov, June 2016, https://yougov.co.uk/topics/politics/articles-reports/2016/06/27/how-britain-voted (Accessed 1 May 2019)

9 The Green Party, @TheGreenParty, Twitter, 9 December 2018, https://twitter.com/thegreenparty/status/1071848908861685760?lang=en (Accessed 10 June 2019)

10 'Understanding the Leave vote', NatCen, December 2016, http://natcen.ac.uk/media/1319222/natcen_brexplanations-report-final-web2.pdf (Accessed 1 May 2019)

11 'EU referendum: I believe in Europe – which is why I rebelled' by Adrian Sanders, *Guardian*, 26 October 2011, https://www.theguardian.com/commentisfree/2011/oct/26/eu-referendum-europe-rebelled (Accessed 24 April 2019)

12 'Sir Frederic Bennett', by Andrew Roth, *Guardian*, 19 September 2002, https://www.theguardian.com/news/2002/sep/20/guardianobituaries.obituaries (Accessed 10 June 2019)

13 'Sir Frederic Bennett', *Telegraph*, 18 September 2002, https://www.telegraph.co.uk/news/obituaries/1407481/Sir-Frederic-Bennett.html (Accessed 10 June 2019)

14 'The United Kingdom's exit from, and new partnership with, the European Union', UK government policy paper, 15 May 2017, https://www.gov.uk/government/publications/the-united-kingdoms-exit-from-and-new-partnership-with-the-european-union-white-paper/the-united-kingdoms-exit-from-and-new-partnership-with-the-european-union--2 (Accessed 24 April 2019)

15 'UK Press Coverage of the EU Referendum' by David A. L. Levy, Billur Aslan and Diego Bironzo, Reuters Institute for the Study of Journalism, 2017, https://reutersinstitute.politics.ox.ac.uk/sites/default/files/2018-11/UK_Press_Coverage_of_the_%20EU_Referendum.pdf (Accessed 24 April 2019)

16 Statement by Kevin Foster, 10 May 2017, https://www.kevinjfoster.com/news/cps-announce-no-charges-over-2015-election-expenses (Accessed 10 June 2019)

17 'Few bright spots in UK traders' sea of red' by Daniel Thomas, James Wilson and Harriet Agnew, *Financial Times*, 24 June 2016, https://www.ft.com/content/ba663574-39fa-11e6-a780-b48ed7b6126f (Accessed 22 April 2019)

18 'Hedge funds win big from Brexit bets' by Miles Johnson, Harriet Agnew and Mary Childs, *Financial Times*, 26 June 2016, https://www.ft.com/content/c02fe256-3aaf-11e6-8716-a4a71e8140b0 (Accessed 1 May 2019)

19 'The Perils of Perception and the EU', Ipsos MORI, 9 June 2016, https://www.ipsos.com/ipsos-mori/en-uk/perils-perception-and-eu (Accessed 25 April 2019)

20 'Perceptions are not reality', Ipsos MORI, 9 July 2013, https://www.ipsos.com/ipsos-mori/en-uk/perceptions-are-not-reality (Accessed 25 April 2019)

21 'It's time to celebrate the Empire, says Brown' by Benedict Brogan, *Daily Mail*, 15 January 2005, https://www.dailymail.co.uk/news/article-334208/Its-time-celebrate-Empire-says-Brown.html (Accessed 25 April 2019)

22 'The British Empire is "something to be proud of"' by Will Dahlgreen, YouGov, 26 July 2014, https://yougov.co.uk/topics/politics/articles-reports/2014/07/26/britain-proud-its-empire (Accessed 25 April 2019)

23 'I love my country so I need to say: Britain, you're being an idiot over Brexit' by Laurie Penny, *New Statesman*, 27 November 2017, https://www.newstatesman.com/politics/brexit/2017/11/i-love-my-country-so-i-need-say-britain-you-re-being-idiot-over-brexit (Accessed 25 April 2019)

24 Winston Churchill, 11 November 1903, International Churchill Society, https://winstonchurchill.org/publications/finest-hour/finest-hour-142/quotations-of-the-season/ (Accessed 25 April 2019)

25 'History Detectives – Red Herrings: Famous Words Churchill Never Said' by Michael Richards, International Churchill Society, https://winstonchurchill.org/publications/finest-hour/finest-hour-141/history-detectives-red-herrings-famous-words-churchill-never-said/ (Accessed 25 April 2019)

Epilogue: Banish the Chill

1 'Haunted by colonial past, Belgium's Africa museum reopens after revamp' by Dave Clark and Matthieu Demeestere, Yahoo! News, 8 December 2018, https://news.yahoo.com/haunted-colonial-past-belgiums-africa-museum-reopens-revamp-165103047.html (Accessed 6 March 2019)

2 'Benin artworks: France to return thrones and statues', BBC News, 23 November 2018, https://www.bbc.com/news/world-46324174 (Accessed 6 March 2019)

3 In June 2019, the museum told me that it had erected a small informational panel at the location of one of the 'villages' – but this had since disappeared due to 'vandalism'.

Acknowledgements

I would like to thank the many people across numerous countries who gave me time and spoke about their lives for this book, particularly those who did so at some risk. I have been lucky indeed to meet and know you.

I am very grateful to the exemplary professionalism, generosity and good company of colleagues from more than twenty years of working with the *Financial Times*, in London and bureaux in Lagos, Abu Dhabi, Bangkok and Brussels.

I am grateful also to the *Financial Times* for permitting the use in this book of certain content from my previous *FT* articles. The *FT* has not seen, and does not endorse, the context in which such content has been published in the book.

The *London Review of Books* kindly gave permission to draw on material in chapter 6 that previously appeared in the *LRB* article 'Small America', published in August 2003.

I greatly appreciate those who read drafts of material in this book or gave other valuable help. They include Antonia Baum, Jacob Borg, Carmen Constantin, Abigail Fielding-Smith, Jonathan Head, Phakarat Ryn Jirenuwat, Barney Jopson, Andrew R.C. Marshall, Vivian Nereim, Thomas Penn, Grace Ramos and Tashny Sukumaran.

I am grateful in particular to my three deepest and most diligent readers, Samantha Lister and Robin and Mary Peel.

I profoundly appreciate the years of encouragement, savvy and excellent advice offered by my agent Will Francis at Janklow & Nesbit. I am also fortunate *The Fabulists* ended up in the skilful hands of editor Alex Christofi and the rest of the Oneworld Publications team, including Jonathan Bentley-Smith, David Inglesfield and Paul Nash.

Finally, I would like to thank all of those, most of all members of my family, who have borne the demands of this book with patience, generosity and an exceptional consideration.

Index